I Know

HE LIVES

HOW *13* SPECIAL WITNESSES CAME TO KNOW JESUS CHRIST

Additional Books by This Author

Bruce R. McConkie: Highlights from His Life and Teachings
Called of God by Prophecy
An Apostle's Record: The Journals of Abraham H. Cannon
Determining Doctrine
Faith to Heal and Be Healed
Latter Leaves in the Life of Lorenzo Snow
The Life of Orson F. Whitney

I Know HE LIVES

HOW *13* SPECIAL
WITNESSES CAME TO KNOW
JESUS CHRIST

DENNIS B. HORNE

CFI

AN IMPRINT OF CEDAR FORT, INC.

SPRINGVILLE, UTAH

© 2017 Dennis B. Horne
Cover art by Rod Peterson

This is not an official publication of The Church of Jesus Christ of Latter-day Saints. The opinions and views expressed herein belong solely to the author and do not necessarily represent the opinions or views of Cedar Fort, Inc. Permission for the use of sources, graphics, and photos is also solely the responsibility of the author.

ISBN 13: 978-1-4621-2115-1

Published by CFI, an imprint of Cedar Fort, Inc.
2373 W. 700 S., Springville, UT, 84663
Distributed by Cedar Fort, Inc., www.cedarfort.com

LIBRARY OF CONGRESS CATALOGING-IN-PUBLICATION DATA ON FILE

Cover design by Shawnda T. Craig
Cover design © 2017 Cedar Fort, Inc.
Edited and typeset by Heather Holm

Printed in the United States of America

10 9 8 7 6 5 4 3 2 1

Printed on acid-free paper

ACKNOWLEDGMENTS

It has been a spiritual joy to research for and prepare this book. My own testimony has been strengthened in searching out and studying the special witness of these Apostles of the Lord Jesus Christ. For this blessing, I will always be thankful.

I performed most of the research myself, but I have also benefited from the previous work of others, both in print and online. My own files on this subject grew over the decades until I realized their contents would make a fine beginning for a book on the subject.

My good wife, Chelsey, has again served as an excellent sounding board. I often ran ideas, problems, and other issues past her, and by doing so was better enabled to find the way forward. She also read and commented on early chapter drafts and made a number of helpful suggestions.

My own dear mother, Linda Horne, was also able to read the entire manuscript just before it was accepted for publication, and just before she passed away. She faced death with unimaginable courage and cheerfulness. I dedicate this volume to her. I will always appreciate the faithfulness and valiance of the women in my life.

Readers will notice that my friend Elder Glen L. Rudd of the Seventy, who passed away on December 30, 2016, is mentioned in the chapter relating Elder Matthew Cowley's special witness, and in several other chapters. In the almost two decades that I knew him, he kindly provided me with many items he had written that included his experiences with Elder Cowley and many other prophets and apostles. He also offered to help me with sources for writing projects, and he read every book I wrote. This particular book was enriched by his materials.

I am grateful for comments I received from a few manuscript reviewers, especially Andrew Hamilton, whose suggestions helped me avoid some mistakes.

ACKNOWLEDGMENTS

Any problems or errors found herein are my fault alone and no one else's. I do not speak for The Church of Jesus Christ of Latter-day Saints or its leaders, past or present.

I also wish to thank Cedar Fort, the publisher, and their editorial board, for having the good sense to recognize the exceptional value and worth of the material presented herein. Also, Shawnda Craig for dust jacket design, and Heather Holm for copyediting and proofreading expertise. Heather is an outstanding professional to work with.

Last, I direct readers to the final section of the introduction, where I have included my personal testimony. I desire this volume to have as much influence as possible in dissolving doubt and strengthening faith in Jesus Christ.

CONTENTS

CONTENTS

Introduction

"There have been special witnesses of this dispensation who have seen Jesus, have talked with Him face to face, and know Him."

A Book about the Apostles' Special Witness of Jesus Christ

This volume delves directly into a central purpose of the apostleship: "The twelve traveling councilors are called to be the Twelve Apostles, or special witnesses of the name of Christ in all the world"—so declared the Lord to His chosen Twelve (D&C 107:23). The Prophet Joseph Smith explained what this means and how critically important it is. He said, "The fundamental principles of our religion are the testimony of the Apostles and Prophets, concerning Jesus Christ, that He died, was buried, and rose again the third day, and ascended into heaven; and all other things which pertain to our religion are only appendages to it."[1]

While it is true that the above revelation states "the *name* of Christ," which means His gospel, herein the focus will lean toward what the Prophet stated—Jesus' death and especially His Resurrection; that He lives now, today, and is known of His Apostles. The devil and his mortal servants hate it, and they do all they can to create doubt and disbelief, but the fact is that there have been special witnesses of this dispensation who have seen Jesus, have talked with Him face to face, and know Him.

Herein I have selected for review thirteen (deceased) Apostles and have woven relevant material into chapters relating in some detail each one's special witness of Jesus Christ. These vignettes therefore contain a measure of their life history, including trials and tribulations, with a generous portion of spiritual experience and powerfully expressive apostolic testimony.[2] The revelation states, "To some it is given by the Holy Ghost to know that Jesus Christ is the Son of God, and that he was crucified for the sins of the world. To others it is given to believe on their words, that they also might have eternal life if they continue faithful" (D&C 46:13–14). The obligation resting upon the Apostles is signified by the first sentence of that verse: they come to know that Jesus Christ is the resurrected, living Son of God with absolute revelatory certainty.

Those inspired words also describe the reason for and the value of this work: to provide readers with the experiences and testimonies of selected special witnesses so that they may, by believing and continuing faithful, also gain eternal life. Such a purpose and hope seems justification enough and a thousandfold more. In substantiation, I quote the reasoning of then-Elder Marion G. Romney:

> Now the revelations that God has given of himself have in every age been intended and given for the benefit of all men, not just for those chosen servants who received the revelation. . . .
>
> God has, from the beginning, seen fit to place a knowledge of himself within the reach of all men. We who are his present witnesses are but discharging our responsibility when we bring these testimonies of the prophets and our own testimonies as to the form and nature of God to your attention.
>
> To the extent we do bring them to your attention, the responsibility passes from us to you to determine the credibility of the witnesses and their testimonies. Let no man underestimate the importance of his decision concerning this matter. To know God and his Son Jesus Christ is life eternal. Without such knowledge, no man can be saved. And the only way to get it is to obtain a personal witness to the truth of the revelations that God the Father and Jesus Christ, his Son, have given of themselves.[3]

THE SACREDNESS OF THE SUBJECT CONSIDERED

Having acknowledged the purposes for this work, some legitimate issues must still be reckoned with.

When examining this subject and these testimonies, there must be appropriate sensitivity for the sacred. For this reason, I determined to only include chapter-length overviews of the special witness of Apostles who have died. President Boyd K. Packer noted that when he heard of sacred spiritual experiences shared in a closed meeting, under conditions where an unspoken obligation was felt to keep something confidential, he would not share such things publicly. Then he commented, "If . . . on some occasion I heard those same things spoken by that General Authority in a public meeting, I felt, thereafter, free to make comment on them."[4] He further mentioned that we have many accounts of spiritual experiences of Brethren in generations past, but that they "generally [were] made known after they were gone." He also noted, "It is not out of order . . . to present some experiences from those who have lived in years past."[5] This counsel became very helpful to me. As I wrestled with the issue, I realized that what would be considered too sacred to share at one time, may well not be so at another time, but would instead become powerfully beneficial. In fact, by not sharing something special and faith-affirming after their death, it may be lost to those who would appreciate and benefit from it the most. Great personal edification and spiritual confirmation can be found in studying the true accounts of experiences with the Divine left by those who have gone before us.

Another helpful view is to consider that we would not know of sacred spiritual experiences unless the Apostles recorded or shared them in some form. Often, they are publicly printed by the Church, or broadcast in audio or video form. Such things are meant to be heard and understood by as many as will receive them. Reflecting on his position as the Prophet of the Lord for all the world, President Gordon B. Hinckley said, "The life of the President of the Church [and we would add that of the Apostles] really belongs to the entire Church. He has very little privacy and no secrets."[6]

Yet recognition of the above considerations does not mean that members of the First Presidency and the Twelve brashly or naively share all their pearls without due caution. I am aware of three statements by Apostles that help us understand their cognizance of what they share and what they do not. Elder Boyd K. Packer stated, "There are many things that the Brethren know, individually and collectively, that they just do not talk about, and there are many scriptures which sustain them in this silence."[7] Elder Bruce R. McConkie likewise noted, "I am sufficiently sensitive to the feelings and minds of many of the Brethren to know that they have seen and heard many [spiritual] things which they do not disclose."[8] Finally, President Marion G. Romney told a group of mission presidents that, "I do not tell all I know. I have never told my wife all I know. I found out long ago that if I told everything I knew, the Lord would cease to trust me."[9]

From these statements, well understood by all their associates, we can be assured that the prophets and apostles divulge only those details of their special witness that the Spirit permits them to declare. They are constrained from revealing more. "It is given unto many to know the mysteries of God; nevertheless they are laid under a strict command that they shall not impart only according to the portion of his word which he doth grant unto the children of men, according to the heed and diligence which they give unto him" (Alma 12:9; see also D&C 63:64; 2 Nephi 28:1; Matthew 7:6; 1 Nephi 14:6; and D&C 41:6). For example, in his last address to students at Brigham Young University, President Harold B. Lee, while mentally searching for the appropriate language in which to express his special witness, said, "Sometime, if the spirit prompts me, I may feel free to tell you more."[10] On another occasion he noted, "There are some witnesses I cannot give now, perhaps sometime later. Many things are too sacred to share at this time."[11]

We should also be aware that these guiding principles mean that there are limitations to what can be deduced from various things that Apostles have said or written at different times and to different audiences. Care must be taken not to assume something that may not be true. For example, if an Apostle at one time says that he has not seen the Lord, such a blessing might later be given him that he may say nothing about. Absence of declaration may not necessarily indicate absence of divine experience.

We should also be deeply and humbly grateful for all that the Spirit of the Lord has permitted them to say. The prophet Nephi taught, "For the things which some men esteem to be of great worth, both to the body and soul, others set at naught and trample under their feet" (1 Nephi 19:7). In the wicked world we live in, there are far more who will *not* believe an apostolic testimony than those who will, and this is according to the prophecies. Yet for those who will believe, who do esteem the Apostles' special witness to be of great worth, the reward is joyous edification, strengthened personal testimony, and blessed guidance along the path to eternal life.

Apostles' Use of Indirect Language for a Reason

One method often employed by the prophets and apostles to provide a glimpse of the extent or detail of their witness for those able to recognize it, is to refer to someone else that enjoyed a special spiritual experience with the Savior, and then indicate that their own experience was like unto it. Such language might refer to Joseph Smith, to the doubting Thomas, to the Brother of Jared, or some other prophet who declared their personal experience with the Christ, and then they indicate that their own experience was the same. This indirect method of declaring their sacred witness helps them convey more to the spiritually attuned and less to the spiritually dead. The Spirit can then individually bear record to those prepared, while others are left ignorant, as they should be. Such indirect expressions by various Apostles are found in these pages.

Some critics have disparaged this indirect method of declaring sacred truth, but they know not what they speak of and they have their reward. These critics and unbelievers can be nonmembers or, sadly, even members of the Church. Elder Packer spoke of the lack of faith that has kept many from receiving the spiritual assurances that might have been theirs. He related that "President Harold B. Lee told me once of a conversation he had with Elder Charles A. Callis of the Quorum of the Twelve. Brother Callis had remarked that the gift of discernment was an awesome burden to carry. To see clearly what is ahead and yet find members slow to respond or resistant to counsel or even rejecting the witness of the apostles and prophets brings deep sorrow."[12]

CONCENTRATION OF TESTIMONY HEREIN

The circumstances under which the apostles and prophets (now numbering over one hundred in our dispensation) have given their special witness are too widely scattered, varied, and numerous to list. Their testimonies are spread throughout Latter-day Saint literature. What this book does is to extract some of them out of this massive collection of material and then concentrate them in one place.

While I have not tried to be exhaustive, still I have assembled many precious gems that I have woven into these accounts. This means this book is filled with apostolic testimony and expressions of absolute assurance, nothing wavering. In these pages, I have purposely sought to concentrate and contextualize the selected Apostles' special witness—not to cheapen, exploit, or sensationalize, but to reassure, reaffirm, and proclaim again. Even though they are now on the other side of the veil, the Holy Spirit still witnesses to the truth of the special witness they have left behind—and that is because, living or dead, then or now, what they said is true.

BEARING WITNESS IN A WICKED WORLD

This train of thought brings up another issue: Should the testimonies of the Apostles be silenced because of the ridicule of the sacred by the wicked? Our answer is that the Apostles follow the promptings and constraints of the Holy Spirit in what they declare, for no matter how wicked the world they live in becomes, they are still called and ordained special witnesses. "Remember that that which cometh from above is sacred, and must be spoken with care, and by constraint of the Spirit; and in this there is no condemnation, and ye receive the Spirit through prayer; wherefore, without this there remaineth condemnation" (D&C 63:64). Sad as it is, some Apostles have received death threats for declaring their special witness of the Savior. We do indeed live in a wicked world that will only get worse as the decades pass.

We can but imagine the humbling and precious details we could be told of how the Apostles received their special witness, if only members of the Church collectively lived today as they will during the Millennium. So often today, if a living Apostle speaks tenderly, forcefully, or frankly about something deeply sacred, a foolish or false member will record it and post it online to be ridiculed by the world. Such unfortunate actions have a way of dampening apostolic expressions about sacred matters.[13]

THE MODERN FAD OF DOUBT AND DISBELIEF

In today's overwhelmingly agnostic and atheistic society where the weakening "Christian" world is failing and falling apart around us, where encroachments from the disbelieving world are being made into the Church and into faithful families, these recorded testimonies of Apostles, these special witnesses of Jesus Christ, as related herein, become ever more important and precious. If read, studied, and pondered with a humble and receptive heart, and in a prayerful and believing attitude, their powerful declarations of truth and conviction can save souls and bless lives and hold back the mounting tide of doubt and disbelief.

In this context, with so many, especially among academics and liberal or activist online voices—even among some supposedly faithful members—expressing their opinion that somehow there is something good or beneficial to be found in doubting, I offer the apostolic declarations quoted in this book as irrefutable refutation. "Look unto me in every thought" commanded our Lord, "*doubt not, fear not*" (D&C 6:36). Anyone teaching otherwise than this plain and simple commandment is wresting the scriptures to their own destruction and leading others astray. President Spencer W. Kimball said, "I know without question that God lives and have a feeling of sorrow for those people in the world who live in the gray area of doubt, who do not have such an assurance."[14]

Repeatedly, without exception, the counsel and plea of the prophets and apostles is to do all one can to dispel doubt and disbelief in one's heart and mind by coming unto Christ. One of the purposes of prophets and apostles is to dispel or dissolve doubt and help other people come to know the Master as they do. Exactly that was said of an Old Testament prophet: "Forasmuch as an excellent spirit, and knowledge, and understanding, interpreting of dreams, and shewing of hard sentences, and *dissolving of doubts*, were found in the same Daniel" (Daniel 5:12). The spiritual gift is to dissolve doubt, not celebrate or coddle it. Doubt is not a prerequisite for choosing faith; desire to believe is (see Alma 32).

Elder M. Russell Ballard noted, "Those who have become lost and confused, and there are many, are typically those who have most often stopped studying, living, and following the doctrine of Christ. They have stopped praying, worshipping, and studying the scriptures and the words of former and living prophets and apostles. Remember . . . that individuals since the beginning of time have accepted the gospel but they have rejected it later."[15] Continuing, he said,

> In every generation there are those who have partaken of the fruit, but later became ashamed of the gospel. Today is no different. To them and to us, Paul boldly declared, "For I am not ashamed of the gospel of Christ, for it is the power of God unto salvation to everyone that believeth" (Romans 1:16). The Lord needs an army of faithful, dedicated, and loyal disciples who are not ashamed of the gospel of Christ and who are willing to speak and stand up for the doctrine of Christ, including all principles and practices that flow from us as announced by The Church of Jesus Christ of Latter-day Saints—even when the principles and practices are not popular with some who may say they are not currently politically correct. . . . Please remember that public opinion is not God. We must be faithful to Him. Additionally, public opinion is not our judge; God is our judge and He will stand by us.[16]

Elder Jeffrey R. Holland put it this way: "I'm not a very neutral person on this subject [of the gospel]. I am not a good person to talk to about whether someone ought to join the Church or not, or whether someone thinks the Church is true or not, or whether or not someone can put up with the imperfections of the Brethren. I'm not a very good person to talk to about that. My fierce loyalty to the divinity of this work is the loyalty I'll take to my grave. If you could . . . hear the last words these lips will ever express, it will be that this is God's eternal truth. This is the truth: Joseph Smith saw the Father and the Son."[17]

President Gordon B. Hinckley stated the case regarding "doubt" well: "There will be those, perhaps not a few, who with the sophistry of beguiling words and clever design will spread doubt and seek to undermine the foundation on which this cause is established. They will have their brief day in the sun. They may have for a brief season the plaudits of the doubters and the skeptics and the critics. But they will fade and be forgotten as have their kind in the past."[18]

THE SUPPOSED REVELATIONS AND TESTIMONIES OF FALSE PROPHETS AND TEACHERS

It is profoundly sad, simply heart-wrenching, when someone is led astray by the teachings of false prophets. Because there must be opposition in all things, it seems that there is always someone who is claiming an unusual spiritual experience, such as a visitation from, or a vision of, Jesus or the Father, that begins leading others astray (out of the Church). They often write a book and put up a website describing their experience and soon gain followers. People who desire the sensational are often attracted to dramatic descriptions of spiritual experiences and find in these false prophets and teachers claims, things that are more interesting to them than what they hear said in church meetings. This is happening in the Church today; even the very elect are being deceived. They let go of the iron rod and are led into forbidden paths. Beware of anyone operating outside of or in opposition to the authorized leaders of The Church of Jesus Christ of Latter-day Saints. Do not follow them or keep their company in any way. To do otherwise can cost someone his or her eternal life. President Boyd K. Packer said, "Claims of special revelation or secret authority from the Lord or from the Brethren are false on the face of them and really utter nonsense!"[19]

PRESERVING AND REMEMBERING THE SPECIAL WITNESS OF THE APOSTLES

President Gordon B. Hinckley once shared some introspective thoughts (as recorded in an old journal) in a general conference talk. In doing so he shared his love and regard for the aging members of the First Presidency and Twelve that he had been blessed to know during his many years of Church employment. His message concluded, "Time has a way of erasing their memory. Another five years and such names [of influential figures among the Twelve] will be forgotten by all but a few. A man must . . . recognize that his family may remember him, that he may count with the Lord, but beyond that, small will be his monument among the coming generations."[20]

Such reminiscing proves that President Hinckley was a wise and perceptive man. Yet such recognition does not mean that we should let the memory of these apostles and prophets pass away without some effort to preserve that which they counted as more valuable to them than all else—their special witness of the living reality of God and His Son. That testimony is repeatedly and collectively declared by them to be their single greatest possession.

As if to prove the point, following his shared recollections, President Hinckley declared, "I hope that all of you will remember that on this Sabbath day you heard me bear my witness that this is God's holy work. The vision given the Prophet Joseph in the grove of Palmyra was not an imaginary thing. It was real. It occurred in the broad light of day. Both the Father and the Son spoke to the boy. He saw Them standing in the air above him. He heard Their voices. He gave heed to Their instruction. It was the resurrected Lord who was introduced by His Father, the great God of the universe. For the first time in recorded history, both the Father and the Son appeared together to part the curtains and open this, the last and final dispensation, the dispensation of the fulness of times."[21] Perhaps the testimonies related herein can help keep the memory of these Apostles and their special witness alive and strengthen the testimony of others.

My Testimony

Some years ago, I had the privilege of attending the retirement program of a prominent and highly positioned Church employee. It was held in a large room on the twenty-sixth floor of the Church Office Building in downtown Salt Lake City.

As I got off the elevator and walked around a corner and through the large doors that opened into the room, I saw that many chairs had been set up and that the front, left row of chairs was occupied by the entire Quorum of the Twelve Apostles. The only missing member was President Boyd K. Packer, whose poor health likely precluded his attendance. I had supposed that a General Authority or two might attend, but I had not expected what I saw. I soon found a seat four rows behind them. President Dieter F. Uchtdorf was also there representing the First Presidency, as were perhaps half a dozen members of the Seventy, and maybe fifty other invited guests.

An associate of the employee conducted the program, and Elder Bruce D. Porter gave a short speech about the retiree's highly valued service to the Church—some forty-six years in all. Then President Uchtdorf presented the employee with a framed letter of appreciation, signed by the First Presidency. (This is a standard gift to Church employees with the appropriate length of service. What was not standard was who presented it.)

Then the retiree spoke and humbly thanked the Twelve and others for coming and honoring him. He bore a marvelous witness to the high and sacred calling of the Apostles and how the Lord sustained them.

As I sat there, observed, and absorbed this once-in-a-lifetime experience, it seemed to me that a spiritual power radiated throughout the room from those men holding the office and keys of the holy apostleship. I could also hear people around me whispering to each other that they had never been so near the whole Quorum as they were then, and what a treat it was, truly powerful and special. Almost all I could think of was how I needed to live better myself and emulate those men in righteous living.

After President Uchtdorf's presentation and a short speech in which he made a few humorous comments, the Twelve lined up, shook the retiree's hand, and wished him well. I (and others present) waited for them to pass before I got in line. Then they ate some refreshments and left. I will always regard that as one of the sweetest, uplifting experiences of my life, to be in the presence of men who knew the Savior so well and from whom emanated spiritual power and love.

I am no Apostle and never will be, but that fact does not preclude me or anyone else from gaining a strong testimony of the gospel. The very reason that Apostles declare their special witness is to increase faith in Jesus Christ in their hearers. I therefore declare the following: It is my spiritual gift "to believe on their [the Apostles'] words [bearing their special witness]" (D&C 42:14).

Over and over, time and again, as I have found and read or heard the testimonies of God the Father and His son Jesus Christ given by the Apostles, I have had confirmed and reconfirmed to my soul their truth by the power of the Holy Spirit. I have had this experience many times in my life, including while researching and writing this book. I felt many instances of both quiet and more forceful spiritual confirmation, or witness, during its preparation. I know that they, the Apostles, know whereof they speak. I know that many of them have seen and heard, and that all of them are the witnesses they proclaim so forcefully to be. They know Jesus personally. I know the Holy Spirit backs up their declarations of their witness. I have repeatedly felt the joy, edification, and assurance of the Spirit in my heart after hearing or reading their testimonies. I know that God the Father lives, Jesus is the Christ, and that Joseph Smith was their Prophet. I know that the gospel is true and that the keys of the sealing power are with the Church. I know I can repent of my sins and be forgiven. I know that those who die in mortality continue to live beyond the veil.

I want to always be a member of the same church and live the same gospel as the apostles and prophets, for I *know* their witness of Jesus Christ is true.

Notes

1. As quoted in *Teachings of the Prophet Joseph Smith*, comp. Joseph Fielding Smith (Salt Lake City: Deseret Book, 1976), 74.
2. In some cases, the availability of desirable and relevant source material dictated who I was able to write about.
3. Marion G. Romney, in Conference Report, October 1967, 134–37.
4. Boyd K. Packer, "Keeping Confidences" (Church Employees' Lecture Series, January 18, 1980), 5.
5. Boyd K. Packer, *Mine Errand from the Lord* (Salt Lake City: Deseret Book, 2008), 134. Brother Packer also noted, "But I know many, many sacred and important things that have been related to me by others that I will not discuss unless I am privileged to do so under the rule stated above" (ibid., 136).
6. Gordon B. Hinckley, "Seek Ye the Kingdom of God," *Ensign*, May 2006.
7. Packer, "Keeping Confidences," 4.
8. *Amelia Smith McConkie: Remembrances for Her Family*, comp. Mary McConkie Donoho (privately published, 2007), 493–94.
9. As quoted in F. Burton Howard's *Marion G. Romney: His Life and Faith* (Salt Lake City: Bookcraft, 1988), 222.
10. Harold B. Lee, "Be Loyal to the Royal within You" (Brigham Young University devotional, September 11, 1973), 11, speeches.byu.edu.
11. *The Teachings of Harold B. Lee*, ed., Clyde J. Williams (Salt Lake City: Bookcraft, 1996), 636.
12. Packer, *Mine Errand from the Lord*, 458.
13. Having said that, I realize that I myself could herein be accused of doing the same thing: placing apostolic pearls where the unworthy and worldly might find them and mock them. Such is why I have reviewed the explanations given in this introduction.
14. In Conference Report, October 1976, 164.
15. M. Russell Ballard, transcription of an excerpt of an address given at the Provo, Utah, MTC, June 17, 2014, n.p.
16. Ibid.
17. Jeffrey R. Holland, "Leading as the Savior Would Lead" (Leadership Enrichment Series, November 9, 2011), 17.
18. Gordon B. Hinckley, "God Is at the Helm," *Ensign*, May 1994.
19. Boyd K. Packer, "From Such Turn Away," *Ensign*, May 1985.
20. Hinckley, "God Is at the Helm." President Hinckley noted, "I read it only to illustrate the remarkable relationship I had as a young man with members of the First Presidency and the Quorum of the Twelve." Remarkable indeed.
21. Ibid.

PART I
THE APOSTLESHIP

I
THE DOCTRINE OF THE APOSTLESHIP

*"The twelve traveling councilors are called to be the Twelve Apostles,
or special witnesses of the name of Christ in all the world."*

WHAT IS THE APOSTLESHIP?

The apostleship is the highest priesthood office in The Church of Jesus Christ of Latter-day Saints. There are generally fifteen men holding that holy office: three in the First Presidency, and twelve making up the Quorum of the Twelve Apostles. The President of the Church is the senior Apostle and directs the ministries of the others.

When asked what an Apostle is, Elder David A. Bednar offered this definition: "An Apostle is a missionary and a special witness of the name of Christ. The 'name of Christ' refers to the totality of the Savior's mission, death, and Resurrection— His authority, His doctrine, and His unique qualifications as the Son of God to be our Redeemer and our Savior. As special witnesses of the name of Christ, we bear testimony of the reality, divinity, and Resurrection of Jesus Christ, His infinite and eternal Atonement, and His gospel."[1]

Elder Neil L. Andersen enlarged on that basic summary of this office of the priesthood. He said,

This is the Lord's pattern. He calls 15 men from "the ordinary pursuits of life" and endows them with the keys and power to guide and direct us. We are not forced to obey; there is no compulsion. But if we will be attentive to their words, if we will be responsive and willing to change our behavior as the Holy Ghost confirms their counsel, we will not be moved out of our place—meaning we will hold fast to the iron rod and will forever remain safely on the path leading to the tree of life. . . .

Their sure witness of the living Christ is one of the greatest blessings to the Church and to the world. The Lord declared that these men are to be "special witnesses of the name of Christ in all the world" (D&C 107:23). Above all else, their voices are raised in testimony of His divinity and His reality. This witness, born in their discipleship and tempered in their ordination, can have a significant influence on our own feelings.

Their testimonies are expressed simply, allowing the Holy Ghost to carry the witness into our hearts. . . . While these statements are powerful, it is the accompanying spiritual confirmation that burns in our hearts and strengthens us.[2]

This volume concentrates on "their sure witness of the living Christ," how they came to have such a witness, and how they share and bear it to the Church and the world. A priesthood ordination to the specified office with the conferral of keys is necessary, but so also is sufficient experience with the Divine. "I would like . . . to speak as an Apostle of the Lord Jesus Christ," stated Elder Richard G. Scott. "There are fifteen men on earth who hold all of the keys of the kingdom. And it is a constant twenty-four-hour a day recognition of the burden and privilege that that apostolic calling comes, that each one of us feels." Further, he said,

And for me the best way is to bear testimony of truth; to express gratitude for that sacred privilege and honor; and to respond to what is in section 46 of the Doctrine and Covenants, where it says, "To some it is given by the Holy Ghost to know that Jesus is the Son of God; that he was crucified for the sins of the world; for others it is given to believe on their words that they also might have eternal life if they continue faithful." That word *know* is a very important word for those fifteen men who are apostles. The sacred experiences and the confirmation that there is a certainty that our Father in heaven lives and that His son Jesus Christ is our Savior. Not a hope; not a belief; not a wish; but an absolute confirmed certainty. . . . Our Father in heaven is real; His son Jesus Christ is real. I know that personally and bear *certain witness* because I know the Savior.[3]

Ordination to the office of Apostle is often referred to figuratively as a mantle, like unto that upon the Old Testament prophets Elijah and Elisha (see 1 Kings

19:19; 2 Kings 2:8). Elder Bednar explained, "President Boyd K. Packer and I were talking one day when he made a most helpful observation. He said the longer one serves as a member of the Twelve, the weightier the mantle becomes and the more overwhelmed you feel. I think this truth also applies to all Church callings. The longer I serve, the more I see and understand the weight of the calling. Consequently, the responsibility drives me to my knees and requires me to rely upon heavenly help instead of the arm of flesh."[4]

Acknowledging the spiritual reality of the presence of the mantle, Elder D. Todd Christofferson testified, "I know He placed President Monson here as the President. I had a witness of that when President Monson stood to speak for the first time as President of the Church. He stood at that pulpit and I perceived, I think almost saw, the mantle come upon his shoulders as he opened his mouth."[5]

In connection with the apostleship come powers, keys, rights, authorities, and obligations. Faith in Christ is the power. The obligation is to become a special witness and missionary and serve the Lord with "unwearyingness" (see Helaman 10:4–5). The authority is the conferral of the priesthood office and setting apart as a member of the Quorum of the Twelve, which includes the authority to do whatever the President of the Church assigns. The rights are endowments of spiritual power through the gifts of the Spirit, such as enlarged teaching capacity and discernment. The keys are the keys of the priesthood or keys of the kingdom (see below). These are all given at the time of ordination and enable any of the Apostles to become the President of the Church if and when they become the senior Apostle.[6]

THE KEYS OF THE PRIESTHOOD

The keys of the priesthood are the right of presidency or the right to preside in the priesthood.[7] Heavenly messengers, such as John the Baptist (see D&C 13), the ancient Apostles Peter, James, and John, and those ancient prophets who appeared in the Kirtland Temple (see D&C 110), bestowed them upon Joseph Smith and Oliver Cowdery, as explained in the revelations (see D&C 27:12 and 128:20). Needless to say, the keys to act in the authority of the priesthood in all things for the salvation and eternal life of mankind are here. The prophets and apostles hold them in their fulness, as directed by the President of the Church (see D&C 132:7). They are what allows the Church to function orderly and by divine priesthood authority. They permit what is sealed and loosed on earth to be sealed and loosed in the heavens. Along with the gift of the Holy Ghost, the priesthood and keys are what give the Church its "living" status (see D&C 1:30). They are part of the heavenly powers currently operating in the Church. The keys direct missionary work, temple work, and the perfection of the Saints. They also authorize and legitimize all gospel ordinances.

As part of their callings, Apostles are witnesses of the use and operation of the keys of the priesthood. As directed, they call and ordain stake patriarchs and temple sealers. They set apart stake presidents and give them the keys of presidency over their stakes. They dedicate temples, meetinghouses, and countries for the preaching of the gospel—anything the President of the Church assigns them to do. An example of being a witness of the keys operating in the Church is found in the experience of Elder Neil L. Andersen, then a member of the Presidency of the Seventy.

> I would like to conclude with an experience we had in March 2000. Sister Andersen and I were invited to attend the temple dedication in Albuquerque, New Mexico. I knew that I would be asked to speak and that my remarks should be brief.
>
> We entered the celestial room dressed in white. President Hinckley sat in the middle chair with a member of the Twelve on his right and with me on his left. As we reverently awaited the first session, I felt a distinct and specific impression that I should adjust the remarks I had prepared. The impression came: "Speak of the keys. Speak of the keys."
>
> I quickly turned to the scriptures to locate the passages that explain the keys of the priesthood being returned to the earth. Then—and I can remember it as if it were yesterday—a powerful spiritual feeling came into my mind and heart. The feeling that burned within me was this: "He who sits next to you holds all the priesthood keys upon the earth. He who sits next to you holds all the priesthood keys upon the earth."
>
> I took a deep breath. I looked over at President Hinckley. I could not deny the powerful manifestation of the Spirit.[8]

Called to Labor for Life

Because the senior Apostle, by date of setting apart as a member of the Quorum of the Twelve, becomes the President of the Church, those so called remain in that office for life. This means they serve under all conditions incident to mortality. It is a constant, never-ending, (mostly) joyous grind, and they would not do it for riches or fame. "It is not easy to be an Apostle," observed Elder M. Russell Ballard. "It is rigorous work. You would not do it for money. But because we know the Lord, and we know that He lives, we look upon our ministry as the greatest privilege and honor that can come to men to go to the four corners of the earth and witness and testify that Jesus Christ is the Son of God."[9]

TRIED BY THE ADVERSARY

The revealed word says, "Ye receive no witness until after the trial of your faith" (Ether 12:3). This means that before (and after) becoming a special witness, those called to the apostleship are subject to all manner of trials and tribulations, but more especially, the temptations, interference, and opposition of the adversary—the devil. Of him and his followers, Elder Joseph F. Merrill taught this basic Church doctrine: "Another closely related teaching . . . is the personality and actuality of Satan, the devil. He is a real person with a spirit body in the image of man. He is here on earth, accompanied by a multitude of other spirit persons who cooperate with him in his evil work. All who sincerely desire to live righteously and resist temptations to do wrong should keep this fact in mind. All such temptations stem right back to the devil and his host of evil spirits, spirit brothers of ours who because of rebellion were cast out of heaven. They are permitted by the Father to be here as a means of testing us to find if in the exercise of our agency we can prove ourselves worthy to return to his presence."[10] Elder Harold B. Lee talked about how those called to be special witnesses of Jesus Christ come to know of the reality of the devil as they come to know the reality of Jesus.

> It is that [evil] power with which seemingly all men who are called to high ministry are tested. I remember an experience of mine on the day that I was ordained a member of the Council of the Twelve. There was a social held at the home of one of the Brethren. The evening was spent by having each one from President Heber J. Grant right down through the First Presidency and the Quorum of the Twelve relate his experience in coming into the Council of the Twelve—the circumstances surrounding his call, his feelings, his testimony. It was to me a most astounding experience because each speaker was relating my story. If we had changed the names, they were all telling the same story. They all had the same feeling of insufficiency, a feeling that they had to overcome. One of the latest to come into our Council said in bearing his testimony, "I have come during this last week to realize that the power of Satan is a very real power."
>
> The next day after the social above referred to, I met President Grant. He was chuckling a bit to himself, and he said to me, "You know, Brother Lee, it beats everything how the old devil tries to make each one of us feel our insufficiency, our unpreparedness for the work to which we are called."[11]

SPECIAL WITNESSES ARE ELIGIBLE TO BECOME SONS OF PERDITION

In seeking to identify who may know the reality of the living Lord well enough to become a son of perdition, some teachings of the Prophet Joseph Smith are commonly quoted:

All sins shall be forgiven, except the sin against the Holy Ghost; for Jesus will save all except the sons of perdition. What must a man do to commit the unpardonable sin? He must receive the Holy Ghost, have the heavens opened unto him, and know God, and then sin against him. After a man has sinned against the Holy Ghost, there is no repentance for him. He has got to say that the sun does not shine while he sees it; he has got to deny Jesus Christ when the heavens have been opened unto him, and to deny the plan of salvation with his eyes open to the truth of it; and from that time he begins to be an enemy. This is the case with many apostates of the Church of Jesus Christ of Latter-day Saints.[12]

Being ordained to the apostleship is a conferral of priesthood office and authority and does not by itself carry within it sufficient spiritual light and knowledge to become eligible to become a son of perdition. Those who become special witnesses of Jesus Christ, on the other hand, which *is* expected of an Apostle, do become eligible through sin and rebellion to become a son of perdition. The very fact of the receipt of their special witness grants them the requisite portion of spiritual knowledge necessary, that were they to turn against light and truth, apostatize, and fight against the work of the Lord, they would become sons of perdition.

The following approved statement is a summary of a discussion by the Council of the Twelve on this subject: "In order to become a son of perdition a man must know the truth by the Holy Spirit, know it as thoroughly as that the sun shines. Every man in this council is under obligation to know that, and when he turns away, fights the work, persecutes the brethren, puts them to death or any kind of abuse, he has turned against the church, against the work, against his priesthood, and when he goes out and denies the faith, then there is nothing that can be done. He becomes a son of perdition. He, of course, loses everything."[13]

Special Witnesses Make Their Calling and Election Sure

The Prophet Joseph Smith taught that caution should be exercised when making suppositions about receiving eternal life as a result of receiving great revelations—the one does not automatically follow the other.

Notwithstanding the apostle exhorts them to add to their faith, virtue, knowledge, temperance, &c., yet he exhorts them to make their calling and election sure. And though they had heard an audible voice from heaven bearing testimony that Jesus was the Son of God, yet he says we have a more sure word of prophecy, whereunto ye do well that ye take heed as unto a light shining in a dark place. Now, wherein could they have a more sure word of prophecy than to hear the voice of God saying, This is my beloved Son, &c.

Now for the secret and grand key. Though they might hear the voice of God and know that Jesus was the Son of God, this would be no evidence that their election and calling was made sure, that they had part with Christ, and were joint heirs with Him. They then would want that more sure word of prophecy, that they were sealed in the heavens and had the promise of eternal life in the kingdom of God.[14]

So while receiving great revelations and visions and manifestations does not guarantee eternal life, it does indicate that the one so blessed is on the right path toward eternal life, and in most cases they will indeed inherit exaltation. Comparatively few are the exceptions to this generality. The more sure word of prophecy, or personal revelation of receiving eternal life comes into effect. Elder Harold B. Lee taught,

Now, what is the spirit of prophecy? The spirit of prophecy is the light of revelation by the power of the Holy Ghost, which reveals it to us. We can receive, and we can know. Brother Charles A. Callis of the Quorum of the Twelve, in a letter that he wrote just before his death and a copy of which came into my hands, made reference to that very thing. He said, "The greatest thrilling experience that you and I can ever have will be on those occasions when deep down in our hearts we receive the witness that our acts and our labors are approved by our Heavenly Father."

To have that witness and that assurance by that power, that we are sealed up unto eternal life, when we have lived our lives and have kept the faith through to the end, will be that which will take us home to the God who gave us life with an assurance and with a joy that can hardly be expressed.[15]

It is true that exceptions to this generality can be found in the history of the Church. In most cases, however, those who serve as special witnesses of Jesus Christ will continue so serving and testifying to the end of their mortal lives, and will thereafter go on to eternal reward, having received *all* of the ordinances of the house of the Lord. The majority of the Apostles of this dispensation had or have their calling and election made sure and are sealed up unto eternal life. This is another reason they become such a force for good for the Church and in the world.

APOSTOLIC BLESSINGS

Apostles have the authority to give special blessings to groups, congregations, and individuals. These are not the same as priesthood administrations on the sick and afflicted. These blessings can be given verbally over the pulpit, or by the laying on of hands, and are done in the authority of the apostleship. They are not for the world or the worldly, but are meant to bless and strengthen and uphold the faithful and righteous in their service toward God and their fellow men and women.[16]

As he concluded a powerful address to teachers in the Church Educational System in 1999, Elder Jeffrey R. Holland took occasion to leave an apostolic blessing on the congregation. On that special occasion, he said,

> I had not thought to do this, but now feel I should. I have read everything I know to read about the apostleship. I have a lot more to learn, but as near as I can tell Apostles are to teach the gospel, bear witness of the name of Christ in all the world, and bless. Because I don't know that I will ever be in a setting with all of you again, I would like to conclude my witness, and some teaching of the gospel, with a brief blessing. And I do so in the name of the Lord Jesus Christ and by the apostolic commission that . . . I have humbly received. . . .
>
> I had not thought to do this; it is a sensitive matter and we don't do it very often. I leave this blessing with you, not through any right or authority of my own but in the name of the Lord Jesus Christ for His glory and goodness, for the kingdom of God and His grace upon the earth. We do so to that end, for that purpose, for that glory and greatness that is His alone. From blessings we can learn much. We learn more than any other thing the goodness of God—the love, the mercy, the grace, and the compassion of God. We may fail Him, but He will never, worlds without end, fail us. Of that I am certain, and of that I bear witness.[17]

Elder Holland then went on to leave a marvelous blessing on the gospel teachers present. These blessings are not advertised before the world (that would mock them) and are only given as the Spirit prompts the Apostle. Therefore, there is no way to quantify how often they have been and are given, nor to whom. They are sacred and available because of the keys of the apostleship, where those holding His authority invoke the Lord's power.

As an example, in 2006, President James E. Faust gave an apostolic blessing to assembled students of the Church Educational System. On this occasion, he said,

> I would like to invoke upon each of you an apostolic blessing, you wonderful young people, you people of promise, and I pray that you will prepare yourselves for your great destiny, that you will stay close to the principles of righteousness and truth, and that you will be guided by the Holy Spirit with the promise you know of the Holy Ghost, that by and through that power you shall know the truth of all things. What greater promise to a student than that—to enjoy the

companionship of the Holy Ghost? I invoke that blessing upon you and pray that our Heavenly Father will watch over you in all of your comings and goings and guide your footsteps in paths of truth and righteousness, that you will be wise beyond your years, and that you will be sensitive to your great destiny and your great promise. I leave this testimony with you and invoke these blessings upon you in the name of the Lord Jesus Christ, amen.[18]

Another example is a blessing (and testimony) given by Elder Richard G. Scott to Church employees.

I would like to exercise a privilege that comes with the honor and responsibility of being one of the Apostles of the Lord, who has the privilege of holding the keys of the kingdom. I know that in and of myself I am not very significant. But I've come to recognize that the Lord does honor the keys of the apostleship He's given 15 of His children. And because of that I would like to exercise those keys in your behalf and invoke a blessing upon you—a blessing of prompting of the Spirit in your professional activities, but beyond that a blessing in your homes, in your personal lives, and for those of you who have companions in your life, with your partner. As you ponder and pray about it, you can identify those things that the Lord feels well about in your life. Things that you're doing well that you often don't give yourself credit for. And simultaneously a feeling of prompting where there are matters that you can strengthen so that you're aware of them and can take that action to be even better.

I don't know if I'll have the chance to be with some of you again. But I would like to leave my testimony. I know that the Church is the Church of Jesus Christ. I feel that through a lot of pondering and prayer I've come to understand the cry that was offered by the Savior just before He laid His life down on the cross, where He said, "My God, my God, why hast thou forsaken me?" (Matthew 25:46). I don't believe the Father ever forsook His Son. That comment may have hurt temporarily the Father's feelings, but what He had done was to remove support the Savior had always enjoyed so that the Atonement could have been wrought totally, completely, fully by reason of the effort of His Beloved Son without additional support from the Father.

I love them both. And I humbly bear witness that They live. They guide the work of The Church of Jesus Christ of Latter-day Saints throughout the world. I know that.[19]

One wonders if one purpose of such a blessing on the true and faithful is for the Apostle to do all in his power to assist those so blessed in sealing them up unto eternal life. Certainly such a blessing in the lives of those striving to live righteously with all their might, mind, and strength would be a great comfort and boon in their efforts, and would do much to help thwart the evil designs of the adversary against them.

THE SEVENTY

The Seventy are also designated by revelation as "especial witnesses" in their ministry (see D&C 107:25). They serve under the direction of the Twelve and are expected to be able to know and testify with power and complete assurance that Jesus is the Christ and lives today. They are commissioned to teach all other essential gospel truths, in concert with their apostolic associates. Various matters relating to the Seventy have evolved somewhat over the decades, and an early precursor to the office was that of Assistant to the Quorum of the Twelve, occasionally referred to herein; however, the duties of the Seventy are not the focus of this work.[20]

NOTES

1. David A. Bednar, "Special Witnesses of the Name of Christ" (*The Religious Educator*, 12:2, 2011), 2; see also at BYU Religious Studies Center, rsc.byu.edu.
2. Neil L. Andersen, "Hold Fast to the Words of the Prophets" (Brigham Young University devotional, March 4, 2007), 3–4, speeches.byu.edu.
3. "Elder Richard G. Scott and daughter Linda Mickle" (excerpt transcribed by author), mormonchannel.org.
4. Bednar, "Special Witnesses of the Name of Christ," 2.
5. D. Todd Christofferson, "The Journey to Lead like the Savior" (Leadership Enrichment Series, November 6, 2013), 16–17.
6. An excellent review of the responsibilities and doctrine of the apostleship is found in Edward J. Brandt, "And He Gave Some, Apostles" (Eph. 4:11), *Ensign*, July 1999. Another fine piece is Joseph Fielding Smith, "The Twelve Apostles" also titled "The Quorum of the Twelve Apostles" (address to seminary and institute faculty, given at Brigham Young University, June 18, 1958); hard copy in author's possession; audio version available at speeches.byu.edu.
   President Gordon B. Hinckley's discussion is also superb, see "Special Witnesses for Christ," *Ensign*, May 1984.
7. See, for example, Bruce R. McConkie, "The Keys of the Kingdom," *Ensign*, May 1983.
8. Andersen, "Hold Fast to the Words of the Prophets," 8.
9. M. Russell Ballard, "You Are Important to the Lord" (LDSSA fireside, April 28, 1990), 18–19; copy in author's possession.
10. Joseph F. Merrill, in Conference Report, April 1947, 132–37.

11. Harold B. Lee, "Satan a Reality" (lecture given to seminary and institute teachers at Brigham Young University, July 9, 1954); see *CES Summer School Talks, 1954 & 1958*, 244.

12. Joseph Smith Jr., *Teachings of the Prophet Joseph Smith*, comp. Joseph Fielding Smith (Salt Lake City: Deseret Book, 1976), 358.

13. Harold B. Lee, "Questions and Answers (I)" (lecture given to seminary and institute teachers at Brigham Young University, June 17, 1954); see *CES Summer School Talks, 1954 & 1958*, 115.

14. Wilford Woodruff journal, May 14, 1843; see rsc-dev.byu.edu.

15. Harold B. Lee, "The Godhead" (lecture given to seminary and institute teachers at Brigham Young University, June 17, 1954), 13–14; hard copy in author's possession. See also Bruce R. McConkie, *A New Witness for the Articles of Faith* (Salt Lake City: Deseret Book, 1985), 498–99.

16. In 2016, Elder Ronald A. Rasband of the Quorum of the Twelve stated that he was prompted to give an apostolic blessing to Latter-day Saints in Ecuador that had been sorely afflicted by a powerful earthquake. Of that occasion: "It was as if my hands were on their heads," he said. "All the words came to my mind at that moment." As quoted in "Elder Rasband Offers Apostolic Blessing to Quake-Weary Ecuadorians," *Church News*, June 24, 2016; see lds.org/church/news.

17. Jeffrey R. Holland, "Our Consuming Mission" (address to Church Educational System religious educators, February 5, 1999), 8–9.

18. James E. Faust, "Beginnings" (Church Educational System fireside for young adults, May 7, 2006), 4; a video presentation is found at lds.org/broadcasts.

19. Richard G. Scott, "Act under the Direction of the Spirit" (Leadership Enrichment Series, February 23, 2011), 16.

20. For those desiring further information about the office and duties of the Seventy, see "The Twelve and the Seventy, Part One: Revelation and the Role of the Seventy," as found on the Church's website at lds.org.

2

THE APOSTOLIC CHARGE

"Never cease striving until you have seen God face to face."

It is not our purpose to give an exhaustive historical treatise on what is known as the charge to the original Twelve. Instead, we only seek to call attention to some items associated with that charge, and also to take note of how elements of the charge have been given in succeeding decades.

In February 1835, at Kirtland, Ohio, the Prophet Joseph Smith appointed a meeting of the members of what was known as Zion's Camp and other elders and members. The purpose of this meeting was to call the Twelve Apostles from among the elders of the Church. The revelation (D&C 18:37–39) designated that Oliver Cowdery and David Whitmer should receive the inspiration of whom to call, and twelve men were then chosen to be ordained the members of the Quorum of the Twelve.

Of this seminal moment in Church history, President Gordon B. Hinckley said, "Following the organization of the first Quorum of the Twelve in 1835, Oliver Cowdery, counselor in the First Presidency, delivered a charge to these men. That statement has become something of a charter for all members of the Twelve who have succeeded that first group."[1]

Among the many things Oliver Cowdery said to the original Twelve on that occasion is the following:

The Lord gave us a revelation that, in process of time, there should be twelve men chosen to preach His Gospel to Jew and Gentile. Our minds have been on a constant stretch, to find who these twelve were; when the time should come we could not tell; but we sought the Lord by fasting and prayer to have our lives prolonged to see this day, to see you, and to take a retrospect of the difficulties through which we have passed; but having seen the day, it becomes my duty to deliver to you a charge. . . .

You have been indebted to other men, in the first instance, for evidence; on that you have acted; but it is necessary that you receive a testimony from heaven for yourselves; so that you can bear testimony to the truth of the Book of Mormon, and that you have seen the face of God. That is more than the testimony of an angel. When the proper time arrives, you shall be able to bear this testimony to the world. When you bear testimony that you have seen God, this testimony God will never suffer to fall, but will bear you out; although many will not give heed, yet others will. You will therefore see the necessity of getting this testimony from heaven.

Never cease striving until you have seen God face to face. Strengthen your faith; cast off your doubts, your sins, and all your unbelief; and nothing can prevent you from coming to God. Your ordination is not full and complete till God has laid His hand upon you. We require as much to qualify us as did those who have gone before us; God is the same. If the Savior in former days laid His hands upon His disciples, why not in latter days?

With regard to superiority, I must make a few remarks. The ancient apostles sought to be great; but lest the seeds of discord be sown in this matter; understand particularly the voice of the Spirit on this occasion. God does not love you better or more than others. You are to contend for the faith once delivered to the saints. Jacob, you know, wrestled till he had obtained. It was by fervent prayer and diligent search that you have obtained the testimony you are now able to bear. You are as one; you are equal in bearing the keys of the Kingdom to all nations. You are called to preach the Gospel of the Son of God to the nations of the earth; it is the will of your heavenly Father, that you proclaim His Gospel to the ends of the earth and the islands of the sea.[2]

Oliver's charge touched on the keys and power of the office, upon preaching the gospel, enduring persecution, exercising faith, and saving souls. But as seen, it also covered the instruction to become special witnesses of Jesus Christ, to strive to see the face of God, to behold the personage of the Lord Jesus Christ, and for Him to lay His hands on them. Perhaps only the Twelve themselves can comprehend the full meaning of these expressions as they purify themselves and approach the sacred throne in humility and mighty faith.

In a follow-up meeting held at the Prophet's home, he asked those of the Twelve there assembled in what way their calling differed from that of other officers in the Church. After some discussion, Joseph pronounced the following: "They are the Twelve Apostles, who are called to the office of the Traveling High Council, who are to preside over the churches of the Saints, among the Gentiles, where there is a presidency established; and they are to travel and preach among the Gentiles, until the Lord shall command them to go to the Jews. They are to hold the keys of this ministry, to unlock the door of the Kingdom of heaven unto all nations, and to preach the Gospel to every creature. This is the power, authority, and virtue of their apostleship."[3] Section 107 of the Doctrine and Covenants contains further revealed instructions to the Twelve.

Members of the Quorum of the Twelve are to familiarize themselves with Oliver Cowdery's charge, with the instructions of the Prophet, and with that found in ancient and modern revelation. Yet, as the many decades have passed, each new member of the Twelve has received a reaffirming charge at the time of his ordination. This charge is usually given by a member of the First Presidency but has occasionally also been given or added to by the President of the Twelve.

We are not privy to the content of the instructions currently given to new members of the Twelve today, but scattered throughout historical sources is enough information to comfortably concur on several elements that have historically made up the apostolic charge. One element is that the Apostles must give up worldly ambitions and consecrate all their time, talents, and resources to fulfilling their calling. They leave behind businesses and their professions to spend their full time in the ministry.[4] Another is that they are expected to fully and freely express their own personal thinking and opinions in council during deliberations, but if, and when, the Council comes to consensus, they are to become of one mind with that decision. They should not hold out against the others or try to persuade others to their viewpoints. There is no lobbying for another course or decision after one has been decided.

Finally, the charge includes the fact that members of the Quorum of the Twelve are expected to become special witnesses of Jesus Christ, including all that entails. In some of the earlier apostolic charges on record, this meant that the Apostle was expected to strive until he prevailed and saw Jesus face to face, whether by dream, vision, or personal appearance. At other times this point has not been stressed or mentioned. It is not known, by this author at least, whether this issue (of striving to see the face of Jesus) is specifically addressed at the time of the ordination of today's Apostles. It is known, however, that some of today's Apostles have indicated that they have seen Him. (See chapter 17 of this volume, "Other Prophets' and Apostles' Special Witnesses of Jesus Christ" for examples.)

In 1889, at the time that three new members of the Quorum of the Twelve were called by President Wilford Woodruff, one of them recorded a highly condensed summary of what was said to them in their charge: "At 3 p.m. I attended a meeting of the Twelve . . . where Bros. Merrill, Lund and myself [Abraham H. Cannon] were set apart as Apostles in the order named. Pres. Woodruff set apart the first, Father [George Q. Cannon] the second and Bro. Joseph F. Smith myself. Our charge was first given us by Father at Pres. Woodruff's instance. The importance of our callings was portrayed, and our privileges were named. Among these were the privileges of having the ministration of angels, and of seeing the Savior Himself; of hearing the voice of God as audibly as we hear a man's voice; of continually being under the direction of the Holy Ghost; of being prophets and revelators; and of many other things."[5]

In 1892, Lorenzo Snow, President of the Quorum of the Twelve at the time, while speaking to the Quorum of the Twelve, stated, "It is the privilege of you brethren to see the Savior, and thus testify of Him, and that you know He lives."[6]

In 1897, in a meeting of the Twelve, "President Joseph F. Smith made some remarks on the calling of an Apostle, which he said required a man to lay aside everything of a temporal character and hold himself ready to respond to any call which might be made upon him. He was to be a special witness of the Gospel and of the Lord Jesus Christ. He must have a witness for himself that Jesus is the Christ, and that he committed the dispensation of the fulness of times to the Prophet Joseph Smith, and be ready to bear that testimony to all mankind. He should not engage in anything that would interfere with these duties without permission from the proper authority."[7]

According to Elder Heber J. Grant, in a Quorum meeting in 1899, the Quorum President Franklin D. Richards said, "If we are faithful, sooner or later we will see the face of the Savior."[8]

In 1899, a new member of the Council of the Twelve noted that he "had earnestly prayed for the gift of faithfulness and wisdom." He then stated that "One of the brethren of this Quorum had said unless a man had seen the face of the Savior he was not worthy of being a special witness of Jesus Christ. [He] Bore strong testimony of his knowledge of God, Jesus Christ and that Joseph Smith was a Prophet. Although he had not seen the face of the Savior, he had seen the Prophet Joseph Smith."[9] Evidently there had been some internal Quorum discussion regarding this matter at that time, and some thoughts had been expressed.

In 1898, at the time of the ordination of Elder Rudger Clawson as an Apostle, all three members of the First Presidency spoke. These statements constitute a fine example of the charge and are therefore given in full.

President Lorenzo Snow delivered the following charge to Brother Rudger Clawson: "A few words I want to say as to the obligations you are placed under now that you have received the Apostleship. The Lord will reveal unto you according to your faithfulness and the circumstances and the duties that will be required of you. You must understand that it is not man that has chosen you; it is not the wisdom of man that has selected you. If it had been man that selected you, or the wisdom of man, there would be a possibility of a failure in the future, and you would not be so well satisfied if you understood that you had been selected by a Council that talked over this matter in a common way, as we generally talk over matters of lesser importance. But you have been chosen because the Lord wanted you to fill this place and because of your faithfulness in the past. You have been placed in circumstances that have been very tempting to you to depart a little from the path of wisdom, and you have resisted those temptations, and you have kept in the path of truth and righteousness, just where the Lord wanted you to keep. You have been wonderfully blessed. I do not know of any young man that has been called to positions like you have been, or any other important positions that the Lord has blessed any more than he has blessed you. It seems that almost every effort you have made has been a success. You were willing to go to the penitentiary for nearly three years, I think. (3 yrs., 1 mo., 10 days.) You had the opportunity of escaping that if you had been pleased to have done so; but you performed your duty under those circumstances acceptably to the Lord and pleasing to your brethren. And now you have been appointed of the Lord to a high and holy calling. Your success depends entirely upon yourself. There is no man that lives and no impediment that you can get into your path, but will be removed, and you will go right along, providing that you preserve your humility, and your meekness, and lowliness, as you have done in the past. Do not think of yourself when important duties are to be performed wherein perhaps there might be advantages to yourself, but think of what the Lord requires of you; think of the good that will be accomplished to others without reference to yourself at all. In this way you can go on and your faith will be increased.

"You are now, of course, the youngest of the Apostles, so far as coming into the quorum is concerned. There are many of this Quorum that have been in this relation to the Church, as apostles, for a great many years, and have had a long experience, and the Lord has blessed them wonderfully. You must not expect that at once you can feel yourself at home and be equal with them in that knowledge which they have obtained through perseverance and a long movement in the path of duty; that you can be as wise and prudent as they, their experience having given them the right to blessings that have been very great to them in the line pertaining to their duties. You will, of course, not feel it your duty to take up all the time, but to let others speak. Let those who have had long experience speak when it comes to matters of high importance and you listen. Do not occupy too much time at first. Wait until you have had the experience and get the wisdom and the understanding the Lord has given to them and will give to you.

"Now, Brother Clawson, we are glad to receive you. President Richards, who is President of the Quorum of the Twelve, is glad to receive you, and all the brethren of the Quorum welcome you to the Quorum with their whole hearts. The more they get acquainted with you, Brother Clawson, the more they will love you; and the more you get acquainted with the brethren, the more you will love them. Move along slowly and pause as you make your steps along; and the Lord will be with you. He will be your leader, and His Spirit will suggest how you should act under the circumstances that may surround you.

"Now, we all feel, Brother Clawson—I speak in the name of my Counselors and the brethren of the Twelve—we all feel to welcome you with all our hearts. God bless you."

President Joseph F. Smith said, "There is one principle that I would like to have presented to Brother Clawson. Perhaps, Prest. Snow, it may not be my place to do that, but as it did not come to your mind, I thought I would like to mention this fact, that one of the great callings and special duties of the Apostles is to become a living witness of the Lord Jesus Christ; to know Him and to be able to testify that He is the Son of God and the Savior of the world. That is essential to the calling of an Apostle of Jesus Christ.

"Another principle is, that the Apostles must acknowledge the order and organization of the Priesthood and the united counsels of the leading presiding quorums of the Priesthood as supreme above his own judgment, his own predilections, choice, or desires, no matter how strong his predilections, desires, or choice may be. All the Apostles and all those holding the Priesthood, especially in the Council of the Apostles and of the First Presidency, we must covenant and agree before God, angels, and men, and with each other, that we will acknowledge this organization that God has instituted as His supreme authority on earth. We must do that in order to preserve the integrity of the work of the Lord and of the organization of the Holy Priesthood. This is one thing that Brother Clawson, as well as each of us, must accede to in order to obtain the spirit of the Apostleship."

President George Q. Cannon: "I would like Brother Rudger Clawson to understand, when he takes upon himself this ministry, that it is the first and most important thing, that he should not set this aside to attend to anything else. His whole life, and all that pertains to his power of life, his talents, and everything should be devoted exclusively to the Apostleship and everything else should be entirely subordinate to that."[10]

At the ordination of Elder George F. Richards as a new member of the Twelve, he noted in his journal that President Smith said, "The Twelve are the Special witnesses of Jesus Christ and should be able to testify that he lives even as if he had been seen by them."[11]

When President Smith called his son, Joseph Fielding Smith, to the Quorum of the Twelve, as part of his charge to his son, he said,

> I merely wish to say in addition to what President Francis M. Lyman has said, (which I endorse thoroughly) that this body of men, this Council of Presidency and Apostles, compose the living constitution of the Church, with power to legislate, judge and decide. A decision rendered here, though it may not meet exactly the mind of an individual member or individual members, will represent of course the mind of the majority, and it therefore becomes binding on each member of the Council, and not one of us can with impunity oppose it or in anywise, directly or indirectly, speak derogatory to it, as to do so would be a transgression, in spirit at least, of the covenant we enter into with the Lord in this Council. I regard this as one of the most sacred obligations resting upon the Presidency and Twelve. We are united here in the bonds of the new and everlasting covenant. We represent the government of the holy priesthood, and besides, we are the special witnesses of Jesus Christ, also of Joseph Smith, and of the divinity of this great Latter-day work.[12]

Contemporary records are not available to give specifics of what is said to new Apostles entering the Quorum of the Twelve today. One might speculate that the essentials of the above related items of counsel remain in place. Some modern Apostles have indicated that they do indeed still receive a charge at the time of their ordination (such as that stated by President Hinckley above), containing instructions regarding their new responsibilities. Because of the scriptural requirements, we can feel assured that the charge to become a special witness, by revelation, will always be given to new Apostles. The specifics of what is said today will remain unknown unless shared by one so called.

Notes

1. Gordon B. Hinckley, *Faith: The Essence of True Religion* (Salt Lake City: Deseret Book, 1989), 51.
2. Joseph Smith Jr., *History of The Church of Jesus Christ of Latter-day Saints* (Salt Lake City: The Church of Jesus Christ of Latter-day Saints, 1932–51), 2:196–98.
3. Joseph Smith, *History of The Church of Jesus Christ of Latter-day Saints*, ed. B. H. Roberts, 2d ed. rev., 7 vols. (Salt Lake City: The Church of Jesus Christ of Latter-day Saints, 1932–51), 2:200.

4. This has not always been the case. In earlier years, the Apostles were expected to support themselves and their families while also performing their duties. As the Church grew, and the demands on the Apostles' time increased, self-support was no longer a possibility, and a "living allowance" was implemented in President John Taylor's day for those of the Twelve who needed it. Today, all General Authorities that are not independently wealthy are given this allowance so they may give their full time to the ministry.

5. As quoted in Dennis B. Horne's *An Apostle's Record: The Journals of Abraham H. Cannon* (Clearfield, Utah: Gnolaum Books, 2004), 99–100 (October 7, 1889).

6. Ibid., 239 (April 1, 1892).

7. Joseph F. Smith, October 7, 1897; see Journal History of the Church, Church History Library, history.lds.org.

8. Heber J. Grant journal, January 11, 1899.

9. Words quoted are those of Abraham Owen Woodruff, son of Wilford Woodruff, as quoted in Heber J. Grant's journal, January 11, 1899.

10. Rudger Clawson journal, October 10, 1898, in *A Ministry of Meetings: The Apostolic Diaries of Rudger Clawson*, ed., Stan Larson (Salt Lake City: Signature Books and Smith Research Associates, 1993), 5.

11. George F. Richards journal, October 6, 1907.

12. As quoted from "Instructions Given to Elder Joseph Fielding Smith Jr., at the Salt Lake Temple, April 7th, 1910, Immediately Prior to His Receiving Ordination as an Apostle," April 7, 1910.

3

TEACHINGS ABOUT WHETHER A MODERN APOSTLE MUST SEE THE SAVIOR

*"The days will come that you shall see him; for he will
unveil his face unto you, and it shall be in his own time,
and in his own way, and according to his own will."*

—D&C 88:68

The question is often asked by curious members of the Church (and even by some outside it) whether apostles and prophets of this dispensation have seen the resurrected Lord Jesus Christ. This chapter cannot fully answer that inquiry, but it does present some reliable information examining the question. As to asking individual living Apostles whether they have received such a transcendent blessing, the counsel to members is to refrain and respect the personal sacredness of the matter. This is especially wise counsel in the Internet age, where the sacred can be so easily sullied.

THE STATEMENTS OF PRESIDENTS SMITH AND MOYLE

Joseph Fielding Smith and Henry D. Moyle are two members of the Quorum of the Twelve who taught that it was not necessary for an Apostle to see the Savior in vision or to receive a personal appearance from Him. President Joseph Fielding Smith, in a lecture given to religious educators, taught,

Let us consider briefly the great responsibilities, which devolve upon the Apostles. They are special witnesses for Jesus Christ. It is their right to know the truth and have an abiding witness, and this is an exacting duty upon them, to know that Jesus Christ is in very deed the Only Begotten Son of God, the Redeemer of the world, and the Savior of all those who will confess their sins, repent, and keep His commandments. The question frequently arises: Is it necessary for a member of the Council of the Twelve to see the Savior in order to be an Apostle? It is their privilege to see Him if occasion requires, but the Lord has taught that there is a stronger witness than seeing a personage, even of the Son of God, in a vision. I wish we could get this clear in the minds of members of the Church. The Savior said:

"Wherefore I say unto you, All manner of sin and blasphemy shall be forgiven unto men: but the blasphemy against the Holy Ghost shall not be forgiven unto men.

"And whosoever speaketh a word against the Son of man, it shall be forgiven him: but whosoever speaketh against the Holy Ghost, it shall not be forgiven him, neither in this world, neither in the world to come" (Matthew 12:31–32).

Therefore the seeing, even the Savior, does not leave as deep an impression in the mind as does the testimony of the Holy Ghost to the spirit. Both Peter and Paul understood this. Here are the words of Paul:

"For it is impossible for those who were once enlightened, and have tasted of the heavenly gift, and were made partakers of the Holy Ghost,

"And have tasted the good word of God, and the powers of the world to come,

"If they shall fall away, to renew them again unto repentance; seeing they crucify to themselves the Son of God afresh, and put him to an open shame" (Hebrews 6:4–6).

What is the lesson to be learned from this? That the impressions on the soul that come from the Holy Ghost are far more significant than a vision. It is where Spirit speaks to spirit, and the imprint upon the soul is far more difficult to erase. Every member of the Church should have the impressions on his soul made by the Holy Ghost that Jesus is the Son of God indelibly pictured so that they cannot be forgotten. We read that it is the Spirit that giveth life.[1]

Several years earlier this question had come up during a stake conference attended by President Joseph Fielding Smith. He then gave a statement on the matter to the Quorum of the Twelve, directly addressing the doctrine. It is similar to the above quotation, but adds further explanation and commentary. Elder Henry D. Moyle read to Church religious educators the statement that President Smith made to the Twelve.

At this point the statement of President Joseph Fielding Smith is pertinent. This is a statement that he made to the Twelve this year in January 1954:

"We are special witnesses, called to bear witness to the life and mission of our Redeemer.

"There are people in the Church—a few, I suppose; I have heard of some of them—who raise a question about our worthiness to act in these callings. They hold to the view, which is held to some extent in the Protestant world, that men cannot be special witnesses and Apostles of Jesus Christ who have not seen Him. I remember one time at a stake conference when a good brother was called on to speak and he made this statement. I think his remarks were aimed at me and most of the other Brethren who were in this Council at that time. He said that there was only one member of the Council of the Twelve who was qualified to be an Apostle, and that was Elder Ballard, because he had seen the Lord. So the rest of the Council were counted out. Of course I had the opportunity to follow this brother and make some remarks and correct this statement.

"When I spoke I read the words of our Savior as recorded in Matthew, chapter 12, verses 31 and 32. They are as follows:

" 'Wherefore I say unto you, All manner of sin and blasphemy shall be forgiven unto men: but the blasphemy against the Holy Ghost shall not be forgiven unto men.

" 'And whosoever speaketh a word against the Son of man, it shall be forgiven him: but whosoever speaketh against the Holy Ghost, it shall not be forgiven him, neither in this world, neither in the world to come.'

"I impressed upon the minds of that congregation that there was a witness far greater than seeing the Lord. A man might see Him in a vision and turn away, deny Him, and sin against His name, but for him, should he truly repent, there would be forgiveness. But denial of Jesus Christ and the blasphemy against the Holy Ghost, after a man had received that testimony of the Spirit, could not be forgiven in this world, neither in the world to come. The assurance that comes from the Spirit, which penetrates the soul and gives the assurance that Jesus Christ is the Son of God and our Redeemer, is more powerful and penetrating than a vision, which may be seen and then in course of time be forgotten. Then I asked the congregation which was the greater—the testimony of seeing, where the vision in course of time becomes dim, or to receive the penetrating influence of the Spirit of God, which penetrates the soul, constantly reassuring.

"Every member of the Council of the Twelve, I feel sure, could testify by the power of the Holy Ghost that Jesus Christ is the Redeemer of the world, and in order to be an Apostle, with all the power and authority and knowledge necessary, did not depend upon having a vision, but it did depend upon the testimony that comes from the source of testimony—the third member of the Godhead. I think I have made my point clear, and this is the fact. Paul has written if a man receives a testimony of the Spirit and then falls away, he cannot be renewed [see Hebrews 6:4–6], and Peter bears similar testimony [see 2 Peter 2:20–22].

"This is the testimony which burns into your very soul which, when it is received, one cannot turn away and put Christ to open shame without receiving this extreme penalty. The testimony of the Holy Ghost is Spirit speaking to spirit, and it is not confined solely to the natural, or physical, senses."[2]

In considering this information, it might be well to remember that although Elder Melvin J. Ballard may have been the only Apostle of that day to publicly share how he received his special witness of the Savior (as described in chapter 13), this does not necessarily mean that others of the Twelve had not received a similar blessing. It's possible that they received it but had not spoken in public about it. They may not have been authorized by the Spirit to speak of it either publicly or privately. The brother mentioned would have no way of knowing and could not state it as fact, nor can we. (Further information about President Joseph Fielding Smith's teachings and views on this question can be found in chapter 10.)

Having finished reading the statement of President Smith to the Twelve, President Moyle went on to give a statement of his own on the question, which harmonized with those of President Smith.

I want to bear witness of my own knowledge that this statement of Brother Smith's is true, and that there is this greater witness that comes into our hearts, a witness that we can no more deny than we can deny that which is absolutely fresh in our mind. It is a witness that continues with us every day of our ministry, regardless of where we are or to whom we bear witness to the truth. . . .

And when that gift comes to us, my brethren and sisters, we do not need any further witness. We have received the highest possible witness that can be given to man from God. . . .

We have a testimony; we who are witnesses have no need of witnesses. Thus should we be qualified for our work in the Church, and I tell you, brothers and sisters, there are others who have not seen the Savior but know that He lives and that He is the Redeemer of mankind. . . .

Now I want to say to you that as I have gone along here today, I have endeavored to bear my testimony to you. I rejoice in the call which has come to me. I have always felt, and I hope that I shall always feel, humble in it. It has been my purpose since this call came to me to serve. I have not wanted to ask anything of anybody. I have just wanted to give. I have felt that there was no service to which man could be called higher than to preach the gospel. There is no work that pertains to the office of a member of the Quorum of the Twelve that is higher than to bear witness to the world that God lives and that the gospel of Jesus Christ has been restored. . . .

Some of us wander over the earth, and sometimes we begin to wonder what need we have of a home or a place to lay our heads, because wherever we go there seems to be some provision made for us. The Lord provides for us, gives us all that we need, and I am sure that we magnify our callings in no higher respect or regard than we do as we go out and fill these assignments throughout the Church and throughout the world and give all that we have and are to the service of the Lord. I know that as this call came to me, there came a witness of the Holy Ghost that I had never possessed before, a change that sometimes I feel was physical as well as spiritual. . . .

I have been given to know that God lives and that Jesus is the Christ, to the point where no vision, no revelation, no divine manifestation could in anywise, as I feel today, add to the assurance that I have in my being that Jesus Christ is the Son of God and that He and the Father appeared to Joseph Smith, and through divine manifestations of the servants of God, he received the keys of the dispensation of the fulness of times.[3]

President Harold B. Lee's teachings on this issue reflected the same line of thought. He stated,

When I came to this position as a member of the Quorum of the Twelve, I was told that my chief responsibility now was to bear testimony of the divine mission of the Lord and Savior of the world. That was almost a crushing realization of what it meant to be a member of the Quorum of the Twelve Apostles. I was assigned to give the Easter talk the Sunday night following the general conference. As I locked myself in one of the rooms of the Church Office Building [Church Administration Building], I took out my Bible and read from the four Gospels the life of the Master, particularly leading down to his Crucifixion and Resurrection. And as I read, I became aware that something different was happening. It no longer was just a story of the doings of the Master, but I realized that I was having an awareness of something I had not had before. It seemed that I was reliving. I was feeling intently the actual experiences about which I was reading. And when I stood that Sunday night, after expressing myself as to the divine mission of the Lord, I said, "And now, as one of the least among you, I declare with all my soul that I know. . ." I knew with a certainty that I have never known before. Whether that was the more sure word of prophecy I had received, I don't know. But it was with such conviction! More powerful than sight is the witness of the Holy Spirit which bears testimony to your spirit that God lives, that Jesus is the Christ, that this is indeed the work of God. I knew it because I had felt it, and there had been a testimony borne to my soul that I could not deny.[4]

Elder Bruce R. McConkie agreed with his father-in-law (President Joseph Fielding Smith) on this question in general, but he varied in his own teachings in that he felt that even after the indelibly imprinted witness of truth by the Holy Spirit on the soul, an Apostle should still thereafter continue striving to see the face of Jesus. He taught that every Apostle should seek for such a blessing.

> There is general awareness in the Church that the latter-day Twelve hold the same office, possess the same priesthood and keys, and bear the same witness of the divine Sonship of him who redeemed us as did their predecessors in days of old. It is true that the witness of the Holy Ghost is sure and absolute and that a man can know with a perfect knowledge, by the power of the Holy Ghost, that Jesus Christ is the Son of the living God who was crucified for the sins of the world. This unshakeable certainty can rest in his soul even though he has not seen the face of his Lord. But it is also true that those who have this witness of the Spirit are expected, like their counterparts of old, to see and hear and touch and converse with the Heavenly Person, as did those of old. . . .
>
> Few faithful people will stumble or feel disbelief at the doctrine here presented that the Lord's apostolic witnesses are entitled and expected to see his face, and that each one individually is obligated to "call upon him in faith in mighty prayer" until he prevails.[5]

Elder McConkie cited both scripture and the teachings of the Prophet Joseph Smith to support his teachings.

President Joseph F. Smith also spoke to the issue, saying of the Apostles, "These twelve disciples of Christ are supposed to be eye and ear witnesses of the divine mission of Jesus Christ. It is not permissible for them to say, I believe, simply; I have accepted it simply because I believe it. Read the revelation. The Lord informs us they must *know*, they must get the knowledge for themselves, it must be with them as if they had seen with their eyes and heard with their ears, and they know the truth. That is their mission, to testify of Jesus Christ and him crucified and risen from the dead and clothed now with almighty power at the right hand of God, the Savior of the world."[6]

These teachings and others seem to suggest that it is preferable, but not necessary, for a member of the Quorum of the Twelve Apostles to behold the Savior by vision or personal appearance. One would suppose that the Holy Ghost would be powerfully involved in whatever means the Lord chose to grant an Apostle absolute assurance.

Having acknowledged such, it is also recognized, absent knowledge of the full facts, that only perhaps three or four of the thirteen Apostles whose special witness is reviewed in chapters 4 through 16 herein may not have seen Jesus, but we simply cannot know for sure. Further, with at least eight of the twenty-eight prophets and apostles named in chapter 17, we can be reasonably sure that they have seen Him. But we still cannot preclude the others from such an experience. The possibility is always present of Jesus Christ manifesting Himself to His Apostles without our knowledge or their preserving (available) record. An indication that such often happens without being made known is this statement from Elder Jeffrey R. Holland, given in the context of the Second Coming having its beginning with Joseph Smith's First Vision in 1820, and various successive personal appearances of the Lord Jesus since then until our day: "We have been in one phase or another, then, of the Second Coming for at least 179 years [now many more], with sacred appearances of the Savior all along that calendar, some of them recorded but *most of them not.*"[7]

THE CURIOUS CASE OF ELDER JOHN W. TAYLOR

When discussing the question of whether an Apostle must see the resurrected Jesus, in vision or by personal appearance, and the qualifications to be a special witness, the strange and sad experience of John W. Taylor, son of President John Taylor, should be noticed.

President John Taylor called his son John W. into the Quorum of the Twelve in 1884 at the age of only twenty-six. He served in that Quorum with widely varying degrees of faithfulness and obedience until 1905, when he resigned his office because of conflicts with his Quorum associates over his continued promotion and practice of plural marriage. He was excommunicated in 1911 for aggravating these same conflicts, and died five years later in 1916.

John W. Taylor was viewed by his associates of the Quorum of the Twelve as something of a frustrating enigma. They knew him to be profoundly blessed with certain gifts of the Spirit, especially those of future prophecy and visions. However, he also often struggled to follow the counsel of his ecclesiastical superiors and spent large amounts of time away from Church headquarters in business pursuits, including land speculation. He was a leader in Mormon colonization efforts in Canada, where he lived during his later years. When it came to the 1890 Woodruff Manifesto and the 1904 Smith Manifesto, first restricting and then completely stopping authorized new plural marriages, he seemed conflicted. At some meetings he would acquiesce to the official documents' authority and that of the First Presidency and the Twelve, and at others he would rebel against them, both openly and privately. He refused to go to Washington, DC, to testify before the congressional committee in the infamous Reed Smoot Hearings of the early 1900s; this after President Joseph F. Smith requested him to do so.

Before these latter troubles, however, he experienced some marvelous spiritual manifestations. In a meeting of the Quorum of the Twelve held in April 1890, Taylor was reported to have told of a vision of the Savior that he had seen.

> He related how he received a testimony of the divinity of the work while engaged at his father's saw mill some years since [before] in Summit County. In a vision he saw the place where he had been at work cutting logs gradually lit up by a brilliant light which seemed to emanate from the east. This light continued to increase in intensity and with the increase he seemed to be pushed further away from its source. Finally he clasped his arms around the stump of a tree for the purpose of keeping himself in position. He saw the Son of God appear in the brilliance of the light, and then his hold upon the stump began to slip, and he knew that should he release his grasp he would be thrust back with such violence that he would be dashed to pieces. As he was holding with grim desperation he awoke. His father [President Taylor] told him that the interpretation of the dream was that the bright light was the truth which would banish all truth-haters from before it, and the tree stump to which he was holding was a similar representation to that of the rod of iron in the Book of Mormon. Bro. Taylor related several other manifestations of God's goodness to him in answer to his prayers.[8]

Some weeks later, he again spoke of his visions or manifestations. "I have seen the Son of God in vision. I have seen the Prophet Joseph, also Brother Brigham Young and my own father since his death." Then he made a very important statement that would return to him and become his own fate since he later lost the spirit of his calling. "I almost fear when I stop to think that I have seen the Lord Jesus Christ knowing as I do that others who have had similar manifestations have fallen away from the truth and I am fearful lest I fall."[9] As an Apostle, he knew there were grave consequences to such a fall after being so blessed.

Several years later, in another Quorum meeting, he "said he had seen the Prophet Joseph and the Savior."[10] Then some six months after sharing that testimony, in another meeting, he "said he did not feel under obligations to sustain the Presidency in anything about which they did not consult him and the Twelve, and he rather complained of their [business-related actions] . . . when they had rebuked him for his efforts to make money out of the sale of lands [in Canada]."[11]

Taylor's land speculations proved unsuccessful, and he spent many months in Canada and Europe unsuccessfully trying to find buyers. While so involved, he was not magnifying his calling in the Twelve. Consequently, "President Woodruff expressed his disapproval of the conduct of . . . John W. Taylor [and another Apostle] in absenting themselves from our Quorum meetings on their private business, without first securing the consent of the Presidency. It is a neglect of their duties as apostles."[12] At a later meeting, Taylor noted that he was "laboring very hard to get means with which to pay his debts, so that he can preach the Gospel."[13] A few months later he was evidently feeling better and "He bore a strong testimony to the divine calling of the First Presidency, of which Quorum George Q. Cannon and Joseph F. Smith are just as good as President Woodruff. [He said] We must sustain these brethren or lose the Spirit of God."[14]

At this point the story moves ahead to the difficulties that John W. Taylor had with ending his support of plural marriage and how that brought him into conflict with his Quorum. His resignation from the Quorum of the Twelve, along with that of Elder Matthias Cowley, was accepted and he was dropped, meaning he was no longer considered one of their number and was not sustained at general conference.

At this point, a comment from Elder LeGrand Richards is worth notice, because it indicates how much Taylor's apostolic brethren knew of and appreciated his gifts of prophecy and revelation.

> Now I will skip to 1906 when my father was called to be a member of the Quorum of the Twelve. . . . I was at that time serving as the secretary of the Netherlands Mission, . . . Then, . . . a cablegram came to our office, the mission headquarters. It was addressed to President Grant, who was then president of the European Mission, and he was up in Berlin. We used to open the telegrams to see if they were important enough to try to relay. As for this telegram, I can quote you the exact words. It read this way: "Cowley and Taylor deposed. Richards, Whitney, and McKay appointed." . . . President Grant was due in Rotterdam the next morning so I went to the station to meet him. I handed him the telegram—I had sealed it up again—and he opened and read it, and he said, "Well, well, Cowley and Taylor deposed. Richards, Whitney, and McKay appointed." [He said, "This man Taylor's had more visions than all the rest of us put together."][15]

This indicates that Heber J. Grant and the other members of the Twelve were well aware of Elder Taylor's spiritual gifts and divine manifestations—yet they also watched him rebel against the counsel and course of the First Presidency and the Twelve regarding plural marriage, resign from their Quorum, and become so disobedient and contrary that he had to be excommunicated. He became insubordinate and rebellious and verbally abused some of the Apostles. One historian stated that the record indicates that "Taylor declared that he wanted nothing to do with any of the Twelve and would prefer not going to heaven if it meant continued association with any of the apostles."[16]

John W. Taylor had fallen low, but just how low is not known. In this murky water the question arises whether Taylor, through rebelliousness and bitterness, had gone so far as to commit the unpardonable sin and become a son of perdition, a fate that he was eligible to receive. Seemingly, the best answer available is that since President David O. McKay and President Joseph Fielding Smith authorized the restoration of his baptism and temple blessings in 1965, they evidently did not view him as such.

Elder Heber J. Grant had a front row seat in the Quorum of the Twelve from which to watch his associate rebel, lose the Spirit, and fall from grace into some unknown degree of personal apostasy. Taylor's saga affected Elder Grant and caused him to become extra sensitive when he heard someone, such as Elder Taylor, testify to seeing a vision of the Savior. Elder Harold B. Lee spoke of Heber J. Grant's anxiety in this regard on several occasions.

> I remember President Grant startled me one time when he said, "You know, whenever I heard one of my brethren who bore testimony that he had had a personal visitation from the Savior, I had an anxiety because I had seen so many who had had such experience who became so puffed up and thought that they were more favored than those who didn't have that personal manifestation that their pride led them away from the Church." He said, "I'm always anxious about a man who's had a personal visitation from the Lord."
>
> One of the members of the Twelve [John W. Taylor] of whom my brethren say had one of the greatest gifts of prophesy that they'd ever seen; his last recorded sermon said, "That person is not truly converted until he sees the power of God resting upon the leaders of this Church and it goes down into his heart like fire." And that's the very thing that cost this man his standing in the Church and, ultimately, his membership in the Church.[17]

Who the other brethren were that had experienced a personal visitation from the Lord is not stated, but, although he never named him, John W. Taylor was he who obtained the blessing and then fell. To a general conference audience, Elder Lee told in some detail of how the plight of Taylor had come to his attention.

> I had a shock and a startling truth borne in upon me by an experience six months ago, when following April conference, the General Authorities and their wives met in a semi-annual party and dinner up at our Institute of Religion near the University of Utah. As a part of the program, the committee in charge had arranged for a recital of the conferences a hundred years ago, from the preceding

October. They read the minutes from the conference of 1849. They then brought quotations from the sermons delivered by the First Presidency and the Council of the Twelve in October 1899. Then they reproduced on the public-address system quotations from the sermons of every one of the present Presidency and the Council of the Twelve. When they put into my hands the quotation from the one in that other Council fifty years ago, whose place [in seniority] I was now filling, I was startled, for I was to read the last recorded statement of a man who lost his standing in the Council and later his membership in the Church of Jesus Christ. And I was more startled when I read this statement from his last recorded sermon. This is what he had said:

"I know that the children of men never were converted till they saw that the power of God rested upon his servants, and the spirit of God went down into their hearts like fire."

He knew, and he came to know by the bitter experience of his own apostasy that the thing which lost him his standing in the Church was that he lost his testimony of the divine appointment of the prophets of God, and that the fire which once burned in his heart had gone out.[18]

The fact that President Lee would take occasion, several times before large congregations, to discuss his and President Grant's cautionary thinking about the pride that can cause someone who had beheld the resurrected Savior to fall and fail is noteworthy and according to the following scripture. "For although a man may have many revelations, and have power to do many mighty works, yet if he boasts in his own strength, and sets at naught the counsels of God, and follows after the dictates of his own will and carnal desires, he must fall and incur the vengeance of a just God upon him" (D&C 3:4).

President Grant's journal contains this record of his thinking:

President Grant took occasion to show . . . that even those who had had the greatest manifestations had been led away when they failed to listen to the counsel of the servants of the Lord placed at the head of the Church; mentioned Oliver Cowdery having seen John the Baptist, Peter, James and John, and even those who had seen the Savior himself, also had fallen away from the Church. He also told of John W. Taylor seeing the Savior when away in the mountains, where he had gone with the idea that he would be free from religious restraint, and that on his return through the gift of tongues it was made known that he had seen the Savior, and he arose and testified to the fact in fast meeting. . . . How Bro. Taylor followed after Moses Thatcher instead of listening to President George Q. Cannon, who had the right to counsel and guide him, and though he [Taylor] was warned by the leading brethren and by dreams and otherwise, yet he followed his own course, which took him out of the church. President Grant

[said] . . . that one living prophet was worth twenty dead ones, and told of Moses W. Taylor who would not be led away even by those who tried to quote the words of his own father to him, and how he became president of a stake, while John W. Taylor, who had tried to lead him away, had himself been excommunicated.[19]

In a testimony meeting in 1942, President Grant told those assembled, "I have never prayed to see the Savior. I know of men—Apostles—who have seen the Savior more than once. I have prayed to the Lord for the inspiration of His Spirit to guide me, and I have told him that I have seen so many men fall because of some great manifestation to them, they felt their importance, their greatness."[20] Obviously Elder John W. Taylor is one of those men whose pride caused them to fall away and disregard counsel. Perhaps there have been others as President Grant hinted. As a historical fact, no other members of the Quorum of the Twelve Apostles has fallen from that group, since the time of John W. Taylor, except for Richard R. Lyman. Moses Thatcher, Albert Carrington, Matthias Cowley, and Amasa M. Lyman also lost their places as Apostles in Heber J. Grant's earlier years in the Twelve, and whether he may have been referring to them, or to people like Sidney Rigdon and Oliver Cowdery, we cannot say.

President Grant himself had a marvelous manifestation regarding his call to the Twelve, received while on a journey.

As I was riding along to meet them on the other side, I seemed to see, and I seemed to hear, what to me is one of the most real things in all my life. I seemed to hear the words that were spoken. I listened to the discussion with a great deal of interest. The First Presidency and the Quorum of the Twelve Apostles had not been able to agree on two men to fill the vacancies in the Quorum of the Twelve. There had been a vacancy of one for two years, and a vacancy of two for one year, and the conferences had adjourned without the vacancies being filled. In this council the Savior was present, my father was there, and the Prophet Joseph Smith was there. They discussed the question that a mistake had been made in not filling those two vacancies and that in all probability it would be another six months before the Quorum would be completed. And they discussed as to whom they wanted to occupy those positions, and decided that the way to remedy the mistake that had been made in not filling these vacancies was to send a revelation. It was given to me that the Prophet Joseph Smith and my father mentioned me and requested that I be called to that position. I sat there and wept for joy. It was given to me that I had done nothing to entitle me to that exalted position, except that I had lived a clean, sweet life. It was given to me that because of my father's having practically sacrificed his life in what was known as the great reformation, so to speak, of the people in early days, having been practically a martyr, that the Prophet Joseph and my father desired me to have that position, and it was because of their faithful labors that I was called, and not because of anything I had done of myself or any great thing that I had accomplished.[21]

In this account, Elder Grant states that he "seemed to see" and "seemed to hear" what took place in the heavenly council, when it was decided by those present to call him into the Twelve. Some negatively biased academic historians have sought to cast doubt on or confuse what President Grant's meaning was in using these expressions. In truth, only those who have had a like experience, where pure and powerful revelation flows into one's mind and heart, can understand how the line between visual and audible sight and sound blurs and fades away into perfect understanding; how the distinctions of sight and sound lose relevance and pure intelligence enters the mind and heart of the recipient. Such is what happened to Elder Grant as a young Apostle. Thereafter he knew and could testify as a special witness himself; a witness that only grew and strengthened throughout the rest of his life.

NOTES

1. Joseph Fielding Smith, "The Twelve Apostles" (lecture given to seminary and institute teachers at Brigham Young University, June 18, 1958), 6–7. Hard copy in author's possession; audio version found at speeches.byu.edu.
2. As quoted in Henry D. Moyle's "Value of a Personal Testimony" (from a lecture given to seminary and institute teachers at Brigham Young University, July 16, 1954); see *CES Summer School Talks, 1954 & 1958*, 307–8.
3. Ibid., 308–9; 311–12.
4. Harold B. Lee, "Objectives of Church Education" (address to Church Educational System religious educators, June 17, 1970), 7.
5. Bruce R. McConkie, *The Promised Messiah* (Salt Lake City: Deseret Book, 1978), 592–93. For further insightful discussion of this subject from Elder McConkie, see *A New Witness for the Articles of Faith* (Salt Lake City: Deseret Book, 1985), 492–99. Herein, Elder McConkie wrote, "Those who see his face ordinarily do not cast this 'pearl before swine' lest men trample it under their feet and rend the recipient of so great a blessing."
6. Joseph F. Smith, *Gospel Doctrine* (Salt Lake City: Deseret Book, 1959), 198.
7. Jeffrey R. Holland, "Our Consuming Mission" (address to Church Educational System religious educators, February 5, 1999), 6; italics added.
8. As quoted in Dennis B. Horne's *An Apostle's Record: The Journals of Abraham H. Cannon* (Clearfield, Utah: Gnolaum Books, 2004), 147–48 (April 9, 1890).
9. Heber J. Grant journal, May 30, 1890.

10. Horne, *An Apostle's Record,* 313 (April 5, 1894).

11. Ibid., 340 (October 3, 1894).

12. Ibid., 423 (September 26, 1895).

13. Ibid., 429 (October 3, 1895).

14. Ibid., 446 (November 7, 1895).

15. LeGrand Richards, "Earth's Crammed with Heaven: Reminiscences" (Brigham Young University devotional, October 11, 1977). The text in brackets was edited from the print version but may be heard in the audio version at speeches.byu.edu.

16. Dale C. Mauritsen, *A Symbol of New Directions: George Franklin Richards and the Mormon Church, 1861–1950* (Brigham Young University Doctor's dissertation, 1982), 101.

17. Harold B. Lee, "Born of the Spirit," June 26, 1962, 9–10. Hard copy in author's possession; audio version available at speeches.byu.edu.

18. Harold B. Lee, "Divine Appointment of Leaders," in Conference Report, October 1950, 130–31.

    Another account shared by Elder Lee of this experience: "I listened to an excerpt of a testimony of a man who was a member of the Twelve and of whom President Grant had said that he never knew a man who had a greater gift of prophecy than did this man. There was put in my hands a quotation from a sermon that he had delivered some fifty years before, which proved to be the last sermon he had ever delivered as a member of the Twelve. Before another conference, he was dropped from the Council of the Twelve and subsequently left the Church. This is what he said in that last sermon: 'That person is not truly converted unless he sees the power of God resting upon the leaders of this Church and it goes down into his heart like fire'" ("Be Loyal to the Royal Within You" [Brigham Young University devotional, September 11, 1973], speeches.byu.edu).

    A third mention from President Lee is this: "I came across, a short while ago, a statement made by a man who was at the time a member of the Council of the Twelve, but because of his misdeeds and his disloyalties, he was dropped as a member of the Council of the Twelve, and was later excommunicated. This was the testimony he bore in his last recorded conference address. He said something like this: 'No person in this world was ever converted until he saw the power of God resting upon the servants of God and the spirit of God went down into their hearts like fire'" ("Divine Revelation" [Oct. 15, 1952]; audio version available at speeches.byu.edu).

19. Heber J. Grant journal, March 15, 1921.

20. Ibid., October 4, 1942.

21. Heber J. Grant, *Gospel Standards,* comp. G. Homer Durham (Salt Lake City: Deseret Book, 1941), 194–96.

PART II
SPECIAL WITNESSES
OF JESUS CHRIST

4

PRESIDENT BOYD K. PACKER'S
SPECIAL WITNESS OF JESUS CHRIST

*"I know Him when I see Him, and I
know His voice when I hear Him."*

President Boyd K. Packer's apostolic associates knew him to be a seer. Elder Russell M. Nelson said of him, "He is a gifted seer," whose teaching from the scriptures was characterized by "deep comprehension. . . . No one has plumbed the depths of this man."[1] Elder Dallin H. Oaks likewise said, "His fervent testimony and his unusual gifts of seership were an inspiring example to all of us."[2]

Boyd Packer was born in 1924 and raised in Brigham City, Utah. He contracted polio as a child and endured the pain it gave him on and off throughout his life, with it returning and crippling him in his last years. He served as a bomber pilot in World War II and returned home to be educated at Weber State College, Utah State University, and Brigham Young University, where he received a doctorate in education. Along the way, he married Donna Smith and started a large family of ten children. Having decided on the teaching profession during the war, he became a seminary teacher in Brigham City. He had only taught seminary for six years when he was hired as a supervisor of seminaries and institutes for the Church, a post he held until 1961, when at the age of thirty-seven he was called as an Assistant to the Quorum of the Twelve Apostles. In 1970 he was called as a member of the Quorum of the Twelve. As the decades passed, he became Acting President of that Quorum (in 1994), and then President of the Quorum of the Twelve (in 2008), serving there until his death in 2015.

Unwilling to Compromise with the Philosophies of Men

Elder Packer's life was one of no compromise with revealed truth. He often spoke out against the vain philosophies of men. For taking this firm approach, he earned many critics (as did his beloved friend Elder Bruce R. McConkie[3]) that were displeased with his condemnation of their liberal, errant, and worldly ideologies. He became noted for speaking against the theory of evolution, extremist feminism, academic intellectual dissidence, homosexual sin and activism, and poorly interpreted or negatively biased Church historical writings. He sought to teach members to follow the Brethren and the promptings of the Holy Spirit. He did much to open members' minds to the idea that those miraculous and supernatural matters proclaimed by the Church were actually real and true and that everyone could know such truths for themselves.

He explained, "The very beginning of this Church was initiated by the veil parting and visitations from beyond the veil. That has not ceased. That process, if anything, has been intensified in our generation, and I bear witness to that."[4] He also wrote, "The fact that sacred spiritual experiences are not discussed widely—for instance, by the General Authorities—should not be taken as an indication that the Saints do not receive them. Such spiritual gifts are with the Church today as they were in years past."[5]

Obtains His Special Witness

When a young Boyd Packer left his home to serve in World War II and become a pilot, he had not yet obtained the testimony he deeply desired. He studied the scriptures, especially the Book of Mormon, discussed the gospel with fellow LDS servicemen, and prayed often with real intent—but for a long time, nothing happened. He had not received the spiritual assurance that he sought. But everything changed one evening as he again sought for conviction and the desire to know welled up within him. He recorded some of his experience.

> During the night, I left my bed and went some distance to a secluded area where a makeshift bunker had been built. It was constructed of fifty-gallon fuel

barrels filled with sand. There was a second row upon the first for the wall. Sand had been pushed up on all sides to the height of the top barrels. One lower barrel at the end was left out to allow a low opening into the bunker, which was perhaps six by eight feet in size. There was no roof.

It was a clear night. After some moments I determined to ask; to really ask for some consolation, some indication to strengthen me. I wanted a testimony. I had studied the scriptures; we had tried to teach one another. I had tried to perfect myself according to the meager knowledge I had. I felt a compelling inward need for some spiritual consolation.

Then I knelt to pray. Almost mid-sentence it happened. I could not describe to you what happened if I were determined to do so—and I am not! It was, as Brother McConkie often said, "beyond my power of expression." I knew it to be a very private, a very individual, manifestation. At last I knew! I knew! I knew for a certainty! I was still unlettered in scriptural studies and all else, but I knew! That which is most worth knowing I knew, for it had been given to me.

After some time I crawled from that bunker under a sky of brilliant stars. I walked, or floated, back to my bed and spent the rest of the night in a feeling of joy and awe.

I did not accept it as a commission or a setting apart. It was a testimony, a witness, *the* witness. From that time to this, my challenge has not been with obedience, nor with resolution or diligence; it has been with restraint! The challenge has been to temper myself and bridle my impulsive Danish personality. It has been to keep sacred and keep private that which each of us must learn for one's own self. Such an experience is at once a light to follow and a burden to carry.[6]

Natural Talent as a Teacher and Leader

After the war, Brother Packer began teaching seminary, and it immediately became apparent that he had great natural ability as a teacher. He wrote his thesis on the Savior's teaching methods and began learning to emulate the Master Teacher and seek for the spiritual gift to teach by the Spirit. His talents soon became known to Church educational leadership, and before long, in his early thirties, he was hired as one of two seminary and institute supervisors overseeing the entire program. It became part of his job to ensure that liberal ideologies and worldly philosophies did not find their way into seminary and institute classroom teaching. He soon found there was cause for concern. It seems that the First Presidency of the Church thought as he did. In 1954 (and again in 1958), they called all seminary and institute men to a special Church educational summer school. He explained,

> There was a purpose for that summer school. Some difficulties had grown up in the institute program, not unlike the difficulties President George Brimhall

had previously faced here at BYU. So they called all the seminary and institute teachers in for a summer school on kind of a mandatory basis to anchor us again. Elder Harold B. Lee of the Quorum of the Twelve Apostles was appointed by the First Presidency to teach us. Our main class was held two hours a day, five days a week, for five weeks. The instructor was Elder Lee. Can you imagine spending two hours a day with him, five days a week for five weeks? Of course, we had visiting professors once in a while—J. Reuben Clark Jr., Mark E. Petersen, and others of the Brethren. That was a marvelous experience to learn from those Brethren.[7]

Decades later, Elder Quentin L. Cook of the Quorum of the Twelve talked about that momentous summer school.

In 1954 the leadership of the Church determined to reinvigorate the teachers of the Church and reestablish the primacy of teaching doctrine instead of significant reliance on secular concepts. Elder Harold B. Lee, then of the Quorum of the Twelve Apostles, gave an introduction to this series of lectures given to seminary and institute teachers. President Boyd K. Packer was 29 years old in 1954. He was teaching seminary in Brigham City and was given certain responsibilities with respect to the seminar. The seminar was continued in 1958, and President Packer was asked to deliver one of the talks. He was assistant administrator of seminaries and institutes. These talks had great significance to him. He kept a record of them and shared them with the current members of the Twelve last spring. These lectures were delivered by Elder Lee, President Joseph Fielding Smith, Elder Henry D. Moyle, Elder Marion G. Romney, President J. Reuben Clark Jr., and others in 1954 and again in 1958. They were very basic doctrinal messages. At the same time, they were both profound and relevant to the issues of that time and refocused Church education.

As one who attended seminary between those years of 1954 and 1958, they were very interesting to me. The doctrinal issues have not changed in the least. They had titles like "The Godhead," "Relationship of God to Man," "The Fall of Man," "The Plan of Salvation," and other similar doctrinal topics. President Packer spoke on "Problems in Teaching the Moral Standard," and it is as applicable today as it was 50 years ago. However, interlaced in the talks were challenges and choices that were very pertinent to that particular time.[8]

Elder Lee required the teachers to submit a term paper for their grade. Boyd submitted his and received the following note from the Apostle:

"Brother Packer, With your engaging personality, your flair for detail, and your foundation of faith you should go far in giving leadership much needed in the Church today and in the future. I shall be watching your progress! Faithfully yours,

Harold B. Lee."[9] As noted, in 2008, President Packer used the lectures as a text to teach the Quorum of the Twelve Apostles in something of a school of the prophets.

ATTACKED BY THE ADVERSARY

The occasional departures from gospel orthodoxy by a few in the Church Educational System would become a cause of serious concern. It was under these conditions that Boyd learned of the power and opposition of the devil. His boss at the time was William E. Berrett, and his companion in the supervisory work was Ted Tuttle, who would soon be called to the Seventy.

An institute teacher, among other things, was counseling young people that repentance was not required and that confession to their bishops for sin was an invasion of their privacy. Complaints from parents and leaders alarmed General Authorities, who called upon Brother Berrett to investigate.

He sent Brother Tuttle to interview the man and to make a decision about him. He and Boyd traveled part way together, then separated, Boyd to meet with teachers in Pocatello.

After Boyd's meetings of the next evening, he returned to his motel at midnight. Without knowing why, he checked out of that motel the next morning and into another before going to his meetings. That night as he opened his motel door the telephone rang. It was Brother Tuttle. "Boyd, I need help!"

"How on earth did you find me?"

"I remembered there is a Utah Motel in Pocatello, so I rang that first." Then he said, "I'm terrified! As I've been praying over what I should do about this man, it is as though all of the hosts of the adversary are working on me. I need your help!"

Promising his best efforts, Boyd hung up, dropped to his knees, and prayed mightily for Ted. "No sooner had I begun to pray than the same heinous power attacked me," he says. "I felt that the room was filled with demons, and I knew that not only Ted's life but mine was in deadly peril." In faith, he continued to plead with the Lord in their behalf, exercising the power of the priesthood to curb and dispel the dark evil. Finally it left.

Anxious about Ted's safety, Boyd joined him as soon as possible. The dread attack upon their persons drew them even closer in spirit. Each had come to know for himself that the power of evil was real.

"Still shaken from our terrifying experience," Boyd recalls, "we determined on our return to Salt Lake to speak of it to Elder Harold B. Lee, our teacher and mentor. He was very sober about it. 'This is very, very meaningful. Perhaps this is prophetic of something that awaits one of you in a call.'"[10]

Within a few years, both Ted and Boyd had been called as General Authorities. Elder Lee always seemed to know what he was talking about and how the devil's displeasure is usually manifest before a call to high Church office.

CALLED AS AN ASSISTANT TO THE TWELVE

In September 1961, Boyd was called as an Assistant to the Twelve. He related the story.

> I was a 37-year-old seminary supervisor. My Church calling was as an assistant teacher in a class in the Lindon Ward.
>
> To my great surprise, I was called to meet with President David O. McKay. He took both of my hands in his and called me to be one of the General Authorities, an Assistant to the Quorum of the Twelve Apostles.
>
> A few days later, I came to Salt Lake City to meet with the First Presidency to be set apart as one of the General Authorities of the Church. This was the first time I had met with the First Presidency—President David O. McKay and his counselors, President Hugh B. Brown and President Henry D. Moyle.
>
> President McKay explained that one of the responsibilities of an Assistant to the Twelve was to stand with the Quorum of the Twelve Apostles as a special witness and to bear testimony that Jesus is the Christ. What he said next overwhelmed me. "Before we proceed to set you apart, I ask you to bear your testimony to us. We want to know if you have that witness."
>
> I did the best I could. I bore my testimony the same as I might have in a fast and testimony meeting in my ward. To my surprise, the Brethren of the Presidency seemed pleased and proceeded to confer the office upon me.
>
> That puzzled me greatly, for I had supposed that someone called to such an office would have an unusual, different, and greatly enlarged testimony and spiritual power.
>
> It puzzled me for a long time until finally I could see that I already had what was required: an abiding testimony in my heart of the Restoration of the fulness of the gospel through the Prophet Joseph Smith, that we have a Heavenly Father, and that Jesus Christ is our Redeemer. I may not have known all about it, but I did have a testimony, and I was willing to learn.[11]

Elder Packer would indeed learn much. He consciously determined to absorb all of the knowledge and vicarious experience that he could from the most senior Brethren who had seen and done so much in their ministries.[12] Also, from 1965 to 1968, he served as president of the New England Mission. He had only been home for a couple of years before further change entered his life.

CALLED AS AN APOSTLE OF THE LORD

In 1970, President Joseph Fielding Smith called him to be a member of the Quorum of the Twelve Apostles. That such would happen was revealed to Elder Packer a few days before the sustaining of the Brethren at the April general conference, when he was in company with President Lee and Elder Romney.

> In connection with the conference, Elder Romney and Elder Packer were attending a seminar for the regional representatives in the seventeenth ward chapel. They were in a classroom alone when President Lee entered the room. "You are looking well," Brother Romney said to President Lee. "Then looks are deceiving," Brother Lee responded. He was weighed down with a critically serious Church matter.
>
> As the two older men talked, Brother Packer saw Elder Romney put his arms around President Lee and assure him, "You are going to be all right." It was then that President Lee reached out to Elder Packer and drew him into that embrace. At that moment, Boyd's heart flooded with sure knowledge that he was to become one of their number.[13]

By Sunday, having endured the intervening time with the private knowledge that he would be called, it came to pass.

> Finally the Sunday afternoon session ended and Boyd had yet to speak to the LDS chaplains. He was doing so when Brother D. Arthur Haycock interrupted the meeting and asked if he could come in with the First Presidency, who were then meeting with a delegation of Japanese people. Brother Packer thought this a natural request because of his experience in Japan, so he turned the chaplains meeting over to another. . . .
>
> . . . When the [Japanese] guests were excused . . . Elder Packer also prepared to leave.
>
> "I think the President wants you to stay," President Tanner said. It was then that President Joseph Fielding Smith delivered to Brother Packer his call to the Quorum of the Twelve Apostles and told him he would be sustained in a solemn assembly the next morning.
>
> It was a very solemn Boyd K. Packer who left the room.[14]

FINDING THE WORDS TO DECLARE HIS WITNESS

As part of his first general conference address in October 1970, he declared, "I come to you now as one of the Twelve, each ordained as a special witness. I affirm to you that I have *that* witness. I know that God lives, that Jesus is the Christ. I know that though the world 'seeth him not, neither knoweth him,' that he lives."[15]

By the time the next (April) general conference arrived, Elder Packer had had time to ponder and think about his call, his special witness, the sacredness of it, and how to deal with the natural curiosity that accompanies the office of the apostleship. With careful and expressive language, Elder Packer explained his qualifications and approach to inquiries about serving among their number.

Occasionally during the past year I have been asked a question. Usually it comes as a curious, almost an idle, question about the qualifications to stand as a witness for Christ. The question they ask is, "Have you seen Him?"

That is a question I have never asked of another. I have not asked that question of my Brethren in the Quorum, thinking that it would be so sacred and so personal that one would have to have some special inspiration, indeed, some authorization, even to ask it. . . .

I have come to know what the prophet Alma meant:

". . . It is given unto many to know the mysteries of God; nevertheless they are laid under a strict command that they shall not impart only according to the portion of his word which he doth grant unto the children of men, according to the heed and diligence which they give unto him.

"And therefore, he that will harden his heart, the same receiveth the lesser portion of the word; and he that will not harden his heart, to him is given the greater portion of the word, until it is given unto him to know the mysteries of God until he know them in full" (Alma 12:9–10). . . .

To one who is honestly seeking, the testimony borne in these simple phrases is enough, for it is the spirit that beareth record, not the words. . . .

I said there was a question that could not be taken lightly nor answered at all without the prompting of the Spirit. I have not asked that question of others, but I have heard them answer it—but not when they were asked. They have answered it under the prompting of the Spirit, on sacred occasions, when "the Spirit beareth record" (D&C 1:39).

I have heard one of my brethren declare: "I know from experiences, too sacred to relate, that Jesus is the Christ."

I have heard another testify: "I know that God lives; I know that the Lord lives. And more than that, I know the Lord."

It was not their words that held the meaning or the power. It was the Spirit. "For when a man speaketh by the power of the Holy Ghost the power of the Holy Ghost carrieth it unto the hearts of the children of men" (2 Ne. 33:1).

I speak upon this subject in humility, with the constant feeling that I am the least in every way of those who are called to this holy office. . . .

Now, I wonder with you why one such as I should be called to the holy apostleship. There are so many qualifications that I lack. There is so much in my effort to serve that is wanting. As I have pondered on it, I have come to only one single thing, one qualification in which there may be cause, and that is, I have *that* witness.

I declare to you that I know that Jesus is the Christ. I know that he lives. He was born in the meridian of time. He taught his gospel, was tried, was crucified. He rose on the third day. He was the first fruits of the Resurrection. He has a body of flesh and bone. Of this I bear testimony. Of him I am a witness.[16]

Twenty years later, he followed up that declaration with further explanation to an audience of missionaries about to leave for the field.

Everywhere we go . . . we are often asked the question, "Have you seen the Lord? You are an Apostle. Have you seen the Lord?"

I always have the same answer. I say that when I was called to the Twelve, I answered that question in a general conference, and I will send you a copy of that talk. In substance it says this: I have not asked that question of anyone. I have never asked that question of my Brethren. I know the answer, but I have never asked it, supposing that would be so sacred and so personal that it would be among the things that the Lord had in mind when He said, "It is given unto many to know the mysteries of God; nevertheless they are laid under a strict command that they shall not impart only according to the portion of his word which he doth grant unto the children of men, according to the heed and diligence which they give unto him."[17]

While it is true that the comparatively young, forty-four-year-old Apostle did not want to say more about his special witness than the Spirit would allow, neither did he desire to say less than permitted, something he also worried about. He wanted no one to be unsure of the sureness of his personal testimony. "There is another dimension also. When one has received *that* witness, and is called to testify, for him to dilute, to minimize, to withhold would be grossly wrong. It is in the face of this that I feel the urgency to bear witness. And I bear my solemn witness that Jesus is the Christ. I say that I know Jesus is the Christ, that the gospel of Jesus Christ was restored to Joseph Smith, a prophet of God, that David O. McKay who presides over this Church is a prophet of God."[18]

His Sense of Protecting the Sacred

A couple of years after his first general conference addresses, he decided to speak to the children of the Church, whom he dearly loved and wanted to teach the best he could. He said, "I know that God lives. I know something of how it feels to have his hand put upon you, to call you to his service. I bear witness and share with you the witness that has been given me, that special witness. He is the Christ! He loves us!"[19]

Elder Packer had drawn a line in spiritual matters, over which he would not go, as much as he wanted to—and he really did want to. "I have had an unquench-able desire to bear testimony of the Father and of Jesus Christ," he told a large gath-ering of BYU students. "Christ said, 'If ye had known me, ye should have known my Father also.' I have yearned to tell what I know about what Christ did and who the Father and the Son are."[20]

And again, to a group of Church college faculty and staff, "I wish there were authorization to say more. I bear witness that the Lord lives, that Jesus is the Christ. This I know. I know that He lives. I know that He directs this Church. Sometimes I wish that there were the authorization to say more, say it plainer, but that is the way we say it . . . that He lives, that we know."[21]

Yet despite the yearning, the deep desire to tell all he knew, he repeatedly emphasized that he would keep the spiritual experiences related to his special witness sacred. To a group of regional representatives, he testified, "I know from experiences too sacred to repeat, that the doctrine is true. That those who have gone beyond live beyond the veil. I know by witness that they have bodies of flesh and bone. I know that resurrected beings are glorious beings; that God directs this work."[22]

To a group of new mission presidents at a training seminar, he likewise de-clared, "I know by experience too sacred to touch upon that God lives, that Jesus is the Christ, that the gift of the Holy Ghost conferred upon us at our confir-mation is a divine gift. The Book of Mormon is true! This is the Lord's Church! Jesus is the Christ! There presides over us a prophet of God! The day of miracles has not ceased, neither have angels ceased to appear and minister unto man! The spiritual gifts are with the Church. Choice among them is the gift of the Holy Ghost!"[23]

To a general conference assemblage, he noted, "I have had too many sacred experiences, of the kind of which we never speak lightly, to feel that the word *dead* describes those who have gone beyond the veil."[24] He thoughtfully noted, "You'd think there would be a better way for one of the Twelve to bear testimony, but we're left to bear it in the same way our little grandkids do in Primary—just to say we know it's true. But I know that He lives. I know His voice when He speaks. I know Him, and of Him I bear witness."[25]

BLESSING THE CHURCH THROUGH HIS SPIRITUAL GIFTS

An occasion when Elder Packer did sometimes feel freer to speak more openly of sacred things was at funerals. He believed a solemn and tender spirit attended a proper LDS funeral, and therefore, on occasion, more might be said than usual, if prompted by the Spirit. At the funeral of his own older brother, he spoke of the ministration of angels he had received. "I saw Mother once since she passed away. I saw her as clearly as I see any of you. There was nothing said. For a time I didn't understand why I had been permitted to see her. And then President Kimball told us in the temple that he had seen his father . . . whom he knew had come to say that he approved of what was happening to his son. Then I knew why my mother had come. It was to say she approved of my life. She was glorious, as others have been who have come to visit."[26]

Summarizing these sacred matters, he taught,

> We lay no claim to being Apostles of the world—but of the Lord Jesus Christ. The test is not whether men will believe, but whether the Lord has called us—and of that there is no doubt!
>
> We do not talk of those sacred interviews that qualify the servants of the Lord to bear a special witness of Him, for we have been commanded not to do so.
>
> But we are free, indeed, we are obliged, to bear that special witness....
>
> Like all of my Brethren, I too come from among the ordinary people of the Church. I am the seventy-eighth man to be accepted by ordination into the Quorum of the Twelve Apostles in this dispensation.
>
> Compared to the others who have been called, I am nowhere near their equal, save it be, perhaps, in the certainty of the witness we share.
>
> I feel compelled, on this 150th anniversary of the Church, to certify to you that I know that the day of miracles has not ceased.
>
> I know that angels minister unto men.
>
> I am a witness to the truth that Jesus is the Christ, the Son of God, the Only Begotten of the Father; that He has a body of flesh and bone; that He knows those who are His servants here and that He is known of them.[27]

As one ponders Elder Packer's spiritual gifts, it becomes thoroughly evident that he saw angels, healed the sick, taught the gospel by the power of the Holy Spirit, conversed with Jesus ("sacred interviews"), and, as mentioned, developed the supernal insight of a seer, one who knows of things yet future. His biographer wrote, "Some of his brethren affirm that Elder Packer has remarkable spiritual perception and the ability to know, by the Spirit in advance, what is to be."[28]

Various comments from those same brethren refer to him as a seer among the prophets.

One example they give of this was his foreknowledge of the floodwaters that would come down from the mountains into the cities along the Wasatch Front in Utah in 1983. His warnings enabled those involved with church, city, and state emergency preparedness to be more prepared than otherwise would have been the case.[29]

Another example is a personal revelation he received in relation to his inquiry of the Lord about noisy liberal intellectual and feminist dissidents that were disciplined by their local leaders in 1993 and thereafter complained loudly in the press. Of this experience, he said,

> Not too many days ago, in a moment of great concern over a rapid series of events that demonstrated the challenge of those within the Church who have that feeling of criticism and challenge and apostasy, I had an impression, as revelations are. It was strong and it was clear, because lingering in my mind was: "Why? Why—when we need so much to be united?" And there came the answer: "It is permitted to be so now that the sifting might take place, and it will have negligible effect upon the Church."[30]

This response proved true. As noisy in the media as the apostates became, their actions and the resultant publicity did indeed "have negligible effect upon the Church" and constituted some necessary sifting.[31]

As to the future of the Church itself, he voiced many prophesies, some mentioned here:

> No matter if the Church grows to be a hundred million (as it surely will!), it will still be no bigger than a ward. . . .[32]

> As we continue on our course, these things will follow as night the day: The distance between the Church and a world set on a course which we cannot follow will steadily increase. Some will fall away into apostasy, break their covenants, and replace the plan of redemption with their own rules.[33]

> Despite opposition, the Church will flourish; and despite persecution, it will grow.[34]

This Church will prevail. There is no power in existence that can thwart the work in which we are engaged. Of that I bear witness.[35]

Not only had he seen into some of what would happen down the road in mortality, but he also stated that he had seen the next life, into eternity, as he declared to students in the Church Educational System in 1995. "I bear witness that Jesus is the Christ, the Son of God, that the gospel of Jesus Christ is true, that you as young members of the Church may look forward to a wonderful life of challenges and happiness and responsibility. It is a wonderful time to live and to be young. I envy you. As I said in the beginning, you are young and I am not. And yet in the eternal scheme of things, I am just as young as you are. Maybe a little closer to the final curtain on Act II, but I know, for I have seen a little behind the curtain into Act III and bear personal witness that the gospel is true, and bear witness of Jesus Christ."[36]

REVEALING HIS SPECIAL WITNESS TO THE SPIRITUALLY RECEPTIVE

The older he got, the more President Packer desired to more plainly bear his special witness of Jesus Christ. With this desire, he seemed to say just a sliver more than he previously had about the details of his special witness—not in every case, and only very carefully for those with ears attuned to his message.

For some, the question arises with the italic use of the word "*that*" in some of Brother Packer's messages and written testimonies ("I have *that* witness"). What did he mean? As for instance, "There are many qualifications that I lack. There is so much in my effort to serve that is wanting. There is only one single thing, one qualification that can explain it. Like Peter and all of those who have since been ordained, I have *that* witness. I know that God is our Father. He introduced His Son, Jesus Christ, to Joseph Smith. I declare to you that I know that Jesus is the Christ. I know that He lives. He was born in the meridian of time. He taught His gospel and was tried. He suffered and was crucified and resurrected on the third day. He, like His Father, has a body of flesh and bone. He made His Atonement. Of Him I bear witness. Of Him I am a witness."[37]

Such use of the word "*that*" was also made in his above-quoted general conference address "The Spirit Beareth Record," and at other times. It seems he intended the word to convey something very important about his special witness.

President Packer loved real, divine, truth—not the world's evolving version of truth, which is usually error—but revealed gospel truth. To a group of Church education teachers, whom he loved and to whom he felt a close kinship, he disclosed some of his thoughts.

"Someday I am going to talk about [the subject of] truth. I have been working on a talk for a few years. Someday when it is right and I feel worthy, and when it's complete, I may give that talk. There is within me a great welling up of joy to know that truth is truth. That it is—and that all the powers of unrighteousness can't change it at all. God lives. Jesus is the Christ, the Son of God, the Only Begotten of the Father. Of him I bear witness. He has a body of flesh and bone as tangible as the bodies that we have. This I know."[38]

Speaking in a sacrament meeting in his home ward in the Sandy, Utah, Cottonwood Creek Stake, President Packer testified of the reality of the Savior and the joy of Christmas to ward and family members. "I want our family to know that they have heard grandpa bear his testimony," he said. "I know that Jesus is the Christ, that He lives, that the gospel is true, and that I know Him when I see Him, and I know His voice when I hear Him. I want you little ones to remember that you heard your grandfather bear a special witness of the Lord Jesus Christ and of the gift of the Holy Ghost."[39] With a little reflection and thought, the sublime meaning of his words becomes apparent.

In one of his last and greatest talks to the Church, knowing that mortality was soon to end for him and that he would be facing his Maker, President Packer returned with some evident emotion to his early account of seeking a witness from the Lord as a young serviceman. He spoke of the time when he received *that* witness, but this time he added a further word of explanation.

> While stationed on the island of Ie Shima, just north of Okinawa, Japan, I struggled with doubt and uncertainty. I wanted a personal testimony of the gospel. I wanted to know!
>
> During one sleepless night, I left my tent and entered a bunker which had been formed by lining up 50-gallon fuel drums filled with sand and placed one on top of the other to form an enclosure. There was no roof, and so I crawled in, looked up at the star-filled sky, and knelt to pray.
>
> Almost mid-sentence it happened. I could not describe to you what happened if I were determined to do so. It is beyond my power of expression, but it is as clear today as it was that night more than 65 years ago. I knew it to be a very private, very individual manifestation. At last I knew for myself. I knew for a certainty, for it had been given to me. After some time, I crawled from that bunker and walked, or floated, back to my bed. I spent the rest of the night in a feeling of joy and awe.

. . . In the years that have followed, I have come to understand that such an experience is at once a light to follow and a burden to carry.

I wish to share with you those truths which are the most worth knowing, the things that I have learned and experienced in nearly 90 years of life and over 50 years as a General Authority. . . .

One eternal truth that I have come to know is that God lives. He is our Father. We are His children. . . .

Another truth I have come to know is that the Holy Ghost is real. He is the third member of the Godhead. His mission is to testify of truth and righteousness. . . .

A supernal truth that I have gained in my life is my witness of the Lord Jesus Christ. . . .

In the Church we know who He is: Jesus Christ, the Son of God. He is the Only Begotten of the Father. He is He who was slain and He who liveth again. He is our Advocate with the Father. . . .

After all the years that I have lived and taught and served, after the millions of miles I have traveled around the world, with all that I have experienced, there is one great truth that I would share. That is my witness of the Savior Jesus Christ.

Joseph Smith and Sidney Rigdon recorded the following after a sacred experience:

"And now, after the many testimonies which have been given of him, this is the testimony, last of all, which we give of him: That he lives! For we saw him" (D&C 76:22–23).

Their words are my words.

I believe and I am sure that Jesus is the Christ, the Son of God, and that He lives. He is the Only Begotten of the Father, and "by him, and through him, and of him, the worlds are and were created, and the inhabitants thereof are begotten sons and daughters unto God" (D&C 76:24).

I bear my witness that the Savior lives. I *know* the Lord. I am His witness. I know of His great sacrifice and eternal love for all of Heavenly Father's children. I bear my special witness in all humility but with absolute certainty.[40]

He had been equally definite in his address the previous year, summing up his apostolic ministry. "Of all that I have read and taught and learned, the one most precious and sacred truth that I have to offer is my special witness of Jesus Christ. He lives. I know He lives. I am His witness. And of Him I can testify. He is our Savior, our Redeemer. Of this I am certain. Of this I bear witness."[41]

President Packer died in 2015 of causes incident to advanced age and the recurrence of childhood polio.

NOTES

1. Don L. Searle, "Elder Boyd K. Packer: Disciple of the Master Teacher," *Ensign*, June 1986.

2. "President Boyd K. Packer: Farewell to a Master Teacher," *Ensign*, August 2015.

3. I think Elder Packer would have fully agreed with these words of Elder McConkie: "The measure of a man is not found in who speaks well of him but who speaks against him. It is just as important to have the right enemies as it is to have the right friends" (Joseph Fielding McConkie, *The Bruce R. McConkie Story: Reflections of a Son* [Salt Lake City: Deseret Book, 2003], 265).

4. *Mine Errand from the Lord*, comp. Clyde J. Williams (Salt Lake City: Deseret Book, 2008), 137; from an address given by Boyd K. Packer for a family history broadcast, November 18, 1999.

5. Boyd K. Packer, *The Holy Temple* (Salt Lake City: Bookcraft, 1980), 243.

6. As quoted in Lucille C. Tate's *Boyd K. Packer: A Watchman on the Tower* (Salt Lake City: Bookcraft, 1995), 60.

7. Boyd K. Packer, "A Teacher of Teachers," *McKay Today Magazine*, Fall 2006, 4; see education.byu.edu.

8. Quentin L. Cook, "Choices and Challenges" (address to Church Educational System religious educators [evening with a General Authority, February 27, 2009], 1). See lds.org/broadcasts.

9. Tate, *Boyd K. Packer: A Watchman on the Tower*, 119.

10. Ibid., 119–20.

11. Boyd K. Packer, "The Weak and the Simple of the Church," *Ensign*, November 2007. In his biography, further information on this experience is given. "I will not forget that day when I stood before President McKay. He sat at the end of the table in the First Presidency's boardroom and said, 'We have explained to you what your obligation will be as an Assistant to the Quorum of the Twelve Apostles. This obligation includes standing with the members of the Quorum of the Twelve as a special witness of the Lord Jesus Christ. Before proceeding with this ordination and setting apart, I want to know if you have that witness. Bear your testimony to us'" (Tate, *Boyd K. Packer: A Watchman on the Tower*, 126).

12. For examples of this, see Boyd K. Packer, "Truths Most Worth Knowing" (Church Educational System devotional, November 6, 2011), speeches.byu.edu.

13. Tate, *Boyd K. Packer: A Watchman on the Tower*, 169.

14. Ibid., 170.

15. Boyd K. Packer, in Conference Report, October 1970, 118–22.
    Also of interest is an experience Elder Packer shared with Elder Neal A. Maxwell. "In October 1983, I returned from South America and left almost immediately for

London to join Elder Neal A. Maxwell at the first regional conference as a substitute for one of the First Presidency. This first conference was something of an experiment. We met in the Hyde Park Chapel for a four-hour priesthood meeting. Elder Maxwell spoke first, quoting King Benjamin, 'Brethren, we did not come here to trifle with words' (see Mosiah 2:9). What he said next changed my life: 'We come to you today in our true identity as Apostles of the Lord Jesus Christ.' Suddenly my body was filled with warmth and light. The weariness of travel was replaced by confidence and confirmation. What we were doing was approved of the Lord" (Boyd K. Packer, "The One Pure Defense" [address to Church Educational System religious educators, February 6, 2004], 1–2).

16. Boyd K. Packer, "The Spirit Beareth Record," *Ensign*, June 1971.
17. *Mine Errand from the Lord*, 579.
18. Boyd K. Packer, in Conference Report, October 1964, 126–29.
19. Boyd K. Packer, "Behold Your Little Ones," *Ensign*, July 1973.
20. Packer, "Truths Most Worth Knowing"; see speeches.byu.edu.
21. Boyd K. Packer, from an address at a Ricks College (now Brigham Young University–Idaho) faculty and staff dinner that the author attended, August 24, 1988.
22. Boyd K. Packer, "That They May Be Redeemed," regional representatives seminar, April 1, 1977; this transcribed conclusion to the talk is not in the pamphlet version published by the Church.
23. Boyd K. Packer, "The Quest for Spiritual Knowledge," *Liahona*, January 2007 (from a talk given at a seminar for new mission presidents, June 25, 1982).
24. Boyd K. Packer, "Covenants," *Ensign*, May 1987.
25. Boyd K. Packer, "How Does the Spirit Speak to Us?" *New Era*, February 2010 (from an address delivered at a seminar for new mission presidents on June 19, 1991); see lds.org.
26. Funeral Address of Leon Claron Packer, Brigham City, Utah, November 29, 1985; as quoted in Tate, *Boyd K. Packer: A Watchman on the Tower*, 286.
27. Boyd K. Packer, "A Tribute to the Rank and File of the Church," *Ensign*, May 1980, 62.
28. As quoted in Tate, *Boyd K. Packer: A Watchman on the Tower*, 281.
29. For a summary of his foresight and involvement in this situation, see Tate, *Boyd K. Packer: A Watchman on the Tower*, 281–82.
30. Boyd K. Packer, "The Great Plan of Happiness," *Teaching Seminary Preservice Readings Religion 370, 471, and 475* (2004), 68–74.
31. Some people confuse media/social media opinion, clamor, and noise with actual substance and occurrence, which is not a good way to really see and understand what is going on with the Church. At President Packer's passing, his son noted, "Dad was always optimistic and positive and not afraid of anything. He said over and over again—we've heard him say—'The Twelve are not afraid of what's going on in the

world.' That brings great peace to the Church and the family." (As quoted in Tad Walch's "President Packer was working on upcoming conference talk when he died" [*Deseret News*, July 7, 2015].)

32. Boyd K. Packer, "The Bishop and His Counselors," *Ensign*, May 1999.

33. Boyd K. Packer, "Out of Obscurity and Out of Darkness," *Ensign*, January 2000.

34. Boyd K. Packer, "The Cloven Tongues of Fire," *Ensign*, May 2000.

35. Boyd K. Packer, "All Church Coordinating Council," May 18, 1993, 7; hard copy in author's possession.

36. Boyd K. Packer, "The Play and the Plan" (address at Church Educational System fireside, Kirkland Washington Stake Center, May 7, 1995).

37. Boyd K. Packer, "The Twelve," *Ensign*, May 2008.

38. Boyd K. Packer, "Teach the Scriptures" (an excerpt from an address to Church Educational System religious educators, October 14, 1977), 4–7; see lds.org.

39. Sarah Jane Weaver, "President Packer shares Christmas testimony: 'Jesus is the Christ'" (*Church News*, Saturday, Dec. 25, 2010); see ldschurchnewsarchive.com.

40. Boyd K. Packer, "The Witness," *Ensign*, May 2014.

41. Boyd K. Packer, "These Things I Know," *Ensign*, May 2013.

5

ELDER BRUCE R. McCONKIE'S

SPECIAL WITNESS OF JESUS CHRIST

"I have a perfect knowledge that Jesus Christ is the Son of the living God and that He was crucified for the sins of the world."

Bruce R. McConkie was, like Nephi of old, born of goodly parents. His father—a lawyer, judge, bishop, mission president, and member of a stake presidency—was a man of mighty faith and deep spirituality, greatly blessed of the Lord, as was his mother, Vivian. Of his father, Oscar W. McConkie, Bruce wrote, "[He] was a very spiritual man. He had many visions and revelations. The Lord entrusted him with much knowledge. . . . [He] would have been qualified to fill any position in the Church but he did not for instance, happen to be called to be one of the General Authorities. I know a number of brethren who are or have been in a similar category."[1]

In a personal memoir, Oscar McConkie wrote, "The week previous to May 21, 1935 . . . I saw a glorious vision in which I saw the Savior of the World."[2] A year later, he received another marvelous vision, containing several separate but related scenes, one of which is relevant here. The overall theme was that of searching intently and diligently for Jesus until finding Him. Oscar wrote,

I was carried in the Spirit to Palestine, next. There, in Palestine, I saw a glorious vision. I suppose that I was carried away in the Spirit. In the vision, I knew that Jesus and John the Beloved were there. . . . I looked and saw one house only in the whole area. It was a Jewish house, small and white, and looked like it would be one room. It was the type of house used in the Meridian of Time, . . . I looked intently upon it, for I was in search of Jesus and John and I felt that they were in the house. In a little while I saw Jesus walk out of the door, followed closely by John. They wore loose turbans on their heads with cloth hanging on the sides and back to below the top of their shoulders. They wore robes and tied them about the waist with sashes. Sandals were on their feet, otherwise their feet were bare. They were dressed alike, in white, but not fine linen or precious fabric. As they came out I observed that Jesus was taller than John, which became sure as they walked together.[3]

With such a father as this, granted sure knowledge and witness, in this manner, of the living reality of Jesus the Christ, it is no wonder that one of their children would become a special witness. Oscar's mother, Emma Sommerville McConkie, possessed great faith herself. Of her, Oscar recorded the following experience:

While mother was president of the Moab [Utah] Relief Society, a nonmember of the Church, who was of a family considered by me to be unfriendly to the Church, but whose wife was a member, and whose children, including a newborn baby, were in poverty and distress. At the time to which I refer, mother was ill, but went daily to minister to the needs of this family. One of these days, she was so weary she could hardly get home. Entering the house, she sat in her rocker and was soon asleep. As she slept she dreamed of bathing a newborn child, which baby she held in her lap. While she held it, of a sudden she saw that it was the Christ child. Her whole being was illumined with a brilliance greater than she had ever before experienced. O what a glorious privilege! she thought. Her soul was exalted as she fastened her eyes upon the Son of God.

She had seen the mysteries of Godliness manifested favorably amongst the people and in her own behalf; and had seen and talked with and been blessed by a disciple of the very Christ, come to comfort her out of the past; and had seen somewhat of the spiritual creation; and had submitted to the watchful teachings of prophets, seers, and revelators of her time; and was intimate with the soothing witness and burning of the Holy Ghost, which, from time to time, had been upon her, all the days of her life, and had, in a dream, shown her the face of her Lord, and in the true sense she had walked and talked with God. . . .

But no experience of her life was so exquisite, nor gave her such consummate joy, as did the occasion of her bathing this child; it being . . . the Christ. It seemed to her that the marrow in her bones would melt, so extreme were the refinements of the warmth, the light, the fire, and the glory that filled every part of her being, and lit up the atmosphere round about. Unspeakable joy awakened her and she saw, open eyed, the brilliance of God's presence, and with her ears heard the gentleness of the audible voice of God, spoken out of the stillness: "In as much as ye have done it unto one of the least of these my brethren, ye have done it unto me."[4]

Bruce McConkie was born July 29, 1915, in Ann Arbor, Michigan, where his father was studying law. He grew up in Monticello and Salt Lake City, Utah. As he neared the time of his mission call, he began courting Amelia Smith, daughter of President Joseph Fielding Smith. On his return from missionary service, they married, and he attended law school at the University of Utah. He also spent some years as an intelligence officer in the Military during World War II. After the war, his interest in practicing law gave way to a greater enthusiasm for writing, and he worked for a short period as a reporter and editorial writer for the *Deseret News*, a major daily newspaper in Salt Lake City. In 1946, President George Albert Smith called him as a member of the First Council of Seventy. In the 1950s he compiled the writings of his father-in-law, Joseph Fielding Smith, issued as the three-volume *Doctrines of Salvation*, and also wrote his own seminal reference work, *Mormon Doctrine*. From 1961 to 1964 he served as a mission president in Australia.

After twenty-six years laboring in the First Council of the Seventy, Bruce was called by President Harold B. Lee as a member of the Quorum of the Twelve Apostles. He served in that capacity from 1972 until his untimely passing on April 19, 1985, at age sixty-nine. During his apostolic years, he continued to write prolifically, producing a three-volume *Doctrinal New Testament Commentary* and a six-volume series on the Messiah, which included the prophecies of His coming, His mortal ministry, and His millennial reign. His final published tome, *A New Witness for the Articles of Faith*, drew upon doctrinal principles found in modern revelation to teach how to develop greater faith in Christ.

EARLY SPIRITUAL TRAINING

Of Bruce, his eldest son, Joseph, said, "If you were to ask my dad where he learned the gospel, he'd say, 'I learned it at the dinner table after Sunday School when my father would review with us what we'd been taught, and correct it.'"[5] Elder McConkie further explained,

> I had a very spiritual home life. My father had a practice in the family of talking about the gospel to the children, with the result that at the dinner table or Sunday dinner or in the evening or what have you, he somehow managed to

get us involved in discussion and everlastingly he taught us the gospel. I would be surprised if there were anyone that I'd ever run across who spent as much time just deliberately discussing and thereby teaching gospel principles to his children as my father did. He was a great conversationalist and he just kept me everlastingly thinking and evaluating on principles of the gospel, and the environment had the effect of getting my mind centered in those channels and the result, obviously, is that when I talk I'm talking on a doctrinal subject.[6]

Such an upbringing paid high dividends, and Bruce became a gospel scholar at an early age, learning to love the scriptures. Later, while walking to law school, he practiced presenting doctrinal material to imaginary audiences. He explained his method to a *Church News* reporter.

When I was going to the university, it took me about 45 minutes to walk there and 45 minutes to walk home. I began to think in outlines. I would arbitrarily choose some subject and imagine that I had been notified to give a talk on that subject. I would then say the first word on the subject and the last word, and then in the 40 minutes or whatever time I allotted myself, I would attempt to cover the subject in some intelligent way, just for the purpose of training myself to think in outlines. So if somebody said "faith," I'd immediately think, well, it's 1, 2, 3, and 1A, 2B, and 3C. . . .

. . . I don't pay any attention to it now except that it had the obvious effect of training me to think in a channel so that I'd keep intelligently on a subject. It set the pattern for the way that I always talk. I don't use notes to speak of. It isn't once in a thousand times I ever have a note, and as I give talks week after week I approach the subject differently. For instance, last Sunday in Moab [Utah] I talked about the family unit with a totally different approach than I had ever talked about the family unit before.[7]

With such disciplined practice guiding him, Elder McConkie's talks became known for their organization, clarity, and scriptural content. When he married Amelia, they began a nightly practice of reading the standard works together, completing them several times.

In 1938, during their early marriage, tragedy struck in the loss of their first-born son, Bruce Redd McConkie Jr., as an infant of only a few weeks. Of this event, Bruce's father Oscar recorded, "He was a beautiful baby. At the [funeral] service, obviously under the direction of the Spirit, Bro. [Joseph Fielding] Smith told of the Prophet Joseph Smith, saying that some spirits were too pure to go through this life, that they had advanced so far in the Spirit World that their only need was to obtain a body and then go back for the work they had to do. He said this was one of those spirits, and I knew that it was so. [Afterward] Bro. Smith and I were [talking] in the backyard. . . . He said . . . that so much faith had been exercised in this case that Lucifer had no power at all, that Lucifer was helpless in this case. And when he said it, I knew that it was true."[8]

CALLED TO THE FIRST COUNCIL OF THE SEVENTY

In relating the events of his call to the First Council of the Seventy, Bruce wrote,

Some weeks, perhaps it was months, before the October Conference in 1946, President John H. Taylor passed away. At the time I was working for the *Deseret News.* . . .

For many weeks thereafter everywhere I would go people would make the comment that I would be the new member of the First Council of the Seventy. Obviously I never did do more than just joke with them and indicated that such would never happen. . . . [I] did not take all this particularly seriously.

However, as the conference approached I began to get somewhat of a feeling that it well might be me after all. . . . By the time the conference came I was beginning to get an idea and somewhat of an inner feeling in my heart that I would be called to the First Council of the Seventy. I do not know if it was inspiration or just the psychological effect of what had been going on all these weeks before the conference came. . . .

I was standing at the press table in the Tabernacle waiting for the final general session . . . to start. Joseph Anderson, clerk of the conference, came down the pulpit stairs, leaned over the banister and whispered in my ear: "President McKay would like to see you."

I knew instantly what was wanted, and so felt somewhat overwhelmed as I followed Brother Anderson back up the stairs. President McKay was standing on the top platform. He said, "Come with me, I want to talk to you.". . .

He took me by the hand, led me over to a chair, had me sit down, and still holding my hand, he sat on the edge of a small table, and said, "Brother McConkie, I have been delegated by the First Presidency to interview you. Your name will be submitted to the conference this afternoon to fill the vacancy in the First Council of Seventy. Do you know of any reason why you cannot serve?"

"No Sir, President McKay, I do not," I replied. . . .

Then he asked a series of questions, to each of which he scarce gave me tine to answer, "You have a testimony of the gospel? You know that Joseph Smith was a prophet? You are in harmony with the General Authorities of the Church as at present constituted?" To each of which I half nodded and half whispered, "Yes."

"You are the unanimous selection of the First Presidency, the Council of the Twelve, and the First Council of Seventy," he said. And then: "It is the voice of the Lord."[9]

UNSHAKABLE TESTIMONY COMES

Immediately after being sustained as a member of the First Council of the Seventy in the Salt Lake Tabernacle, Elder McConkie encountered President George Albert Smith. The Prophet said to him, "We have a lot of work for you to do. You will have to be good to live up to all the good things I have heard about you."[10]

On October 10, 1946, Bruce met for the first time in the temple with his new quorum, the First Council of Seventy. Their meeting was interrupted by President J. Rueben Clark, asking them to meet with the First Presidency and Twelve in order to have Bruce set apart. During the ensuing meeting, President Smith spoke to those present on several subjects. Thirty-one-year-old Elder McConkie recorded his feelings: "Seated in that council meeting, I felt the calm and joy of the Spirit of the Lord as I have never felt it. It seemed as though Pres. Smith was speaking the word of the Lord, or even as though the Lord himself was there before us telling us his will." After President Smith spoke, he ordained Bruce and set him apart, promising him joy and blessings through service.[11]

Elder McConkie found himself working among the finest of tutors in spiritual matters, and as he served and studied and prayed with them and in private, his sensitivities sharpened. We are not privy to most of the spiritual experiences he received, but he felt proper to relate some. For example, "May I just tell you one experience that I had?" he asked a general conference assemblage in October 1951. "I have never told this to any person before, except my wife. Six months ago in the Solemn Assembly, where the First Presidency of the Church were sustained, as I sat down here behind one of these lower pulpits, the voice of the Lord came into my mind as certainly, I am sure, as the voice of the Lord came into the mind of Enos, and the very words were formed, and it said, 'These are they whom I have chosen as the First Presidency of my Church. Follow them'—those few words." He then added, "I have had a testimony of the divinity of this work from my youth. I was reared in a family where love was the motive force, where my parents taught me righteousness, and I have grown up with a testimony. But that witness was an added assurance. It meant to me, if I hadn't known before, which I did know before, that this is the Lord's Church; that his hand is over it; that he organized it; that these men who preside are called of him; that they are his anointed; that if we will follow them as they follow Christ, we will have eternal life."[12]

Enduring the Trial of Internal Criticism over the Book *Mormon Doctrine*

In 1958, Elder McConkie's seminal encyclopedic work, *Mormon Doctrine,* was published. Because it explained gospel doctrines clearly and forcefully, it quickly became a popular book with Latter-day Saints. However, the breadth of subjects covered (some outside the range of LDS doctrine), the authoritative tone in which they were explained, and the controversial nature of some of the content, caused the First Presidency to take a close look at it. Both Elders Marion G. Romney and Mark E. Petersen were assigned by the First Presidency to submit written reports on their findings after reviewing the book. These reports eventually led to a meeting between the First Presidency (then consisting of David O. McKay, J. Reuben Clark, and Henry D. Moyle), Elder Mark E. Petersen, and Elder McConkie, to discuss his best-selling book.

When they called Bruce in, they asked him to take a seat, but he said he would prefer to stand. Elder Mark E. Petersen of the Quorum of the Twelve, present and accounted for during this meeting, did most of the talking. President Henry D. Moyle (the second counselor) indicated that on this occasion, the First Presidency gave Bruce a "horsewhipping." They were really hard on him and "raked him over the coals" for a period of time. He further indicated that it was the worst criticism that that First Presidency had ever given a General Authority; that he went home feeling bad that they had been so hard on Bruce—it was basically Mark E. Petersen doing the talking and the First Presidency going along with and backing him up in his criticisms of Bruce's book; that Elder Petersen was the real force behind the (temporary) discontinuance of *Mormon Doctrine*; and that he was the reason the First Presidency gave it so much attention and why Bruce got into so much trouble over it. President Moyle indicated that Bruce simply listened to what they had to say, didn't offer any arguments or protestations, said he had no questions at the end of the meeting when he was asked if he did, and he left.

President Moyle indicated that he felt bad enough about their horsewhipping of Bruce that he resolved to make it up to him someday. Then a year later, when the time was right and a mission president was needed in Australia, President Moyle decided to call Bruce to serve there as a way to make up for what they had done, and he called him. The service as a mission president was the greatest thing that could have been done for Elder McConkie, because he became the boss, the president. He could make his own decisions, could sign the checks, and could run things his way. Bruce had never been in a position of authority where he could run things, but as a mission president, he finally had it. The mission experience really helped and changed and improved Elder McConkie. Elder Marion G. Romney didn't think that much was doctrinally wrong with *Mormon Doctrine*, and President Joseph Fielding Smith didn't think anything was wrong with it.[13]

Around 1965–66, President David O. McKay gave Elder McConkie permission to revise his book under the supervision of Elder Spencer W. Kimball, and an improved, second edition of *Mormon Doctrine* was published in 1966.

Elder McConkie's experience with the senior Brethren regarding his book was the single most difficult experience he ever endured with his ecclesiastical leaders. He was obedient and circumspect about what he was told to do, and though a severe trial, it became a great lesson and learning experience for him.[14]

GREATER SPIRITUAL ASSURANCE COMES

After serving in the First Council of the Seventy for over two decades, he reflected on the choice experiences that were his and wrote, "Over the years, I have felt the spirit of inspiration many times and have had great truths revealed to me. There have been a few times when I have prevailed upon the Lord to speak to me and give counsel and direction in direct words." One of those instances was in July 1966, and another was in July 1970. Elder McConkie did not indicate whether there was a veil between himself and the Lord or not on those sacred occasions, but he did record what he was told. One of the things that the resurrected Lord said to him was, "Thou art one of those whom I have chosen out of the world to stand as a witness of my name in all the earth and before kings and rulers." Another was, "Thou art called to testify of my name unto the ends of the earth."[15]

At the April 1972 general conference, Elder McConkie spoke of another impression he had received. "I asked the Lord what he would have me say on this occasion and received the distinct and affirmative impression that I should bear testimony that Jesus Christ is the Son of the living God and that he was crucified for the sins of the world. I have what is known as 'the testimony of Jesus,' which means that I know by personal revelation from the Holy Spirit to my soul that Jesus is the Lord."[16]

In commenting on his remarks in conference that day, Elder McConkie later wrote that the Lord "poured out upon me and the whole congregation his Spirit in a manner far exceeding anything else that had ever happened to me in connection with any talk or sermon I have ever delivered. What I said on that occasion came from him so that the attending spirit carried the message into the hearts of people with convincing power."[17] His wife, Amelia, confirmed this statement with her own experience and impressions. She said, "Bruce later shared with me that he felt the spirit rest upon him as it never had before in his life's experience. About halfway through his talk, I became aware that there was an absolute stillness in the whole Tabernacle. The cameras that incessantly clicked during every other talk were quiet. There was not a cough or a movement, and every ear seemed tuned to each word he spoke. President Lee told him he had lifted up [the spiritual level of] the whole conference." Amelia felt that the hand of the Lord was evident. She added, "In light of all that happened after that speech was given, it would appear that this particular conference address marked the beginning of the announcement by the Lord that Bruce would one day receive the call to be an especial witness of Christ."[18]

A similar event occurred later that July when Elder McConkie spoke at the funeral of President Joseph Fielding Smith. A marvelous outpouring of the Spirit of the Lord attended his comments. Elder McConkie humbly gave the credit and his gratitude to the Lord. The veil had become thin for Elder McConkie, and he related to extended family members that President Joseph F. Smith had been present at the funeral of his son.[19] Later that August, Elder McConkie attended the Mexico City area conference, where the new First Presidency was sustained for the first time. Of this experience he recalled, "When the Brethren read [the names of] the members of the Council of the Twelve for a sustaining vote, eleven names were read, stopping with Marvin J. Ashton. I, however, heard the twelfth name. It was mine. From that day I [knew] I was to fill the vacancy [in the Twelve]."[20]

With such unexpected foreknowledge given him, Elder McConkie desired to obtain divine confirmation. "Finally on Friday, September 29, I determined that I needed some peace of mind about the matter, and so I went alone to the seventies room on the fourth floor of the Salt Lake Temple. I talked the matter over with the Lord and told him I was not asking to be called to the Council of the Twelve and that I wanted it clearly understood that my sole interest was in having him choose the person he wanted and who would do the most for the building up of his kingdom and the rolling forth of his work, and I then asked him to give me the knowledge of what his mind and will was."[21] Regarding this, he wrote,

> Following my petition, the Lord gave me the following answer, which in this instance I did not write down, in the verbatim words, but in which these points were covered:
> That I had been called to fill the present vacancy in the Council of the Twelve;
> That I had been foreordained to this position;
> That one of the reasons for the call was to honor my father, Oscar W. McConkie;
> And that my father on the other side of the veil had intervened in my behalf on the same basis upon which President Grant's father had intervened in his behalf.[22]

(When Elder McConkie spoke to the Brethren in council during the time that President Lee died and Elder Spencer W. Kimball became the President of the Church, he told them, "I said I had been made aware that my father had been involved in my call to the Council of the Twelve. . . ."[23])

Amelia shared her own reflections: "The call was not entirely unexpected. Though Bruce had not shared with me all his thoughts and previous experiences regarding this calling, many people had suggested to us that they felt Bruce would fill the vacancy. But more significant to my mind was the exceptional feeling of peace, tenderness, and harmony we had experienced in our home for the past several days. We felt, rather than saw, that we had visitors from beyond the veil."[24]

CALLED AS A SPECIAL WITNESS

On October 4, 1972, Bruce was called by President Harold B. Lee as a member of the Council of the Twelve, an Apostle and special witness "of the name of Jesus Christ in all the world" (D&C 107:23). Having been called away from a meeting with the First Council of the Seventy, Elder McConkie explained what happened next.

I left and never returned to the meeting. When I got out in the hall [my secretary] said, "President Harold B. Lee is on your telephone." I came down to my office and answered the phone, and he said, "This is Harold B. Lee. Will you please come down to my office?" I went down and he put his arms around me and said, "The Lord and the Brethren have just called you to fill the vacancy in the Council of the Twelve." I said, "I know it, President Lee. This is no surprise to me. I have known it for some time."

In spite of my prior knowledge, it was a great emotional shock, and he said to me, "Tell me about it," and I told him of my experience in Mexico City and in the temple the previous Friday. He said, "I am glad the Lord is confirming my inspiration." We sat and talked for about half an hour. He told me that he had known for three months that I was to fill the vacancy and that he had had the matter reconfirmed the previous Sunday when he spent an hour in the Holy of Holies discussing the matter with the Lord. . . . Then he said, "I counseled with the Lord about the matter and . . . the Lord made it very plain what he wanted." In our conversation, he also told me that it was what he wanted and that when he presented my name on Tuesday to the First Presidency, they were delighted, and that when he presented it earlier that day (Wednesday) there was universal approval and pleasure manifest by the Brethren.[25]

At that October conference, Elder McConkie bore his witness. "The first of these gifts listed in our modern revelation on spiritual gifts is the gift of testimony, the gift of revelation, the gift of knowing of the truth and divinity of the work. This gift is elsewhere described as the testimony of Jesus, which is the spirit of prophecy. This is my gift. I know this work is true. I have a perfect knowledge that Jesus Christ is the Son of the living God and that he was crucified for the sins of the world."[26] Having so stated, he then referenced the personal revelations he had received from the Lord in 1966 and 1970, stating, "I know there is revelation in the Church, because I have received revelation. I know God speaks in this day because he has spoken to me."[27] Then he added further words of testimony, in which he quoted his personal revelation shared with the 1951 conference nearly two decades before.

> I rejoice in the privilege and opportunity to serve as a witness of his name, to teach the truths of salvation which he has revealed, and then to testify that these doctrines are true. God has given us the truths of salvation in this day on the same basis he has revealed them in every dispensation of the past. His system is now and always has been to reveal to apostles and prophets and righteous men the doctrines and truths of salvation and to command them to teach those truths and to bear witness of their verity to the world. They are to bear testimony that they know their teachings come from the Lord. His representatives and servants are always witnesses of the truth. I rejoice in the privilege of standing as a witness of the truth in this day. With reference to these brethren who hold the keys of the kingdom of God at this hour, the voice of the Lord to his people is "These are they whom I have chosen as the First Presidency of my Church. Follow them."[28]

Having been called, sustained, and ordained (on October 12, 1972, by President Lee acting as voice), Elder McConkie approached his apostolic work with zeal, diligence, and a greater endowment of spiritual power. He had faith he could succeed. He wrote, "I reread Section 18 and 112 relative to the calling of the Twelve and what is expected of them; also Matthew 10 and the account of the Nephite disciples in Third Nephi. Needless to say, the whole matter is completely overwhelming, and yet, because it is the Lord's work and his hand is in it, the counsel given in these revelations can be followed, and the success that should attend the Lord's work will result from such a course." He also affirmed, "As I said in my acceptance speech in the Solemn Assembly, I have a perfect knowledge of the truth and divinity of this work. It is the Lord's work, and it is destined to triumph. There is an eternal principle that truth will prevail."[29]

As he moved into his ministry, he was magnified in his apostolic office. Amelia remembered, "[In South America] he counseled with a man on a problem he was having. Bruce began to tell him that he didn't know the answer to his problem and that the man should write to the brethren for an answer, but as he thought this, he said, 'It came to me very clearly just what should be done.' Bruce told me he had never had such a strong, clear impression as he had at that time, and he knew the mantle had fallen."[30]

His duty shone clear before him. At the next general conference, he stated,

> I do not minimize in any degree or to any extent the obligation that rests upon us to be gospel scholars, to search the revelations, to learn how to reason and analyze, to present the message of salvation among ourselves and to the world with all the power and ability we have; but that standing alone does not suffice. When that is all over, we have to comply with the command the Lord gave for us in this day: "Ye are my witnesses, saith the Lord, that I am God" (Isa. 43:12). We have to put an approving, divine seal on the doctrine that we teach, and that seal is the seal of testimony, the seal of a personal knowledge borne of the Holy Ghost. . . . And I attempt with all the vigor of my soul so to do on this occasion, because I am one, among many great hosts in latter-day Israel, who has this knowledge. I know of myself of the truth and the divinity of this work and of the doctrine I now teach.[31]

Because he sought the Lord humbly and with great faith, spiritual impressions and direction came. At the October 1973 general conference, he noted,

> I had it impressed upon me, when President Lee opened the conference yesterday, and again when President Romney bore the persuasive and powerful and true witness that has just come from his lips, that if the Lord himself were here, those statements which came from them are the very things that he would say at this time. . . . There may be those who have special gifts and needs to serve in other fields, but as far as I am concerned, with the knowledge and testimony that I have, there is nothing I can do for the time and season of this mortal probation that is more important than to use all my strength, energy, and ability in spreading and perfecting the cause of truth and righteousness, both in the Church and among our Father's other children.[32]

With continued spiritual experience came absolute assurance. In 1973, while speaking to a group of priesthood leaders, he stated, "I shall speak about the doctrine of revelation and shall lay before you some of the great and wondrous principles which enable man to commune with his Maker. These are matters about which I can speak with some confidence and surety because I have received revelations and learned by experience to recognize the voice of the Spirit."[33]

SEEKING THE FACE OF JESUS

As he magnified his calling, a new dimension entered his messages, centered around Doctrine and Covenants 93:1, and those with eyes to see, and ears to hear, and hearts to understand were enabled to catch a deeper vision of this Apostle's witness. His words spoken at the dedication of the Washington DC Temple carried great meaning.

This Washington [DC] Temple, as with all our other temples, is . . . a house to which the Lord himself will come personally when he has occasion to visit this part of his vineyard. It is a house to which he will send his angels as his purposes may require. It is a house where he will pour out his Spirit upon all those who here assemble to worship the Father in Spirit and in truth. It is a house where the visions of eternity shall be seen and the revelations of his mind and will shall be given. . . .

As we assemble here in worshipful reverence to wait upon the Lord and to partake of his Spirit, we might well ponder this great promise in our hearts. How long will it be before we, either as a people or as individuals, have attained that perfection which will enable us to see the face of Him whose we are? When will we receive a fulfillment of that eternal decree that says, "Verily, thus saith the Lord: It shall come to pass that every soul who forsaketh his sins and cometh unto me, and calleth on my name, and obeyeth my voice, and keepeth my commandments, shall see my face and know that I am" (D&C 93:1).

God grant that we may use this holy house, not alone for ordinance work, but to commune with him face to face, as was the case with holy men in days of old, and has been the case with some among us in this last dispensation.[34]

This subject—of striving to so live as to obtain the privilege and blessing of seeing the face of the Lord Jesus while yet in mortality—so occupied Elder McConkie's thoughts that he devoted two chapters to it in his book *The Promised Messiah*, naming them, "Seek the Face of the Lord Always" and "Who Has Seen the Lord?" His comments therein are telling and enlightening. "As believing saints it is our privilege . . . to see the Lord face to face; to talk with him as a man speaketh with his friend." Also, "The fact is that the day of personal visitations from the Lord to faithful men on earth has no more ceased than has the day of miracles." And, "When the Lord has a house on earth, it is the natural and normal place for him to use in visiting his earthly friends." Further, "This means that if we obey the law that enables us to see the Lord, so shall it be, but if we do not meet the divine standard, our eyes shall not behold him."[35] Continuing, "These accounts have been preserved for us as examples and patterns of what has been, what is, and what yet shall be. They let us know the manner in which the Lord works, and they show us that other men, with passions and faults like ours, have yet overcome the world and gained surpassing outpourings of spiritual enlightenment." And last, "We shall now collate and comment upon some of the more important manifestations of Deity to man so as to have before us what we may expect if we have faith like the ancients."[36]

On June 1, 1978, Elder McConkie enjoyed, with his Brethren of the First Presidency and ten of the Twelve, the most spiritual experience of his life, at least to that point.[37] It came in the house of the Lord at the time of the receipt of the revelation to President Spencer W. Kimball extending priesthood and temple blessings to all worthy men regardless of race (see D&C Official Declaration 2). On June 28, 1978, Elder McConkie related the event to family members while vacationing in Nauvoo and visiting in the home of a Kimball relative. A family member present, who took notes from Bruce's narration, later described what he said.

> When we were all seated . . . Bruce began to tell us some of the events and details about this revelation. . . . One thing that he cautioned us not to do was to make it more than it was, even though I can't imagine a greater thing than this in this life. . . . With President Kimball the preliminaries for this [revelation] started at least two years [before it was received]. There were many, many, discussions, returning to the subject from time to time in their quorum meetings in the temple. There was much fasting and there was much praying and many prayers were offered pleading to the Lord for a resolution of this problem. During the last three or four months there had been extended discussion during the quorum meetings regarding offering all of the blessings of the gospel to all the people of the earth.
>
> Now the various members of the quorum were asked to express themselves briefly and did. . . . The Prophet had told the quorum that this was a problem that he had been wrestling with for many hours and had spent many hours going to the upper rooms of the temple, wrestling [in prayer] with the Lord. He had not received a revelation but he wanted a revelation. . . .
>
> This particular Thursday (this was on June 1) President Kimball asked the members of the Quorum [of the Twelve] to stay; he said that he had some things that he wanted to discuss further. All of the members of the quorum were there except [two].
>
> President Kimball began by saying that there was a matter that had been discussed many times and he would like to discuss it again. He said, "We would like to get an answer to it. I would like to get a revelation one way or the other. If it is to remain as it is, I will defend it with my life. But if the Lord feels that the time is come to give the priesthood blessings to all worthy men, I want that

revelation." And then he called another prayer . . . in which he asked the Lord to give them an answer. . . . Bruce said, President Kimball, in his modest way, asked the Brethren if it would be alright if he were mouth, that is, if he were the one who lead the prayer. And he said before the prayer, "Are there any questions that any of you would like to ask?" It was an informal meeting, and in an informal meeting, the Brethren do not have to follow seniority.

Bruce raised his hand, and for ten minutes he discussed points that were known to the Prophet—that he had written in his memorandum to him—but they weren't necessarily known to the other members of the quorum. Elder Packer then spoke, and there were no new extensions of the discussion; there were no duplication of ideas. Then the Brethren began to speak freely, and there was a discussion and clarification of ideas and talk that was going forward. Then they had the prayer circle, and the prayer given by the Prophet, Elder McConkie said, were the words of the Lord and it was given by the Spirit. He prayed perhaps five or ten minutes, and he asked the Lord for an answer, to reveal to the brethren in a simple way, His desires.

Bruce said he had often wondered what Paul had meant in Acts [2:3] by "cloven tongues of fire"—these were the words that Paul used, because he had no other words to describe it. But he said since this experience in the temple, when the Lord revealed to the ten members of the quorum of the Twelve and the First Presidency His will concerning the giving of the priesthood to all worthy men, he now understood what Paul meant, because he had experienced it. But even having experienced it, he couldn't put into words what happened except to say that he now understood what Paul meant when he said, "cloven tongues of fire fell upon the congregation," and he said it did upon each of the members present. . . .

Someone asked Bruce, "was it like the day of Pentecost in the restored Church when some saw angels, some saw others, and so forth?" He said, "It was like that." They tried to get him to say who was present. He was very careful to say it was like that day and would not go into detail. . . .

Bruce says that this was the most spiritual experience he had ever had, and that, if you will remember back to his conference address when he was called to be an Apostle, he indicated that he had talked with the Lord prior to his being called; that he had direct communication with the Lord, and the Lord let him know that he was approved, and what was in store for him. And yet, despite all of that, he said that this was the greatest spiritual experience he had ever had.[38]

President Kimball heard of the informal McConkie family meeting and soon thereafter asked Elder McConkie to write for him an account of his statements to his family at that time. Responding, Elder McConkie wrote a formal memorandum for the Prophet, dated June 30. This account confirms the substance of the above family recitation and adds further details.

In recent years the counselors in the First Presidency and all members of the Council of the Twelve and Presidency have had an acute awareness of the desire of President Spencer W. Kimball to learn the mind and will of the Lord relative to conferring the Holy Priesthood upon worthy males of every race and color. In recent months one aspect or another of this matter has come up for informal discussion in various regular meetings of the First Presidency and the Twelve. . . .

On two occasions in recent months President Kimball has invited the members of the Twelve, if they felt so inclined, to give him written memorandums expressing their personal views together with any doctrinal explanations as to whether it would be appropriate to give the priesthood to worthy members of all races and colors. Some of the Brethren responded to this invitation and sent documents to the President. . . .

On Thursday, June 1, 1978, the Twelve met as usual at 8 a.m. All of the Brethren came in at 9 a.m., and the normal meeting, including testimonies, was held. There were about fifteen Brethren invited to speak and bear testimony. . . . The meeting on this day seemed to have a particularly high spiritual tone. All of the Brethren who expressed themselves did so with faith and testimony, and the spirit of the Lord was present in manifold abundance.

At the conclusion of the prayer . . . President Kimball took the unusual step of inviting the members of the Presidency and the Twelve to remain in the room . . . and then excused the other Brethren. Always on these first Thursdays, all of the Brethren come to the meeting fasting. On this occasion, on the first of June, President Kimball said to the Twelve that he would like them to continue during the balance of that day to fast with the Presidency and that the normal luncheon at the end of the business meeting had been cancelled. President Kimball then advised the members of the Presidency and the Twelve that in recent months he had been giving extended serious, prayerful consideration to the matter of conferring the priesthood upon the Negroes and that he felt the need for divine guidance. He said that in recent weeks he had spent many hours alone there in the upper room in the temple, pleading with the Lord for counsel and direction. He said he hoped the Lord would give a revelation one way or another and re-solve the matter. He indicated that if it was the mind and will of the Lord that we continue in the present course, denying the priesthood to the descendants of Cain, that he was willing to sustain and support that decision and defend it with all its implications to the death. He said however, that if the Lord was willing to have the priesthood go to them, he hoped for a clear affirmation of this so there would be no question in anyone's mind.

There followed a near two-hour period in which there was complete, extended and free discussion on the matter. President Kimball began by asking for expressions of opinion and feeling from members of the Twelve. The Brethren responded freely and without hesitation. None were in any way inhibited in setting forth their views. Each one spoke. Some questions were asked by the counselors in the First Presidency as various of the Brethren expressed their views. These were answered to the seeming complete satisfaction of all. There was a wondrous and marvelous feeling and spirit of unity in the meeting. All of the expressions of all of the Brethren leaned and tended toward the view that it would be a wholesome and beneficial thing if the Lord felt inclined to approve the giving of the priesthood and temple blessings to worthy men of all races and colors. There was no divisive feeling whatever. A strong, compelling spirit of unity was in the meeting. It seemed as though all of the Brethren were, in effect, joining in the prayers that President Kimball had recently been making in the same room on this tremendously important matter.

After full discussion and full expression on the part of all concerned, President Kimball suggested that we go forward with the prayer. . . . He said that if it was agreeable with the Brethren, he would be mouth. President Kimball then importuned the Lord with great fervor and faith. All the Brethren joined in his prayer as it was recited at the altar. He asked that a revelation might be given manifesting the Lord's mind and will on this matter so that the issue could be resolved. It was one of those occasions when the one who was mouth in the prayer prayed by the power of the Spirit and was given expression and guided in the words that were used and the sentences that were said. The spirit of unity that had prevailed first in the meeting with all the Brethren and then in greater manifestation and degree when the Presidency and the Twelve met alone, continued to increase in the hearts of all present.

While President Kimball prayed, the revelation came. When he ceased to pray, there was a great Pentecostal outpouring of the Spirit such as none of those present had ever before experienced. There are no words to describe what then happened. It was something that could only be felt in the hearts of the recipients and which can only be understood by the power of the Spirit.

When the Spirit of the Lord fell upon certain Nephite congregations, they were unable to write in language what happened and indicated that the outpouring of the Spirit could only be understood by the power of the Spirit. On the day of Pentecost in the Old World, it is recorded that cloven tongues of fire rested upon the people. It is thought that this is an attempt to find language which would describe the overwhelming power and impact of the Holy Ghost upon the hearts of people. On this occasion, in the upper room of the temple, something akin to the day of Pentecost occurred. All of the Brethren at once knew and felt in their souls what the answer to the importuning petition of President Kimball was. All knew with one voice what the intent and purpose of the Lord was with reference to the priesthood. Nothing could have been more clearly and forcibly presented. Some of the Brethren were weeping. All were sober and somewhat overcome. When President Kimball stood up, several of the Brethren, in turn, threw their arms around him, and each of the Brethren knew that an answer had been received and that the voice of the Lord had been heard. All knew what should be done. At this point they retired. . . . All of the Brethren felt subdued and sobered.

Subsequent to the meeting, President Kimball and each of his counselors and President Benson, representing the feelings of all who were present, expressed themselves to the effect that never in their experience in the Church had they ever felt or experienced anything in any way comparable to what occurred on this first day of June in 1978 in the upper room in the Salt Lake Temple.[39]

Elder McConkie's life was filled with supernal spiritual experiences. Who knows what visions he saw or heavenly beings he entertained during his apostolic service? He did not say. He did say this: "God is no respecter of persons. . . . Every soul is precious in his sight and he is just as anxious to give the visions of eternity to me and to you as he was to Enoch and Abraham and Moses."[40] He taught that one measure of truly spiritually experienced, mature, and faithful Latter-day Saints is to determine "What fellowship we have with holy beings on both sides of the veil."[41]

His April 1979 and April 1980 general conference messages were filled with prophecies about the future.[42] Such also filled his book *The Millennial Messiah*. The future was not all dark for him. Whether some of his utterances and writings reflected independent personal revelations to him or constituted his inspired interpretations of scripture, we cannot say.

When it came to the most sacred spiritual experiences he had enjoyed, he noted, "There have also been some other matters which I will not mention."[43] He wanted his teachings and example to build faith in others, yet he did not cast pearls before swine. He loved spiritual truths and desired others to catch the same spirit of hungering and thirsting after righteousness that he possessed. He invited a group of regional representatives (somewhat commensurate with today's Area Seventies) to follow his example, saying, "I would hope that all those called to teach and preach the gospel have had the same experience that has been mine on many occasions. In the spirit of prayer, while reading and pondering the holy word, new views, added concepts, truths theretofore unknown, have suddenly dawned upon me. Doctrines that were dim and hidden and little known, have, in an instant, been shown forth with a marvelous clarity and in wondrous beauty."[44] To a similar group he also testified, "These principles are true. Some may not believe them; others may feel they are expressed too strongly. So be it. But remember that God is the

Judge and someday all of us will stand before his bar and be judged by how fully we have believed and how strictly we have lived his law. And I for one am a witness that he speaks today and reveals his mind, his will, and his purposes to every living soul who abides the law which enables him to commune with the Infinite."[45]

Truly, a matter of utmost importance to him was to so live in righteousness as to pierce the veil and behold Jesus and speak with Him face to face. Elder S. Dilworth Young, a member of the First Council of the Seventy, who labored with Bruce for many years and knew him well, understood this and therefore wrote, "Other matters of life have importance, of course, and receive attention, but nothing can interfere with his search to find out about God. Like Nephi of old, his thirst is to receive the vision of his tree of life and to live to pierce the veil himself."[46] At Bruce's funeral, then-Elder Boyd K. Packer said, "Brother McConkie and I shared a witness that I have come to believe few men share. I could and I did speak more openly to him of sacred things than any other man."[47] (See chapter 4 on Elder Packer's special witness for further information.)

An Apostle's privilege is to so live in humility, righteousness, and faith that he may prevail and behold the face of the Lord Jesus.[48] Explaining how this works in conjunction with the abiding witness of the Holy Ghost, Elder McConkie wrote, "It is true that the witness of the Holy Ghost is sure and absolute and that a man can know with a perfect knowledge, by the power of the Holy Ghost, that Jesus Christ is the Son of the living God who was crucified for the sins of the world. This unshakeable certainty can rest in his soul even though he has not seen the face of his Lord. But it is also true that those who have this witness of the Spirit are expected, like their counterparts of old, to see and hear and touch and converse with the Heavenly Person, as did those of old."[49] And further, "Few faithful people will stumble or feel disbelief at the doctrine here presented that the Lord's apostolic witnesses are entitled and expected to see his face, and that each one individually is obligated to 'call upon him in faith in mighty prayer' until he prevails."[50]

As previously noted, most Thursdays the Quorum of the Twelve Apostles meet and counsel together in an upper room (fourth floor) of the Salt Lake Temple. The purpose of these meetings is to transact important Church business, pray, partake of the sacrament, and to teach and bear testimony to each other. They also meet with the First Presidency and members of the Seventy. In such sacred and holy environs, the Spirit is abundantly present. On such occasions and when requested, Elder McConkie took his turn and taught his Brethren with great power.[51] Elder Mark E. Petersen related one such occasion (in 1980) to students at BYU.

> This morning at seven o'clock, the Counsel of the Twelve met in their fourth-floor assembly room in the Salt Lake Temple. We were there from seven until

twelve in a very moving, spiritual meeting. The sacrament was passed, and we all partook of it in a most solemn manner and were grateful for the privilege. . . .

Behind the pulpit in that little meeting room is a beautiful mural depicting the Savior in the Garden of Gethsemane. We talked about Gethsemane and about the Savior. Brother Bruce R. McConkie spoke at length about the tremendous suffering that the Savior went through. He did it in a very touching way and with great solemnity, reminding us how the Savior went into the Garden of Gethsemane. . . .

Brother McConkie called our attention to the fact that the suffering incident to the Atonement began there in Gethsemane and that the Savior suffered so dreadfully that drops of blood came from his pores. . . .

Brother McConkie then told us that the Savior was not kneeling in that prayer. The suffering that he endured was so infinite, so much beyond our understanding, that even he fell prostrate upon the ground.[52]

It becomes apparent that, as he stated, Elder McConkie had paid a price and been blessed to have certain spiritual truths revealed to him even beyond that contained in the scriptural record.

Elder Rex C. Reeve, a member of the First Quorum of the Seventy in the late 1970s and '80s, recorded his impressions of being taught by Elder McConkie: "The First Quorum of the Seventy met today with the Council of the Twelve, and we were taught by Elder Bruce R. McConkie on the Son of God—that He was actually the son of the Father, conceived in the natural manner. I received a strong witness to my soul that it was true. It is a special privilege to be taught by the Twelve."[53] When it came to the doctrine and reality of Jesus the Christ, the Only Begotten Son of God in the flesh, this special witness knew whereof he spoke—and the Holy Spirit bore record.

Another General Authority remembered, "I was present in a gathering of the Saints where Elder Bruce R. McConkie preached a powerful doctrinal discourse. As he concluded, he asked the following question: 'How do you prove that Jesus is the Christ?' There was a complete silence. Then, he declared, 'It all centers in the Resurrection!' Then he asked, 'How do you prove the Resurrection?' Once again there was a profound silence. He then declared, 'It all centers in witnesses!' There, standing before us, was an Apostle of the Lord Jesus Christ, a special witness."[54]

The powerful and expressive language Elder McConkie used in his famous last general conference address in April 1985 is especially convincing. "And now, as pertaining to this perfect atonement, wrought by the shedding of the blood of God—I testify that it took place in Gethsemane and at Golgotha, and as pertaining to Jesus Christ, I testify that he is the Son of the Living God and was crucified for the sins of the world. He is our Lord, our God, and our King. This I know of myself independent of any other person. I am one of his witnesses, and in a coming day I shall feel the nail marks in his hands and in his feet and shall wet his feet with my tears. But I shall not know any better then than I know now that he is God's Almighty Son, that he is our Savior and Redeemer, and that salvation comes in and through his atoning blood and in no other way."[55]

Those closest to him knew that his special witness was a pearl of great price whose luster need not be dimmed by death or time. His brother Brit prayed with faith for such. "We're grateful for Elder McConkie who has been 'a voice in the wilderness,' who has borne testimony of the divinity of Jesus Christ wherever he has gone. . . . We're grateful for those things that he has taught us, for those things which he has written, and for his testimony that has been instilled in our hearts."[56] Likewise, President Ezra Taft Benson testified, "His testimony bears repeating because his was a sure witness as an Apostle of the Lord Jesus Christ and as a special witness of his name."[57]

With some doubtful voices today seeking to diminish the validity, legitimacy, and solidity of Elder McConkie's teachings and witness, we might ask what the current leadership of the Quorum of the Twelve Apostles thinks of him. In a September 2015 newspaper article, President Russell M. Nelson related some of his experience with Bruce: "Occasionally, I would have an idea I wanted to discuss or had a question. I would knock on his door, and he was always gracious, always warmly welcoming. When I could see this was an opportunity to learn from him, I would ask him to put his remarks on pause for a minute while I called Elder Oaks and asked him to come up so we could converse with Elder McConkie together. That was a rare privilege."[58]

Surely such respect, humble deference, and esteem fully answers the question.

Notes

1. *Amelia Smith McConkie: Remembrances for Her Family*, comp. Mary McConkie Donoho (privately published, 2007), 491.
2. Oscar W. McConkie, *Memorabilia* (privately published, n.d.), 280.
3. Ibid., 197. Date of vision is March 29, 1936.
4. Ibid., 20–21. See also the account as given by Elder McConkie in Dennis B. Horne's *Bruce R. McConkie: Highlights from His Life and Teachings*, 2nd ed. (Salt Lake City, Utah: Eborn Books, 2010), 24. This rendering omits the fact that Emma saw, open eyed, the Eternal Presence. See also Oscar W. McConkie Jr.'s "Ye

Are My Witnesses . . . That I Am God" (LDS Institute of Religion Devotional, October 29, 1971), 5–6; copy in author's possession.

5. Dennis B. Horne, *Bruce R. McConkie: Highlights from His Life and Teachings* (Roy, Utah: Eborn Books, 2000), 36.

6. Dell Van Orden, "Bruce R. McConkie: A Challenging Future" (*Church News*, 1973), 3; see also Horne, *Bruce R. McConkie*, 36.

7. Ibid., 3.

8. *Amelia Smith McConkie*, 124.

9. Ibid., 484–86.

10. Ibid., 482.

11. Ibid., 489.

12. Bruce R. McConkie, in Conference Report, October 1951, 146–50.

13. The details of Elder McConkie's meeting with the First Presidency and Elder Petersen are taken from notes of an interview with Elder Glen L. Rudd, by the author, Dennis Horne, August 27, 2009. President Henry D. Moyle told Elder Rudd about their meeting with Bruce and what happened therein. For narration of a similar experience involving an author, the First Presidency, and Elder Mark E. Petersen, see Leonard J. Arrington, *Adventures of a Church Historian* (Urbana and Chicago: University of Illinois Press, 1998), 146–47.

14. For further information about Elder McConkie's experience regarding the first edition of *Mormon Doctrine*, see Horne, *Bruce R. McConkie*, 2nd ed., 427–33. This material is found in the epilogue, near the back of the book, and contains much detailed information not found in the first edition. See pages 399–462.

15. *Amelia Smith McConkie*, 493.

16. Bruce R. McConkie, "The Testimony of Jesus," *Ensign*, July 1972.

17. *Amelia Smith McConkie*, 493.

18. Ibid., 314–15.

19. See Robert L. Millett and Joseph Fielding McConkie, *The Life Beyond* (Salt Lake City: Bookcraft, 1986), 81.

20. *Amelia Smith McConkie*, 494.

21. Ibid.

22. Ibid., 495. President Grant related the following, which he experienced while on a journey, that concerned his call to the Twelve:

"As I was riding along to meet them on the other side, I seemed to see, and I seemed to hear, what to me is one of the most real things in all my life. I seemed to hear the words that were spoken. I listened to the discussion with a great deal of interest. The First Presidency and the Quorum of the Twelve Apostles had not been able to agree on two men to fill the vacancies in the Quorum of the Twelve. There had been a vacancy of one for two years, and a vacancy of two for one year, and the conferences had adjourned without the vacancies' being filled. In this council the Savior was present, my father was there, and the Prophet Joseph Smith was there. They discussed the question that a mistake had been made in not filling those two vacancies and that in all probability it would be another six months before the Quorum would be completed. And they discussed as to whom they wanted to occupy those positions, and decided that the way to remedy the mistake that had been made in not filling these vacancies was to send a revelation. It was given to me that the Prophet Joseph Smith and my father mentioned me and requested that I be called to that position. I sat there and wept for joy. It was given to me that I had done nothing to entitle me to that exalted position, except that I had lived a clean, sweet life. It was given to me that because of my father's having practically sacrificed his life in what was known as the great reformation, so to speak, of the people in early days, having been practically a martyr, that the Prophet Joseph and my father desired me to have that position, and it was because of their faithful labors that I was called, and not because of anything I had done of myself or any great thing that I had accomplished" (Heber J. Grant, *Gospel Standards*, comp. G. Homer Durham [Salt Lake City: Deseret Book, 1941], 194–96). See also Horne, *Bruce R. McConkie,* 120, and Joseph Fielding McConkie, *The Bruce R. McConkie Story: Reflections of a Son* (Salt Lake City: Deseret Book, 2003), 322–28.

23. McConkie, *The Bruce R. McConkie Story,* 368.

24. *Amelia Smith McConkie,* 314.

25. Ibid., 496.

26. Bruce R. McConkie, "I Know That My Redeemer Lives," *Ensign,* January 1973.

27. Ibid.

28. Ibid.

29. *Amelia Smith McConkie,* 498.

30. Ibid., 317.

31. Bruce R. McConkie, "Upon Judea's Plains," *Ensign,* July 1973.

32. Bruce R. McConkie, "Think on These Things," *Ensign,* January 1974.

33. Bruce R. McConkie, "Revelation," unpublished address given in 1973, 1; hardcopy in author's possession.

34. As quoted from the remarks of Elder McConkie at the Washington (DC) Temple dedication, November 22, 1974, 5–7; hardcopy in author's possession. See also Bruce R. McConkie, *A New Witness for the Articles of Faith* (Salt Lake City: Deseret Book, 1985), 497.

35. The sentence quotations and others like them are found in Bruce R. McConkie, *The Promised Messiah* (Salt Lake City: Deseret Book, 1978), 570–95.

36. McConkie, *The Promised Messiah,* 596–97.

37. In substantiation of this statement, Elder McConkie wrote, "In the days that followed the receipt of the new revelation, President Kimball and President Ezra Taft Benson—the senior and most spiritually experienced ones among us—both said, expressing the feelings of us all, that neither of them had ever experienced anything of such spiritual magnitude and power as was poured out upon the Presidency and

the Twelve that day in the upper room in the house of the Lord" (Mark L. McConkie, *Doctrines of the Restoration: Sermons & Writings of Bruce R. McConkie* [Salt Lake City: Bookcraft, 1989], 161–62).

38. "Address of Bill Jordan Pope" (brother-in-law of Elder McConkie), given shortly after the 1978 revelation was received (LDS Church Archives, Salt Lake City, Utah).

39. Memorandum to President Spencer W. Kimball from Elder Bruce R. McConkie, June 30, 1978, entitled "The Receipt of the Revelation Offering the Priesthood to Worthy Men of All Races and Colors," 1–7; copy in author's possession.
   Elder McConkie is elsewhere quoted as saying, "On the day of Pentecost in the Old World it is recorded that cloven tongues of fire rested on the people. They were trying to put into words what is impossible to express directly. There are no words to describe the sensation, but simultaneously the Twelve and the three members of the First Presidency had the Holy Ghost descend upon them and they knew that God had manifested his will. . . . I had had some remarkable spiritual experiences before, particularly in connection with my call as an apostle, but nothing of this magnitude." This wording is incorrectly cited in Edward L. Kimball's "Spencer W. Kimball and the Revelation on Priesthood," *BYU Studies*, 47:2 (2008), 56, as coming from the McConkie memorandum to President Kimball, but it does not. I speculate this wording may have come from an interview Edward Kimball conducted with Elder McConkie at a later date.

40. McConkie, "Revelation," 6.

41. Bruce R. McConkie, "A Convert Called Peter" (address prepared for the General Authority training meeting held August 31, 1983, but not given), 25.

42. See Bruce R. McConkie's "Stand Independent above All Other Creatures," *Ensign*, May 1979, and "The Coming Tests and Trials and Glory," *Ensign*, May 1980.

43. *Amelia Smith McConkie*, 494.

44. Regional representatives' seminar, April 2, 1982; in *Doctrines of the Restoration*, 243–44.

45. McConkie, "Revelation," 8.

46. S. Dilworth Young, "Elder Bruce R. McConkie of the Council of the Twelve," *Ensign*, January 1973.

47. As quoted in "Funeral transcript of Bruce R. McConkie," 7; copy in author's possession. Most recently, and before his passing, President Packer asked that quotations from various talks he had given wherein he bore his apostolic witness be published for the Church in the *Ensign*. (See "A Witness of the Savior Jesus Christ," *Ensign*, December 2015, on LDS.org.)

48. See explanation given in McConkie, *The Promised Messiah*, 592–94.

49. Ibid., 592.

50. Ibid., 594.

51. In a general conference talk, Elder L. Tom Perry referred to these marvelous teaching experiences: "We [the Twelve] are a class as we study the doctrines of the kingdom together. Can you imagine what a special experience it would be to be in a quorum meeting and be taught gospel doctrine by Elders Ezra Taft Benson, Mark E. Petersen, LeGrand Richards, Howard W. Hunter, Bruce R. McConkie, David B. Haight, or Neal A. Maxwell?" See "What is a Quorum?," *Ensign* or *Liahona*, November 2004.

52. Mark E. Petersen, "The Covenant People of God" (Brigham Young University fireside, September 28, 1980), speeches.byu.edu.

53. As quoted in the journal of Elder Rex C. Reeve, December 6, 1978 (unpublished); copy in author's possession.

54. John M. Madsen, "The Gospel" (Brigham Young University—Idaho devotional, March 8, 2011), byui.edu.

55. Bruce R. McConkie, "The Purifying Power of Gethsemane," *Ensign*, May 1985.

56. As quoted in "Funeral transcript of Elder Bruce R. McConkie," 1–2.

57. Ibid., 2.

58. Gerry Avant, "President Nelson reflects on being an Apostle of the Lord, discusses possible announcement of 3 new apostles," *Church News* (September 30, 2015); see deseretnews.com.

6

President Harold B. Lee's

SPECIAL WITNESS OF JESUS CHRIST

*"When I see Jesus, I cannot mistake His
identity. I know that He lives!"*

Of President Harold B. Lee, Elder Marion G. Romney observed,

> In one aspect of Harold B. Lee's life and his character, he was different
> from any other man that I've ever been associated with. I felt with him like I'd
> imagine the Prophet Joseph Smith was, with respect to the inspiration that
> came to him. Joseph Smith spoke by the power of the Spirit out of a personal
> knowledge and association with the Father and the Son. Brother Lee, in my
> judgment, was more like the Prophet Joseph Smith in this respect than was
> any other man I've ever associated with. He seemed to get the inspiration of
> the Lord spontaneously. Harold just seemed to me to speak directly from in-
> spiration and could jump, as it were, from peak to peak as he went along in his
> teachings and his interpretations of the gospel and in his answering of ques-
> tions. He obtained his knowledge from God by revelation. He was a seer.[1]

WARNED BY AN UNSEEN SPEAKER

Born in Idaho in 1899, Harold Lee was an impressive individual from the start. Even as a child he was obedient to the warning voice of an angel.

> I have a believing heart because of a simple testimony that came when I was a child, I think maybe I was around ten—maybe eleven—years of age. I was with my father out on a farm away from our home, trying to spend the day busying myself until father was ready to go home. Over the fence from our place were some tumbledown sheds which had attracted a curious boy, adventurous as I was. I started to climb through the fence and I heard a voice as clearly as you are hearing mine—"Don't go over there!" calling me by name. I turned to look at father to see if he were talking to me, but he was way up at the other end of the field. There was no person in sight. I realized then, as a child, that there were persons beyond my sight and I had heard a voice. And when I had heard and read these stories of the Prophet Joseph Smith, I, too, know what it means to hear a voice because I've heard from an unseen speaker.[2]

Harold became a schoolteacher at seventeen and a principal at eighteen. At twenty he served a mission, returning to get married (to Fern Tanner), go to school, and work, again as a principal. At twenty-eight he was called to the Salt Lake Pioneer Stake high council, and at thirty-one he was the Pioneer Stake president. He served for five years, at which time he was released by the First Presidency to become the managing director of the Church's new welfare plan. He also taught seminary and served on the Salt Lake City Commission. He dabbled in politics, and some prominent friends tried to draft him to run for governor or the United States Senate, but service to the Church became his highest priority, and he left politics behind.

WORK AND INSPIRATION IN THE CHURCH WELFARE PROGRAM

Church welfare work would engage a substantial portion of his life. As Pioneer Stake president, and with the great depression in its disastrous depths, Harold and his counselors sought help from the First Presidency of the Church. "When they had finished [explaining their needs], the prophet [Heber J. Grant] asked his counselors, Anthony W. Ivins and J. Reuben Clark, if they agreed with him that the Church should care for the needy. After receiving an affirmative response, he pounded the table with his fist for emphasis and, according to

President Lee's record, he said, 'This is the decision of The Church of Jesus Christ of Latter-day Saints: If necessary we will close every seminary, and church school, and temple, and take care of our people if it takes the hide off of the Church.' The First Presidency then made additional funds available for the Pioneer Stake welfare program."[3]

Later, as Harold continued as Pioneer stake president and actively did all he could to relieve the severe needs among his many stake members, a major life change came to him personally. While the President of the Church, he related the essentials of his experience to a general conference audience.

It was from our humble efforts that the First Presidency, knowing that we had had some experience, called me one morning asking if I would come to their office. It was Saturday morning; there were no calls on their calendar, and for hours in that forenoon they talked with me and told me that they wanted me to resign from the city commission, and they would release me from being stake president; that they wished me now to head up the welfare movement to turn the tide from government relief, direct relief, and help to put the Church in a position where it could take care of its own needy.

After that morning I rode in my car (spring was just breaking) up to the head of City Creek Canyon into what was then called Rotary Park; and there, all by myself, I offered one of the most humble prayers of my life.

There I was, just a young man in my thirties. My experience had been limited. I was born in a little country town in Idaho. I had hardly been outside the boundaries of the states of Utah and Idaho. And now to put me in a position where I was to reach out to the entire membership of the Church, worldwide, was one of the most staggering contemplations that I could imagine. How could I do it with my limited understanding?

As I knelt down, my petition was, "What kind of an organization should be set up in order to accomplish what the Presidency has assigned?" And there came to me on that glorious morning one of the most heavenly realizations of the power of the priesthood of God. It was as though something were saying to me, "There is no new organization necessary to take care of the needs of this people. All that is necessary is to put the priesthood of God to work. There is nothing else that you need as a substitute."[4]

CALLED TO BE AN APOSTLE

Harold's efforts with the Church welfare program, with the help of others, were successful and lasted for decades to come. However, after approximately six years directing and expanding the program, at the age of forty-two, he was called as a member of the Council of the Twelve Apostles. In his journal, he described what happened.

> I was sitting in the audience attending the general priesthood meeting as the managing director of the Church Welfare Program. At the conclusion, President J. Reuben Clark, who was conducting the meeting, called my name out and asked that I come to the stand to meet Bishop Joseph L. Wirthlin. Bishop Wirthlin did have a matter of business to mention to me, but it was really a way to have me meet with President Heber J. Grant.
>
> When I arrived at the stand, Elder Joseph Anderson said that the President was waiting for me in the General Authorities' room. It amazed me, and I immediately sensed that there was something more than just a social visit that President Grant had in mind. It was then that he announced to me that I had been named to be elevated to the Quorum of the Twelve to fill the vacancy which had been created by the death of Senator Reed Smoot.[5]

According to President Lee's biographer, "After learning of his appointment, he said, 'Oh, President Grant, do you really think I am worthy of such an exalted calling?' The plain-spoken President replied simply, 'If I didn't think so, my boy, you wouldn't be called!'" In his journal, Harold also wrote, "I went to lunch with President Clark, where he gave me careful and detailed explanation of the procedures on Thursday, where I was to be ordained an Apostle in the temple and accept a charge from the President of the Church as to my duties, obligations, and responsibilities as a member of the Quorum of the Twelve." And then, "I attended my first meeting in the Salt Lake Temple with the First Presidency and the Council of the Twelve. I was ordained an Apostle and set apart as a member of the Council of the Twelve by President Heber J. Grant, with his counselors and the eleven members of the Council assisting. Before the ordination, I was given a charge by each member of the Presidency in which they stressed important matters pertaining to activities of General Authorities."[6]

Obtaining His Special Witness

One element of the apostolic charge (that we presume Elder Lee was given) was a commission not to cease striving until he had obtained his special witness. According to Elder Lee's several accounts, this happened the week following the conference. He recalled the experience:

It was on the day or so following conference that President Stephen L. Richards, who was then chairman of the Church radio and publicity committee, approached me and said, "Brother Lee, next Sunday is Easter, and we have decided to ask you to give the Sunday night radio talk, the Easter talk, on the Resurrection of the Lord." And then he added, "You understand now, of course, that as a member of the Council of the Twelve, you are to be one of the special witnesses of the life and mission of the Savior and of that great event." The most overwhelming of all the things that have happened to me was to begin to realize what a call into the Council of the Twelve meant.

During the days which followed, I locked myself in one of the rooms over in the Church Office building [Church Administration Building], and there I read the story of the life of the Savior. As I read the events of his life, and particularly the events leading up to and of the Crucifixion, and then of the Resurrection, I discovered that something was happening to me. I was not just reading a story; it seemed actually as though I was living the events; and I was reading them with a reality the like of which I had never before experienced. And when, on the Sunday night following, after I had delivered my brief talk and then declared, simply, "As one of the humblest among you, I, too, know that these things are true, that Jesus died and was resurrected for the sins of the world," I was speaking from a full heart, because I had come to know that week, with a certainty which I never before had known.

I do not know whether that experience was the realization of the workings of the gift of the more sure word of prophecy, but this much I came to know: neither the Prophet Joseph Smith, nor any who have followed since, have ever received a personal visitation from the Master, nor have they ever received a special witness of his life and mission, except they have had a supreme faith. Until that faith had been tried and tested, only then did they receive the witness.

This much more I know, and bear humble witness, that only shall I receive a greater witness than I today have, that he is, when my faith through trial shall have become the more perfect.

I know with all my soul today, God being my witness, that the Savior died, was resurrected, and lives today.[7]

On another occasion and to a different audience, he phrased his experience thusly: "As one of the humblest among you, and occupying the station I do, I want to bear you my humble testimony that I have received by the voice and the power of revelation, the knowledge and an understanding that God is. It was a week following the conference when I was preparing myself for a radio talk on the Life of the Savior, when I read again the story of the life, the Crucifixion and the Resurrection of the master, there came to me as I read that, a reality of that story. More than just what was on the written page. For in truth, I found myself viewing the scenes with a certainty as though I had been there in person. I know that these things come by the revelations of the living God."[8]

OPPOSITION AND ATTENTION FROM THE ADVERSARY

As has been mentioned by other Apostles, a common occurrence they experience is displeasure manifested toward them by the adversary. While each is unique in their life stories and varied circumstances, there are also ways in which their apostolic office unites them in sameness of experience. Elder Lee explained, "As I have listened to every member of the Twelve that has come in since I became a member of that body, each has repeated my own experience. Within a week after my installation as a member of the Twelve, I sat in a social gathering and listened to all who had preceded me who were then living relate their experiences in being called to be apostles, and all of them were also telling *my* story. It was put in language by one of the brethren who said, 'One thing that I *have* learned since I came into the Council of the Twelve, and that is that there *is* a devil.' "[9]

As though fate sought to prove the point, not long into his apostolic ministry, Elder Lee was faced with a situation in which the power of the devil was manifested.

I think that I might add my own testimony that came shortly after I was called into the Council. A young man whose marriage I had performed sometime previously came hurrying into my backyard (on a Saturday) where I was working and urged me to come quickly, that his wife was acting strangely. When I dressed and went with him, I found this girl seemingly all right physically, but she was talking about strange things. She said she had had a visitation from angels. She had seen Elijah. She had seen Moses. She claimed to have had some great experiences. She said they had told her that she couldn't live longer with this husband, that she should sever her connections with him. She had six or seven little children.

I sat down and began to try to soothe her in conversation. She smiled sweetly. I had been her stake president for a number of years before this time. I said, "Now, you have always been willing to take counsel and to listen to the counsel of your stake president."

And she smiled and listened as I tried to calm her, and then she said, "But, President Lee, I'm not who you think I am. I am not who you think I am."

Then her voice changed, and she grew more severe, and she said, "And do you know who you are? You are the head of the Church."

"No, I am not the head of the Church, although I sit with those who are the heads of the Church."

Then, seeing that our conversation was resulting in nothing, I said to her husband, "Let's administer to her."

He anointed her head with oil, and just at the moment our hands touched her head she was transformed into almost a demon of rage. She jumped to her feet, her eyes flashing, and she uttered a phrase that chilled me from the top of my head to the soles of my feet: "Oh, no, you are not going to send me out of this world!"

Every hair in my head felt like a pinprick, and yet before me was this little defenseless girl whom I had known from her childhood. Someone was speaking through her. Rather forcefully then we took hold of her and rebuked the power of the devil, commanded it to depart, which it did, leaving her weak and limp. . . .

There is a devil, and we had better pray God that we never have to have that personal encounter with him. There are legions of his emissaries round about us, contending for our souls and the souls of all of Adam's children. Let us make no mistake about it, Satan is a reality.[10]

In reflecting on what the evil spirit possessing the woman had said about him being the "head of the Church," Elder Lee thought it might mean that the devil knew he would someday become the head or President of the Church.[11]

Developing into a Seer

Elder Lee's apostolic ministry was like unto that of others of his quorum, visiting the stakes, blessing people, speaking constantly, reorganizing stake presidencies, and for him, continuing to work in the Church welfare program. He grew in grace and spiritual stature, gradually developing the reputation among his associates of being very close to the Lord and becoming a seer in their eyes. Knowing this, as Elder Marion G. Romney commented about some of the members of the Twelve in his first address after his own call as an Apostle, he noted, "Brother Lee is a seer. I know I'll never go wrong if I'm with him."[12] Elder Marvin J. Ashton agreed, saying, "President Lee was one of the most spiritual leaders I have ever known. He seemed to have continuous possession of the whisperings of the Spirit."[13]

Tried as by Fire, Rewarded with Confirming Witness

In some of his talks, Elder Lee told of what he felt to be one of the most difficult but spiritual experiences of his life. He did not give many contextual details, being primarily interested in relating how his spiritually strenuous efforts to help a friend brought to him a trial that drew him very close to the Lord. Several of the accounts or comments, which are presumed to be the same experience, and which he used to emphasize his testimony of how diligence and faith brought him divine guidance and reaffirmed witness, follow.[14]

We read about Enos, struggling in prayer all day and all night. . . . I've been in that circumstance where it wasn't all one day and one night, but the next day and the next night, and the next day. I'd fast until my strength was fast going, then I'd get a little nourishment and I'd go on fasting. I wasn't always on my knees, but I was praying. I remember the blessing I was seeking for one I was trying to save. I was all alone in this house where I was staying, and so I was left to my own. I had to go before a judge the next day, in the morning. And so, all day Sunday I made an outline of what I might say when I got before that judge as carefully as I knew how to document it. But in the middle of the night (apparently I had slipped off into a little slumber), suddenly I was awakened (I was as much awake as I am now) and it was as though someone had pulled up a chair and was there right beside me and dictated into my mind exactly what I was to do. It wasn't what I had planned and what I had written on this paper in outline. I didn't need any outline. All because I had been close to the Lord. I knew I could trust Him. And I saw a miracle happen, . . . and that judge made a decision. . . .

I felt confident that if I had to struggle much longer there would have been no veil. I would have seen as well as I heard dictated to my mind. So that I *know* in whom I can trust when I have nowhere else to go.[15]

My own testimony: I was faced with a difficult, trying problem. I know what Enos means when he said, "My soul hungered, and I went out by myself where I could pray." I had a spiritual experience. I saw no light. I heard no voice to my physical senses, but I knew then as surely as I know now that I live, that on that night, when I was struggling, seeking, I had done everything in my power to prepare myself for the great responsibility that lay ahead. I knew in my own soul that that night my mind was being directed by an omnipotent power which pierced my very soul. . . .

As one of those who feels himself the least among you, and having a right as a member of this Church, and my appointment, to testify of these things of which I have spoken to you this morning, in all solemnity, and with all my soul, I bear you my testimony that I know that Jesus lives, that he is the Savior of the World. I know that he reveals himself and is revealing himself to his prophets.[16]

I was once in a situation where I needed help. The Lord knew I needed help and I was on an important mission [to save a friend]. I was awakened in the hours of the morning as though someone had wakened me to straighten me out on something that I had planned to do in a contrary course, and there was clearly mapped out before me as I lay there that morning, just as surely as though someone had sat on the edge of my bed and told me what to do. Yes, the voice of the Lord comes into our minds and we are directed thereby.[17]

I bear you my testimony that I know that God hears and answers prayers. I have been close to him in the hours of some of my greatest trials, and surprisingly they are the times that I have drawn closest to Him. In fact, in a certain trial that was one of the most severe tests of my life, I feel that if the trial had gone on for a few more hours His presence was so near that I could have seen Him face to face.[18]

A Witness of Revelation to the Twelve

As he sat in council with the First Presidency and the Twelve, he often observed revelation at work among them, guiding and inspiring. He wanted members of the Church to understand that this occurred, and it occurred often, so he bore testimony and shared occasional insights.

As I come to you this morning with a humble heart to talk to you about revelation, I come to you as one who sits in the company of men who live close to their Heavenly Father. There have been occasions when I have had within me a feeling of sureness about things. I have seen matters come before the First Presidency and the Council of the Twelve in our weekly meetings. I've seen a decision reached, not based upon reasoning, but upon an impression which after that decision had been made has been found to have been a heaven-sent direction to protect and to guide.

I recall an incident a little over six months ago when an important matter had been decided upon, and the Presidency had called the Twelve to announce the decision. After the decision had been made, it was a thrilling thing to hear the President of the Church say, "Brethren, the Lord has spoken."[19]

To a group of Church religious educators, he explained,

Brother John A. Widtsoe used to tell us about a group who gathered around him between meetings at a stake conference, and someone said, "Oh, Brother Widtsoe, how long has it been since the Church received a revelation?" And Brother Widtsoe stroked his chin for a moment and said, "Oh, probably since last Thursday." When he said Thursday, he was referring to the meeting that is held in an upper room of the temple—the Presidency and the Twelve meet each Thursday. Brother Widtsoe knew, as I know, and as all who attend those meetings know, that there we see in perspective the whole Church brought to review. We see wisdom beyond human wisdom, decisions prompted by powers beyond ourselves. We left our meeting a week ago last Thursday and I walked out of the meeting with President Hugh B. Brown. He said, "Wasn't that marvelous to see that display of intelligence as we presented these very difficult problems?" Maybe it's only been since last Thursday that the Church has had a revelation.[20]

Sometimes while bearing his special witness, he would describe a little about how he received revelation. "With all my soul and conviction, and knowing the seriousness and import of that testimony, I tell you that I know that He lives. I am conscious of His presence much of the time when I have needed Him most; I have known it out of the whisperings of the night, the impressions of the daytime when there were things for which I was responsible and on which I could receive guidance. So I testify to you and tell you that He is closer to the leaders of this Church than you have any idea. Listen to the leaders of this Church and follow their footsteps in righteousness, if you would learn not only by study but also by faith, which testimony I bear most humbly and sincerely."[21] And again, to a different audience, he said, "I bear you my testimony that I have that witness; I know that it is true and that Joseph was a prophet and the gift of prophecy is among men today. I know it and thank God that I have had a simple enough faith that from my childhood I too have had a theophany. I've heard a voice of an unseen spirit. I've received witnesses and testimonies that I could not have received except by that gift by which we too might continue to know the truth."[22]

Explaining the Witness of Modern Apostles

Elder Lee once had a question come to him, indirectly, as a challenge from a minister of a sectarian church, of what constitutes a modern Apostle or special witness of Jesus Christ. He gave the following explanation to the missionaries who inquired.

May I impose to bear my own testimony. I was visiting in one of the missions some years ago when two missionaries came to me with what to them was a very difficult question. A young Methodist minister had laughed at them when they said that apostles were necessary today in order for the true church to be upon the earth. And the minister said, "Do you realize that when they met to choose one to fill the vacancy caused by the death of Judas that they said it had to be one who had companied with them and had been a witness of all things pertaining to the mission and the Resurrection of the Lord? How can you say you have apostles if that is the nature of an apostle?" And so these young men said, "What shall we answer?" I said, "Go back and ask your minister friend two questions. First, how did the Apostle Paul gain what was necessary to be called an Apostle? He didn't know the Lord, had no personal acquaintance, he hadn't companied with the Apostles. He hadn't been a witness of the ministry nor the Resurrection of the Lord. How did he gain his testimony sufficient to be an apostle? Now the second question: You ask him how does he know that all who are today apostles have not likewise received that witness?" I bear witness to you that those who hold the apostolic calling may and do know of the reality of the mission of the Lord—to know which is to be born and quickened within the inner man.[23]

Becomes President of the Church

Most of three decades passed as Elder Lee served in the Quorum of the Twelve, with the senior Apostles older than him passing away. Then the aged President David O. McKay died in January 1970, and President Joseph Fielding Smith called Elder Lee to be his first counselor in the First Presidency, where he served for about two and a half years. Then President Smith died, and Elder Lee became President Lee, when on July 7, 1972, he was ordained the President of the Church by the Quorum of the Twelve. In a conversation with a friend, President Lee told of obtaining confirmation for his choice of counselors.

He said, "When I realized I was to be President of the Church I immediately thought of counselors. I was certain I wanted to keep President Tanner as first counselor and I wanted Marion [meaning Marion G. Romney] as second counselor." Then he said, "After a little while it dawned on me that I had not cleared this with the Lord. I was sitting here in my office and thought I better go over to the temple and find out for sure." He said, "I grabbed my hat and told Francis [Gibbons, his secretary] I would be back in a very short time. I walked over to the temple, went up to a room that I can go in whenever I want to [the Holy of Holies]. There I asked the Lord if I could have as my counselors President N. Eldon Tanner as first counselor and Marion G. Romney as my second counselor." He then looked at me and said, "I got an immediate answer and I knew that it was alright with the Lord. I came right back to the office. I wasn't gone much over twenty minutes."

He then bore testimony to me of how wonderful it was to be close to the

Lord. He said, "If all my problems could be answered as quickly and positively as that one, I shouldn't have much trouble as President of the Church."[24]

Along with counselors, President Lee needed to call a new Apostle to fill the vacancy in the Twelve created by President Smith's passing and Elder Marion G. Romney's inclusion in the First Presidency. "President Lee was concerned about the coming conference . . . with the selection of one to fill the vacancy in the quorum. He told [a friend] that he had received the revelation he was seeking. 'When it came, I trembled. I couldn't write it down fast enough.'" The name he received as part of that written revelation was Bruce R. McConkie. After formally calling Elder McConkie, President Lee told him that he had "known for three months that [Bruce] was to fill the vacancy and that he had had the matter reconfirmed the previous Sunday when he spent an hour in the Holy of Holies discussing the matter with the Lord."[25] President Lee also received revelation to call James E. Faust as an Assistant to the Twelve (see chapter 9, President Faust's special witness), and Rex D. Pinegar as a member of the First Quorum of the Seventy. Both Elder McConkie and Elder Faust had their calls revealed to them in advance by the Spirit.

In his final address at the general conference in which he was sustained as the President of the Church, President Lee indicated that he felt the Lord had made of him a new man ("I am different than I was before Friday morning"), and then he declared,

> There has come to me in these last few days a deepening and reassuring faith. I can't leave this conference without saying to you that I have a conviction that the Master hasn't been absent from us on these occasions. This is his church. Where else would he rather be than right here at the headquarters of his church? He isn't an absentee master; he is concerned about us. He wants us to follow where he leads. I know that he is a living reality, as is our Heavenly Father. I know it. I only hope that I can qualify for the high place to which he has called me and in which you have sustained me.
>
> I know with all my soul that these sayings are true, and as a special witness I want you to know from the bottom of my heart that there is no shadow of doubt as to the genuineness of the work of the Lord in which we are engaged, the only name under heaven by which mankind can be saved.[26]

He later reflected further on the experience of becoming *the* President and Prophet.

> On the day when I came to this call, which imposed a greater responsibility

to be a witness of the mission of the Lord and Savior, Jesus Christ—I suppose no one ever came to such a position without a lot of soul-searching, realizing his own inadequacy, and without the help of the Almighty—after a long night of searching and days of spiritual preparation that followed, I came to know as a witness more powerful than sight, until I could testify with a surety that defied all doubt, that I knew with every fiber of my soul that Jesus is the Christ, the Son of the living God, that He lived, He died, He was resurrected, and today He presides in the heavens, directing the affairs of this church, which bears His name because it preaches His doctrine. I bear that testimony humbly and leave you my witness.[27]

President Lee soon found that being the President of the Church meant that personal temptations increased. To a group of college, Church, and community leaders in Idaho, President Lee mentioned this fact, as recorded in the journal of Henry B. Eyring (then president of Ricks College, which is now BYU—Idaho). "President Lee began to speak. . . . He spoke with power, emotion, and informality that I cannot recreate on this page. He spoke of his own calling, saying, 'If you think Satan doesn't try to tempt the prophet, you're wrong. I'm his prime target on earth.' "[28]

DECLARING HIS SPECIAL WITNESS AS THE PROPHET OF GOD

During his brief tenure as President of the Church, President Harold B. Lee accomplished much, including taking opportunity to declare his special witness. To a group of temple workers, he disclosed more about that witness than he perhaps ever had before, and he noted he would have liked to reveal even more. He said, "Jesus lives! I bear my witness to you this morning. There are some witnesses I cannot give now, perhaps sometime later. Many things are too sacred to share at this time. I have received a witness that I cannot or dare not deny. When I see Jesus, I cannot mistake His identity. I know that He lives!"[29] He used similar language in one of his last messages, given to the BYU student body, testifying in that large venue for the last time. "I bear you that sacred testimony, that I know with a witness that is more powerful than sight. Sometime, if the spirit prompts me, I may feel free to tell you more, but may I say to you that I know as though I had seen, that He lives, that He is real, that God the Father and his Son are living realities, personalities with bodies, parts, and passions—glorified beings."[30]

President Lee only served for a year and a half as President of the Church, when death took him in late December 1973 at age seventy-four—a comparatively young age that shocked the membership of the Church. Having been relatively healthy and vigorous, it was expected that he would serve with energy and vitality for many years to come.

Since his death, it has become known that President Lee returned in a dream given to a trusted friend and associate, and therein explained the reason for his surprising demise.

> In the dream [of September 16, 1978] there were two vivid messages: first, that if President Lee had gone on living, a very severe affliction would have developed in his body which, if allowed to progress, would have given him great pain, suffering, and incapacity. The medical details of this were dreadful and distressing. He said his sudden death in December 1973 was brought about as an act of love and mercy, for the Lord wished to spare him and the Church the misery that otherwise would have ensued. His second message was that the revelations received and the actions subsequently taken by President Kimball were the very same as would have been received and performed by President Lee had he remained as the prophet. President Lee exclaimed that the Lord gives His will to His living prophet regardless of who the prophet is at the time, for the Lord indeed is directing his Church.[31]

The revelation President Lee referred to, received by President Kimball, but which would have been received by him had he lived, is the June 1, 1978 revelation granting the priesthood and temple blessings to all men of any race, depending on worthiness. It seems that date was when the Lord, in his own provinces, desired to lift the restriction.

NOTES

1. Marion G. Romney, as quoted in *Thoughts on Welfare from the Words of President Harold B. Lee*, comp. Glen L. Rudd (Salt Lake City: privately published, n.d.), 71.
2. Harold B. Lee, "Divine Revelation" (talk, October 15, 1952), 6; hard copy in author's possession, audio version available at speeches.byu.edu.
3. Francis M. Gibbons, *Harold B. Lee: Man of Vision, Prophet of God* (Salt Lake City: Deseret Book, 1993), 117–18.
4. Harold B. Lee, "Admonitions for the Priesthood of God," *Ensign*, January 1973. President Lee also noted, "With my mind completely, shall I say, subdued and humbled to the dust, my view of the Church was limited within the boundaries of the

Pioneer Stake. I had hardly traveled outside of my own stake. We knew what our problems were and they were great. One of the reasons why I had been called in, so President Grant said, was because the Church statistics showed that in our stake we had probably the greatest burden of welfare need of any stake in the Church; the second reason was that we had tried to do something about it" (Harold B. Lee, "Use the Priesthood in the Welfare Program" [1968]; in Glen L. Rudd's *Thoughts on Welfare from the Words of President Harold B. Lee*, 10).

5. Harold B. Lee journal entries given as quoted in L. Brent Goates' *Harold B. Lee: Prophet & Seer* (Salt Lake City: Bookcraft, 1985), 157–64.

6. Ibid.

7. Harold B. Lee, "Special Witnesses," in Conference Report, April 1952, 126–27.

8. Lee, "Divine Revelation," 10.

9. Harold B. Lee, "Sweet Are the Uses of Adversity," 10; audio version available at speeches.byu.edu.

10. Harold B. Lee, "Satan Is a Reality" (lecture given to seminary and institute teachers at Brigham Young University, July 9, 1954); see *CES Summer School Talks, 1954 & 1958*, 257–59.

11. There is some question as to the overall timing of this incident, whether it occurred when Brother Lee was a stake president or an Apostle. For Elder Lee's thoughts on the devil knowing he would become President of the Church, see Oscar W. McConkie Jr.'s "God Spoke to Harold Every Day" in *He Changed my Life: Personal Experiences with Harold B. Lee*, ed. L. Brent Goates (Salt Lake City: Bookcraft, 1988), 29. For another account of this experience and conclusion, see Goates' *Harold B. Lee, Prophet & Seer*, 219–20. The date for the blessing is here given as 1943.

12. Marion G. Romney, "A Testimony of the Redeemer," *Improvement Era*, December 1951, 893.

13. Marvin J. Ashton, "A Still Voice of Perfect Mildness" (Brigham Young University devotional, February 20, 1990), 3, speeches.byu.edu.

14. For background information on this matter, see Goates' *Harold B. Lee: Prophet & Seer*, 312–14.

15. Harold B. Lee, "To Be on Speaking Terms with God" (Salt Lake Institute of Religion devotional, October 12, 1973), 11–12; hardcopy in author's possession.

16. Harold B. Lee, "But Arise and Stand upon Thy Feet" (talk, February 7, 1956), 11–12; hardcopy in author's possession, audio available at speeches.byu.edu.

17. Lee, "Divine Revelation," 7.

18. Harold B. Lee, "Prayer" (address to seminary and institute faculty at Brigham Young University, July 6, 1956), 20; audio available at speeches.byu.edu.

19. Lee, "Divine Revelation," 9–10.

20. Harold B. Lee, "Loyalty" (address to religious educators, July 8, 1966); see *Charge to Religious Educators*, 2nd ed. (Salt Lake City: Church Educational System and The Church of Jesus Christ of Latter-day Saints, 1982), 64.

21. Elder Harold B. Lee of the Council of the Twelve, April 1968; as quoted by Elder Marvin J. Ashton in "A Still Voice of Perfect Mildness," February 20, 1990, 3; speeches.byu.edu.

22. Harold B. Lee, "The Church and Divine Revelation" (address to seminary and institute teachers, Brigham Young University, July 13, 1954); see *CES Summer School Talks, 1954 & 1958*, 273.

23. Harold B. Lee, "Born of the Spirit" (October 15, 1952), 10–11; hardcopy in author's possession; audio available at speeches.byu.edu.

24. *Thoughts on Welfare from the Words of President Harold B. Lee*, 66.

25. As quoted in *Amelia Smith McConkie: Remembrances for Her Family*, comp. Mary McConkie Donoho (privately published, 2007), 496–97. See also chapter 5 on Elder Bruce R. McConkie's special witness.

26. Harold B. Lee, "A Blessing for the Saints," *Ensign*, January 1973.

27. "British Area Conference Report" (August 29, 1971), in *The Teachings of Harold B. Lee,* comp. & ed. Clyde J. Williams (Salt Lake City: Bookcraft, 1998), 637.

28. Harold B. Lee (late 1973), as quoted in Robert I. Eaton and Henry J. Eyring's *I Will Lead You Along: The Life of Henry B. Eyring* (Salt Lake City: Deseret Book, 2013), 257.

29. "Meeting for the Temple Workers of the Provo Temple" (July 9, 1972), in Williams' *The Teachings of Harold B. Lee,* 636.

30. "Be Loyal to the Royal Within You" (Brigham Young University devotional, September 11, 1973), 11, speeches.byu.edu.

31. As quoted in Russell Marion Nelson's *From Heart to Heart: An Autobiography* (Salt Lake City: Quality Press, 1979), 159–60.

7

President Marion G. Romney's

SPECIAL WITNESS OF JESUS CHRIST

*"I have heard the voice of God in
my mind, and I know His words."*

"I cannot remember when I did not have a testimony. It has, of course, been strengthened through the years, but I can never remember when I did not believe."[1] So declared Elder Marion G. Romney, who valued his testimony above all else.

EARLY ADVENTURES

Before a group of students at a Salt Lake Institute of Religion devotional, Elder Marion G. Romney reminisced about his childhood and early days.

> I'm a Mexican by birth. I was born in Colonia Juarez, Chihuahua, Mexico. My parents happened to be down there at the time. I was raised there until I was about fifteen years old. During the last two or three of those years, the Madero Revolution was in progress. The rebels and the federalists were chasing each other through the country; each taking everything we colonists had, by way of arms

and ammunition and by way of supplies. Finally we were forced to leave. I came out of Mexico with the Mormon refugees in 1912.

I remember I had a very thrilling experience on the way from where we lived to the railroad station about eight miles south of Colonia Juarez. We went in a wagon. Most of the men remained in the colony for a while. Just a few came out with the women and children. I was riding with my mother and her seven children and my uncle (her brother) and his family of about five or six children. We were in a wagon box. . . . My mother and my uncle and his wife sat in the spring seat. We had one trunk—that was all we were able to bring. I was seated on the trunk in the back of the wagon. We were going south and I was looking north up the road we were traveling. The Mexican rebel army was coming up the valley from the railroad station toward our town. They were not in formation. They were riding their saddle horses. Their guns were in the scabbards. Two of them stopped us and searched us. They said they were looking for guns. We didn't have any guns or ammunition. They did find $20.00 on my uncle—pesos, not dollars. A peso then was worth 48 cents on the dollar. They took that and then waved us on. They went up the road about as far as from here to the back of this room, stopped, turned around, drew their guns from their scabbards, and pointed them down the road at me. As I looked up the barrels of those guns, they looked like cannons to me. They didn't pull their triggers, however, as evidenced by the fact that I am here to tell the story. That was a very thrilling experience! One of my maturing experiences.

The rebels blew up the railroad track after the train we were on passed over it. Later, Father and the rest of the men came out to El Paso, Texas, on horseback. We never returned nor did we recover any of our property while my father lived.

Father and I went to work to earn a living for his large family. There were no welfare programs then. We had a difficult time making a living. We had to . . . or die.

That Fall Father and Mother went with their family to Los Angeles, California, to find employment. Father was a carpenter and there was a building boom in California. I stayed out of school that year and learned carpentering as a carpenter's helper. . . .

In 1916 we came to Salt Lake where he obtained a bachelor's degree at the University of Utah. I worked as a carpenter to help sustain the family.

In the fall of 1917, we moved to Rexburg, Idaho, where Father presided over Ricks Academy, which he helped develop into a junior college.

Going to school but part time, it took me from 1918 to 1932 to get through college.

Well, so much for my maturing. My going on a mission might be interesting to you. It was so difficult for Father to earn a living for his family, that we never talked about a mission for me after we came out of Mexico, until 1920. I had participated in athletics at Ricks, football and basketball, and had been urged to attend the University of Idaho at Moscow and participate in athletics. When I graduated from Ricks Junior College, I learned that a man with a junior college certificate, when it came to jobs, could take his pick; and that's what I did. I took my pick and shovel and went to work digging a sewer trench in Rexburg.[2]

Elder Romney continued, "Toward the end of the summer, just before school started, a stake conference was held in the Rexburg Tabernacle. The choir seats in that building formed a half circle. The pulpit was on a line with and between the ends of the seats. I sat on the end seat in the choir, straight across from the podium. Apostle Melvin J. Ballard conducted the conference. As he stood at the pulpit, he told of seeing the Savior on an occasion when as president of the Northwestern States Mission, he had visited an Indian reservation in Montana."[3]

On that occasion, Elder Melvin J. Ballard testified,

> As I approached He smiled, called my name, and stretched out His hands toward me. If I live to be a million years old I shall never forget that smile. He put His arms around me and kissed me, as He took me into His bosom, and He blessed me until my whole being was thrilled. As He finished, I fell at His feet, and there saw the marks of the nails; and as I kissed them, with deep joy swelling through my whole being, I felt that I was in heaven indeed. The feeling that came to my heart then was: Oh! if I could live worthy, though it would require four-score years, so that in the end when I have finished I could go into His presence and receive the feeling that I then had in His presence, I would give everything that I am and ever hope to be![4]

Marion related, "His account so impressed me that I immediately went to my father and told him that if he would help me borrow the money to sustain me in the mission field, I would use what money I'd saved during that summer to get into the mission field. This he agreed to do. That fall [of 1920], in November, I went to Australia, where I served on a mission for two years and a half. The bank loaned me $35.00 a month. When I returned I went to work and paid off the loan."[5]

RECEIVING A WITNESS AS A MISSIONARY

It was while on his mission that Elder Romney enjoyed one of the great anchoring spiritual experiences of his life; one that left him forever changed. Serving at a time when there was less emphasis on companionships, he spent part of a preparation day alone at the library of the University of Sidney. On this occasion, among all the shelves and stacks of worldly books, he found himself turning to his own copy of the Doctrine and Covenants, soon becoming deeply absorbed in section 76 in particular, which is the vision of the degrees of glory given to the Prophet Joseph Smith and Sidney Rigdon. Having lost track of time, his study of that section took him into the evening.

Young Elder Romney finished reading, left the library, and was overcome with the impressiveness of what he had been reading. He later described what happened next.

> One Saturday I went to the University of Sydney and spent the afternoon in the library. When I got tired looking in the books, I sat down at a table with my Doctrine and Covenants and read the 76th Section where the Lord talks about the three degrees of glory and so forth. As I read it, I got tremendously interested, and when I finished and got up to go, it was dark. As I stepped outside and down the steps of the library building, I looked into the heavens and saw the stars in that southern sky, the Southern Cross and other constellations. They seemed unusually bright. As I gazed into the heavens and walked across the lawn to the street, I seemed to see the things I'd been reading about. That experience had such an effect on me that never since then have I been able to find complete satisfaction in any work other than the work of the Lord.
>
> I don't know that I remember when I didn't have a testimony, but this experience gave me an emphasis that I've never forgotten. From then on, even though I did many things, practiced law for example and received a great deal of satisfaction in winning lawsuits and doing other things, I didn't ever feel that I could give them my full wholehearted devotion.[6]

MARRIAGE, SCHOOLING, AND DISCIPLINED SCRIPTURE STUDY

Upon returning from his mission, Marion married Ida Jensen, and after years of hard work and schooling, he obtained a law degree. He explained, "It was my intention to be an engineer, but in the meantime, I had gotten married, and we had to make a living as we went through school. Consequently I did not have time to do the required laboratory work for engineering; I, therefore, changed over to history and political science. I worked my way through college and then through the law school here at the University of Utah. I finally obtained a law degree in 1932."[7]

With marriage, the Romneys wanted to bring children into their family, but found their desires and hopes in that direction would constitute a test of faith for them.

During the early years of our married life, my wife and I intensely desired what we considered to be a particular blessing. We set about through fasting and prayer to obtain it. . . . We asked, we believed, we thought we had faith, but though we fasted often and prayed fervently, the years rolled by without bringing us the desired answer to our prayers. Finally, we concluded that we had not fully understood somehow—that we were concentrating our faith and prayers upon receiving the particular thing, which by predetermination we had set our hearts upon. We had to consider the conditions of the promise. . . . We had to learn to be as earnest in praying "if it be Thy will," as we were when presenting our personal desires and appeals. We have no need to fear that our well-being will not be served by such an approach. . . . Submitting to His will in every instance will be for our own good. And this we must do in faith if we would have peace and happiness in our present state of imperfect living.[8]

The Romneys eventually had three children, but only one, George, named after his father (Marion George), grew to adulthood. They also adopted a son. Although Marion had learned carpentry as a trade and also worked for the post office, as stated above, he eventually decided to become a lawyer. That profession can sometimes challenge one's ethics, and he knew it. He said, "I decided that I would not be anything but an honest man, and so I made a resolution and followed it through for the twelve years I practiced law. I went to my office each morning thirty minutes earlier than my associates. There I read the scriptures for thirty minutes and prayed about what I'd read. I pleaded with the Lord to give me strength to be an honest man while I practiced law. I read through the Book of Mormon nine times during that period and through the Pearl of Great Price, New Testament, and Doctrine and Covenants about the same. That's where I really got acquainted with the Book of Mormon."[9]

Marion also dabbled a little in politics, but found his loyalty to the gospel intervening and interfering. One experience especially tested him and put him on the right course in his life. His biographer wrote,

As the 1936 election neared, it was viewed by both Republicans and Democrats as a referendum on the record and the objectives of the Roosevelt administration. Opponents pressed the nation's president to declare himself with regard to his willingness to abide by the decisions of the Supreme Court. When he would not do so, the *Deseret News* published an unattributed front-page editorial on the Saturday before the election, without mentioning Roosevelt by name, suggesting that the record of one of the candidates could be construed to indicate that he would continue to press for unconstitutional legislation. It urged Church members to vote to protect the Constitution.

Marion had been asked to serve on the campaign committee of Governor Henry H. Blood. When the editorial appeared, he felt as if his political life had collapsed around him. As a Democratic politician, working on the campaign committee of the man who would be re-elected governor of Utah, and committed to vote for the incumbent Democratic president of the United States, he was stunned. It was only an editorial and it was not addressed to him. Furthermore, it was a legal matter not an ecclesiastical one, but there it was— on the front page of the newspaper he considered the voice of the Church. He called some of his friends, who suggested that it was just a political trick.

Marion began to fast. He went to his law office, locked the door, and when he left after three hours of anguished prayer, he had received an assurance that the editorial was inspired and had been written by Heber J. Grant, the President of the Church. Marion believed he had no choice but to resign from the governor's committee. This he did and then spent all of his efforts from that time until the election (to no avail) trying to dissuade his friends from voting for Franklin Roosevelt.

As a result of the election, Democratic Party candidates were swept into power at all levels of government. Marion soon realized he had made a costly political decision, but he believed it was correct and that was enough for him.[10]

CALLED AS AN ASSISTANT TO THE TWELVE

After serving as a bishop and stake president, at the age of forty-four, Marion was called as an Assistant to the Quorum of the Twelve Apostles. He related,

> At the time I was called to be an Assistant to the Twelve I was a stake president, and was seated in the tabernacle at conference. President Clark was presenting the General Authorities for the vote of the people. There was a vacancy in the Council of the Twelve. President Lee was called to fill the vacancy. I had long been a friend of his and was thrilled. Then Brother Clark went on to say something to the effect that the work of the Twelve had become so heavy that a decision had been made to add more help. It was therefore proposed that we sustain the following five high priests as Assistants of the Twelve. I was sitting in the audience between my stake patriarch and my second counselor. Marion G. Romney was the first name. . . . I hadn't heard about it; nobody else had heard about it. I didn't hear the other four names.[11]

On May 21, 1941, Elder Romney and the other newly called Assistants were given their charge and an explanation of what was expected of them by President

Heber J. Grant. Elder Romney came to have a great love for the prophet of the Lord. He loved to hear him bear testimony and wrote, "I remember the times I thrilled as I listened to President Heber J. Grant bear his testimony. When he used to close a conference, he would say, 'I know as I know that I live that God lives, that Jesus is the Christ, the Son of the living God, the Redeemer of the world, and that Joseph Smith was a prophet of the true and the living God, and that Mormonism, so called, is in very deed the plan of life and salvation.' I never heard him say these words without getting a tingling feeling up and down my spine."[12]

After his call as an Assistant to the Quorum of the Twelve, Elder Romney was assigned to travel to southern Utah on Church business, in company with two senior members of the Twelve—both of whom he had idolized and esteemed with the highest respect. To travel in their company was somewhat intimidating to him. As they were driving, they decided that they would stay in the area and hold one more meeting for the youth. Since the other brethren had each already spoken, they decided Elder Romney should do the speaking. This decision filled Elder Romney with sudden fear. "As he struggled to control his feelings, the voice of the Lord came into his mind saying, 'You received your calling from the same source from which they received their callings. If they call on you to speak, stand up and rely on me.' Marion would later say that the peace that came into his soul on that occasion, and which sustained him thereafter on many similar occasions, had to be experienced to be appreciated."[13]

In the 1940s, with the passing of a few of the Apostles, speculation arose as to who would fill the vacancies in the Quorum of the Twelve. Some of that speculation found its way to Elder Romney's ears, which he did not appreciate. During these years, Elders Spencer W. Kimball, Ezra Taft Benson, and Mark E. Petersen were called to fill the vacancies in the Quorum. Even though he disliked hearing his name mentioned by friends as one who would one day be called as an Apostle, he had to admit to himself that he had still entertained the idea. He was consequently annoyed with himself.

At that time he made a firm commitment to keep his mind on what he had been assigned to do and shut out all ambitious thoughts. He had no wish to aspire to office. His prayer became that the Lord would help him to do only that which he had been called to do, and do it the best he could.

After the last general conference, in which Elder Petersen was called to the Twelve, Marion began to fast once a week, every week, for twenty-four hours, over the span of seven years, with the purpose in mind to pray in faith to ask the Lord to take from his mind unworthy thoughts of aspiring to office. He told no one but his wife of this lengthy and concerted effort to put his heart right before the Lord.

Then in 1951, the matter he had prayed and fasted about for so long came to a head. His biographer wrote,

> This practice continued, unknown to anyone save Ida, until October 4, 1951. Early that morning President David O. McKay called and asked Marion to give a three- or four-minute talk in the meeting the Brethren were to have later that day in the temple.
>
> Marion complied. During the meeting the impression was repeatedly and strongly suggested to his mind that he would be called to fill the existing vacancy in the Council of the Twelve. He fought it desperately. After repeated prayer, in which he pleaded with his Heavenly Father to take the thought out of his mind and to forgive him for entertaining it, it left him. The meeting ended, and from 3:30 p.m. to 5:30 p.m., Marion enjoyed perfect peace.
>
> About 5:30, President McKay called him into his office and told him that he had been enthusiastically and unanimously chosen by the First Presidency and the Twelve to fill the vacancy in the Quorum. Marion was completely overcome. He phoned Ida and when she came at 6:00 to his little office in the Welfare Department, they wept together.[14]

Bearing Testimony as a Special Witness

In his first conference talk thereafter he said, "This call has set up a tremendous emotional reaction in me. I didn't think there could be such a big tempest in such a little teapot. I suppose that I need the help of the Lord now more than I ever needed it in my life. . . . The great respect I have always had for the office to which I am now called contributes greatly to the emotional strain I am experiencing. . . . I have always thought of this office as the office of a special witness of the Redeemer of the world." He continued, "When I think about being a special witness of him, and I remember that Peter, James, and John could not stay awake through his last suffering in Gethsemane, I think of some who have failed. I don't want to fail. I think of those who have given their lives for the witness. I have counted that. If it should be necessary, I hope I will not falter to give my life for the testimony of Jesus. I know he lives. I doubt if I will know it better when I meet him."[15]

Two years later, he amplified and expanded on his testimony as a special witness.

> I would like to say just a word about my testimony of the mission of Jesus Christ. I want to go a little farther back for a moment, if I can be given guidance by the Spirit of the Lord to speak the truth accurately, and mention the great condition precedent to the efficacy of the mission of Jesus Christ. That

condition precedent is the mission of Father Adam, because without the mission of Adam there would have been no need for the mission—the Atonement—of Jesus Christ.

I have an assignment from the First Presidency to serve on the Church publications committee. This committee is expected to read and pass upon the literature proposed for use in the study courses of our auxiliary organizations. It would please me immensely if, in the preparation of this literature, we could get away from using the language of those who do not believe in the mission of Adam. I have reference to words and phrases such as "primitive man," "prehistoric man," "before men learned to write," and the like. We sometimes use these terms in a way that offends my feelings; in a way which indicates to me that we get mixed up in our understanding of the mission of Adam. The connotation of these terms, as used by unbelievers, is out of harmony with our understanding of the mission of Adam.

"Adam fell that man might be" (2 Ne. 2:25). There were no pre-Adamic men in the line of Adam. The Lord said that Adam was the first man (D&C 84:16; Moses 1:34; Moses 3:7). It is hard for me to get the idea of a man ahead of Adam, before the first man. The Lord also said that Adam was the first flesh (Moses 3:7) which, as I understand it, means the first mortal on the earth. I understand from a statement in the book of Moses, which was made by Enoch, that there was no death in the world before Adam (Moses 6:48; see also 2 Ne. 2:22). Enoch said,

"Death hath come upon our fathers; nevertheless we know them, and cannot deny, and even the first of all we know, even Adam.

"For a book of remembrance we have written among us, according to the pattern given by the finger of God; and it is given in our own language (Moses 6:45–46)."

I understand from this that Enoch could read about Adam in a book which had been written under the tutelage of Almighty God. Thus there were no prehistoric men who could not write, because men living in the days of Adam, who was the first man, wrote.

I am not a scientist. I do not profess to know anything but Jesus Christ, and him crucified (1 Cor. 2:2), and the principles of his gospel. If, however, there are some things in the strata of the earth indicating there were men before Adam, they were not the ancestors of Adam.

Adam was the son of God. He was our elder brother, not older than Jesus, but he was our brother in the same sense that Jesus was our brother, and he "fell" to earth life. He did not come up through an unbroken line of organic evolution. There had to be a fall. "Adam fell that men might be" (2 Ne. 2:25).

Some men speak of the ancients as being savages, as if they had no intelligence. I tell you this man Enoch had intelligence, and Adam had intelligence, as much as any man that ever lived since or that lives now. They were mighty sons of God.

"And he said unto them: Because that Adam fell, we are; and by his fall came death; and we are made partakers of misery and woe" (Moses 6:48).

If Adam and Eve had not partaken of the forbidden fruit, they would have had no children, and we would not have been (2 Ne. 2:23–25; Moses 5:11).

I do not look upon Adam's action as a sin. I think it was a deliberate act of agency. He chose to do that which had to be done to further the purposes of God. The consequences of his act made necessary the Atonement of the Redeemer.

I must not go into a longer discussion, but I say again that I would be very pleased if, in our teaching of the gospel, we could keep revealed truth straight in our minds and not get it confused with the ideas and theories of men, who do not believe what the Lord has revealed with respect to the Fall of Adam.

Now, I believe with Enoch, "Because that Adam fell, we are; and by his fall came death" (Moses 6:48); that every man must die, as Brother Petersen said yesterday. I believe that to meet the demands of justice, it took the Atonement of Jesus Christ to redeem men from that death, that they may be raised again and have their spirits and their bodies, which are separated through death, reunited. I believe that through the Atonement of Jesus Christ whatever "transgression" Adam committed was paid for, and that as in Adam all die, even so in Christ shall all be made alive, every living creature (1 Cor. 15:22; D&C 29:24; D&C 77:2). I believe, too, that through the Atonement of Jesus Christ my individual sins, your individual sins, and the individual sins of every human being that ever lived or ever will live upon the earth were atoned for, upon condition that we accept the gospel and live it to the end of our lives.

I know that my Redeemer lives. I shall not know it better when I stand before the bar of God to be judged. I know that Jesus is the Redeemer. I bear that witness to you, not from what people have told me; I bear it out of a knowledge revealed to me by the Holy Spirit. As to this knowledge, the Lord, after commanding the early Apostles of this dispensation to testify that the words he had spoken to them were of him, said:

"For it is my voice which speaketh them unto you; for they are given by my Spirit unto you, and by my power you can read them one to another; and save it were by my power you could not have them;

"Wherefore, you can testify that you have heard my voice, and know my words" (D&C 18:35–36).

I am willing to bear this witness to all the Saints and to all men and women everywhere, saints and sinners, in all the world, for it is the eternal truth.

I know that the Prophet Joseph Smith was a prophet of God. I know he saw God, the Eternal Father, and his Son, Jesus Christ, as he says he did. I was not there, but I have read his account many, many, many times. From his account

I get in my mind a mental picture, but I did not get my knowledge that he had the vision from that source. I received it from the whisperings of the Holy Spirit, and I have had those whisperings in my mind the same as Enos had when he said, "The voice of the Lord came into my mind" (Enos 1:10).[16]

Elder Romney concluded his address with a statement about testimony in general. "Get the testimony of the gospel. I think it is a disgrace for men and women to stand on the same ground day after day in their testimony, their knowledge of the gospel, and their work in the Church. We should go forward."[17]

At the next conference, he spoke of the intense suffering of Christ. "Jesus then went into the Garden of Gethsemane. There he suffered most. He suffered greatly on the cross, of course, but other men had died by crucifixion; in fact, a man hung on either side of him as he died on the cross. But no man, nor set of men, nor all men put together, ever suffered what the Redeemer suffered in the garden. He went there to pray and suffer. One of the New Testament writers says that it 'was as it were drops of blood falling down to the ground' (Luke 22:44)."[18] Also,

> There is another phase of the Atonement which makes me love the Savior even more, and fills my soul with gratitude beyond expression. It is that in addition to atoning for Adam's transgression, thereby bringing about the Resurrection, the Savior by his suffering paid the debt for my personal sins. He paid the debt for your personal sins and for the personal sins of every living soul that ever dwelt upon the earth or that ever will dwell in mortality upon the earth. But this he did conditionally. The benefits of this suffering for our individual transgressions will not come to us unconditionally in the same sense that the Resurrection will come regardless of what we do. If we partake of the blessings of the Atonement as far as our individual transgressions are concerned, we must obey the law.[19]

At the April 1955 general conference, he related how, at least to that particular point in his life, he had strengthened his spiritual knowledge, his witness.

> My office is that of a special witness (D&C 107:23) of the Redeemer and of the gospel. I desire to have the spirit of that office and to testify to you of some eternal truths which are worthwhile to my brethren and sisters in the Church . . . . What I have to say I did not learn through my five senses. . . . The truths to which I testify I have learned through revelation.
> Now, do not misunderstand, I do not propose to give a startling account of an open vision. I have not seen one. Neither have I heard an audible voice. Revelation comes through three or four channels. One is the open vision;

another is the audible voice; another is the witness of the Spirit. Enos spoke of this method—the witness of the Spirit—when he said that he heard the voice of God say unto him, "Thy sins are forgiven thee" (Enos 1:5). And then a little later, after he had prayed for his brethren, the Nephites, he said,

"The voice of the Lord came into my mind again, saying: I will visit thy brethren according to their diligence in keeping my commandments" (Enos 1:10).[20]

During his early apostolic years, Elder Romney's messages seemed to largely consist of bearing his testimony of Jesus Christ and explaining His plan and gospel, focusing especially on the Atonement and Resurrection, and also teaching about and promoting the Church welfare plan, for which he had been assigned some significant responsibility by the First Presidency.

A Trial of Faith Followed by Marvelous Blessings

As the years passed, the Romneys got older and had to deal with age-related issues, such as dimming vision and hearing loss, but also more serious health issues. In 1965 Marion's wife Ida tripped over a cord in their living room, breaking her back and a bone in her hand. This caused her great pain for an extended period.

In the October 1965 general conference, Elder Romney spoke on the subject of "Making Your Calling and Election Sure," in which he said that "To do this one must receive a divine witness that he will inherit eternal life." He further said that "The fullness of eternal life is not attainable in mortality, but the peace which is its harbinger and which comes as a result of making one's calling and election sure is attainable in this life."

He further taught, "Now in conclusion, I give you my own witness. I know that God our Father lives, that we are, as Paul said, his offspring. I know that we dwelt in his presence in pre-earth life and that we shall continue to live beyond the grave. I know that we may return into his presence, if we meet his terms. I know that while we are here in mortality there is a means of communication between him and us. I know it is possible for men to so live that they may hear his voice and know his words and that to receive 'the Holy Spirit of promise' while here in mortality is possible." Elder Romney then went on to encourage all to call upon God until they received the witness in their souls that they had obtained the revealed promise of eternal life.[21] It would not be long before Elder Romney would be given a more personal knowledge of what he had spoken about to the Church.

In 1967 Ida had recovered from her back injury, but was again stricken, this time by a serious stroke. She was immediately hospitalized and often administered to by members of the General Authorities and family members. Her condition often varied, from being able to converse and recognize people, to being incoherent and comatose. As the days rolled by, Elder Romney spent all of his time either fulfilling his apostolic duties or sitting by her bedside hanging onto hope. Eventually her condition deteriorated. The attending doctors thought her case critical and gave Marion little hope for her recovery. As time passed she eventually came to recognize no one, and the prognosis was that even if she lived, it would probably only be in a vegetative state. She was repeatedly blessed by the power of the priesthood, but it began to seem to Elder Romney that she was perhaps appointed unto death. He continued fasting for her as much as his health would permit. He prayed much and studied the scriptures much. He pondered and wrestled within himself about what he could ask the Lord for, and wondered what the Lord's will for her actually was. "What right do I have," he said, "to have Ida healed? The Lord hasn't healed the Prophet, he hasn't healed others who are in as great a need as I. Who am I to ask for a blessing? Why should the Lord answer my prayers?"

Elder Romney's biographer described what happened next.

One evening, shortly after returning from an assignment, he visited Ida in the hospital, where he found her unchanged. She did not recognize him, and the likelihood that she would never speak to him again left him deeply depressed. With nowhere to go and no one with whom to share his grief, he went home. There, following a lifelong pattern, he turned to the scriptures in an effort to commune with the Lord. He picked up the Book of Mormon and continued where he had left off the night before.

He had been reading in the book of Helaman about the prophet Nephi, who had been condemned and charged with sedition because he dared point out the wickedness of the rulers of that day. In a dramatic trial, in which the ancient prophet was charged with the murder of the chief judge, he fearlessly taught the gospel and with inspired insight revealed the identity of the murderer. In the confusion surrounding the collapse of the trial, the people and court officials went their separate ways, leaving Nephi free to do whatever he desired to do. He returned home pondering the things which he had experienced. As he did so he heard a voice.

Although Marion Romney had read the story many times before, it now struck him as a personal revelation. The words of the scripture so touched his heart that for the first time in weeks he felt a tangible peace. It seemed as if the Lord was speaking directly to him. The scripture read,

"Blessed art thou [Marion] for those things which thou hast done; for I have beheld how thou hast with unwearyingness declared the word, which I have given unto thee, unto this people. And thou hast not . . . sought thine own life, but hast sought my will, and to keep my commandments.

"And now, because thou hast done this with such unwearyingness, behold, I will bless thee forever; and I will make thee mighty in word and in deed, in faith and in works; yea, even that all things shall be done unto thee according to thy word, for thou shalt not ask that which is contrary to my will."

There it was—the answer not only to the question of how to show his faith, but also, it seemed, to Ida's illness. He knew that the Lord was pleased with him. He knew that by refusing to ask a special favor without first ascertaining the will of the Lord, he had unknowingly demonstrated the quality of his faith. He knew that it had not been found wanting.

With awe Marion fell to his knees. The scripture was the direct answer to many prayers. More than anything else he wanted to know the Lord's will for Ida. He was willing to let her go; or, if need be, he would care for her in whatever condition the Lord wanted her to be in. As he concluded his prayer with the phrase "Thy will be done," he seemed to feel or hear a voice that said, "It is not contrary to my will that Ida be healed."

Marion then rushed to the hospital to bless his beloved Ida. She did not stir as he placed his hands upon her pale forehead. With undeviating faith, he invoked the power of the priesthood he had been given by his father so many years before. He pronounced a simple blessing and then uttered the incredible promise that she would recover her health and mental powers and yet perform a great mission upon the earth.

Even though he did not doubt, Marion was astonished to see Ida's eyes open as he concluded the blessing. He sat down on the bed and listened to her frail voice ask, "For goodness sakes, Marion, what are you doing here?" In total surprise he responded, "Ida, how are you?" With a flash of humor, which showed that she was not totally unaware of her circumstances, Ida Romney replied, "Compared to what, Marion? Compared to what?"[22]

Ida Romney steadily recovered until well, and Elder Romney, as part of this humbling and sanctifying experience, received his calling and election made sure and was sealed up to eternal life. His apostolic ministry had the effect of softening and enlarging his soul in meekness and he felt he was receiving the blessings of the Lord in his work. To his Brethren of the Twelve in a temple meeting, he stated, "I hope I can be true to the gospel and to you Brethren. I have been one that could see weaknesses in other men, but they are getting a little dimmer. As I get acquainted with you, I am beginning to love you with a love I did not know one and one-half years ago. I don't know whether I am overemotional or not, but I seem to feel the voice of the Lord directing me in his ministry. I feel to be conscious that the Lord is closer to me now than he has ever been before."[23]

Inwardly pondering on his special witness as an Apostle of the Lord Jesus

Christ, Elder Romney wrote the following in his journal: "I don't know just how to answer people when they ask the question, 'Have you seen the Lord?' I think that the witness that I have and the witness that each of us [Apostles] has, and the details of how it came, are too sacred to tell. I have never told anybody some of the experiences I have had, not even my wife. I know that God lives. I not only know that he lives, but I also know him."[24]

His Spiritual Gift: Hearing the Voice of the Lord

In explaining to the young people of the Church how to gain a testimony, he reflected on his own personal experience. "I know that God lives and that Jesus Christ lives. I shall not be more certain when I stand before them to be judged of my deeds in the flesh. The Holy Ghost has revealed these truths to me. I know that God can hear prayers; he has heard mine on numerous occasions. I have received direct revelation from him. I have had problems that did not seem to have a solution, and I have suffered in facing them until it seemed that I could not go further if I did not have an answer to them. After much praying, and on many occasions fasting for a day, a week, over long periods of time, I have had answers revealed to my mind in finished sentences. I have heard the voice of God in my mind, and I know his words."[25]

Hearing the voice of God in his mind was one of Marion G. Romney's greatest spiritual gifts as a special witness, and he spoke and testified of it often. In a 1961 general conference address, he stated, "I know, for example, what Enos was talking about when he said, 'the voice of the Lord came into my mind again, . . .' He did not say it came into his ear, but that it 'came into my mind again, saying. . . .' I know what that voice is like, because I have had it come into my mind and give me names when I have had to select stake presidents. There is nothing mysterious about it to people who learn to be guided by the Spirit. The voice of the Lord has come into my mind, in sentences, in answer to prayer."[26]

To another group he explained,

> In my own life, I have had answers, as a result of long periods of faithful fasting and prayer. I have had the answers of God come into my mind with the same distinctness that Enos had when the answer came to his mind and he said, "The voice of the Lord came into my mind again, saying." I have had that experience; sentences, names, have been given to me. I know this is true and in my soul is an absolute certain witness. I know if it were necessary for us to do it, we could go into our secret chambers or on the mountaintop and hear the voice of God as plainly as the Prophet Joseph did. I know that to be a truth.[27]

Standing before an audience of Church Educational System instructors, he taught, "I just talk to the Lord. And I want to testify that you can pray that way so you can hear his answer, as Enos heard it. Enos said that the voice of the Lord came into his mind (see Enos 1:10). I know that is possible because I have heard it on many occasions as plain as if it were in my ear; the voice of the Lord comes into my mind."[28]

To a general conference audience, he gave a specific example, similar to others given in this chapter.

> Enos says, "The voice of the Lord came into my mind again, saying: I will visit thy brethren according to their diligence in keeping my commandments." (Enos 1:10)
>
> I can personally testify to this form of revelation because I have experienced it.
>
> For example: I was once concluding a talk I had given at the funeral of a fine Latter-day Saint mother and was almost ready to say amen and sit down. There came into my mind the words, "Turn around and bear your testimony." And this I did. I thought no more about the event for several months until my sister, then living in a neighboring stake, paid us a visit and told us this incident:
>
> She said: "There lives in our ward a woman who for many years has taken no interest in the Church. Our efforts to activate her have been fruitless. Recently she has completely changed. She pays her tithing, attends sacrament meetings regularly, and participates in all Church activities. When asked what caused the reformation, she said, 'I went to Salt Lake City to the funeral of my mother. During the services, a man by the name of Romney spoke. After he had given an ordinary talk, I thought he was going to sit down; but instead he turned around to the pulpit and bore a testimony which greatly impressed me. It awakened in me a desire to live as my mother had always taught me.'"
>
> Now I know, my brothers and sisters and friends, and bear witness to the fact that revelation from the Lord comes through the spoken word, by personal visitation, by messengers from the Lord, through dreams, and by way of visions, and by the voice of the Lord coming into one's mind.[29]

Elder Romney's Special Witness

Elder Romney was ready, willing, and eager to bear his witness at all times and in all places, but he knew he could reach the largest number of people in his general conference addresses. On these occasions he tried to weave his witness into his messages as often and strongly as possible. On a few occasions he also declared that having given his witness, it therefore became binding on his listeners. They would from then on be accountable for how they received it. He testified,

> I know these things are true. I know them by the witness of the Spirit to my soul, and I bear you that witness. I know Jesus Christ lives. When I think of him, my Redeemer, I am always moved. In my mind's eye, I see him in that great council before the world was, when he said in effect to his Father, "I will go. Mine be the willing sacrifice, the endless glory thine."
>
> I view him as the Creator of this world and of the starry heavens. In this respect it is difficult for us to realize the greatness of Jesus. . . .
>
> I think of this man—this Son of God, Jesus—as he stood on Mount Shelem before the brother of Jared in his full-length spirit body. . . .
>
> That was 2,200 years before he appeared on earth as the infant son of Mary. I think of his coming into this world, the Son of Mary and God the Eternal Father.
>
> I think of him as he went through his life, teaching and blessing the people.
>
> And, oh, I think of him in Gethsemane, when he suffered the pain of all men, that we might be forgiven of our sins on conditions of repentance. . . .
>
> By his suffering he put into effect the plan of mercy, the merciful gospel plan of redemption by which all men may be cleansed of their sins.
>
> And then I think of him on the cross. I think of him in the garden, when he spoke to Mary, following which the light and knowledge broke through upon his disciples that he in reality had won the victory over death, bringing about not only his own, but the resurrection of all people.
>
> I think of him with the Father in the grove with the Prophet Joseph. I know he lives.
>
> I know my Redeemer lives. "Hear, O ye heavens, and give ear, O earth, and rejoice ye inhabitants thereof, for the Lord is God, and beside him there is no Savior" (D&C 76:1).
>
> I bear you my testimony that this statement is true, and this witness which I bear will be binding upon you; for I, like my brethren of the presiding councils of the Church, am a called and ordained personal witness of the Lord Jesus Christ.[30]

A few years later at another conference he stated, "Now, in conclusion, as a special witness, I want to leave my testimony with each of you. . . . I personally know 'that there is a God in heaven, who is infinite and eternal . . . that he created man, male and female, after his own image and in his own likeness . . .'; that in these latter days he has revealed himself anew; and that he is 'the only living and true God . . .' (D&C 20:17–19). I have obtained this knowledge and testimony through the same means that Peter, Paul, Joseph Smith, and tens of thousands of others have received it—by the witness of the Holy Spirit to my soul."[31]

To a congregation assembled at BYU, he testified, "I won't know any better on that great day, not too far distant, when I shall stand before my maker to give an account of the deeds done in the flesh, and put my fingers in his side and feel the wounds in his hands; that he lives, that the gospel is true, than I know it now."[32]

One of Elder Romney's most direct and revealing declarations of how his witness of the Savior had grown and strengthened and solidified beyond all doubt or question found expression in a 1967 conference address.

> Now as for myself, the Holy Ghost has borne and continues to bear witness to me that the words of the prophets are true. I know that God lives, that he is my Father, and that Jesus Christ is my Redeemer and that he spoke the truth when he said,
>
> "It shall come to pass that every soul who forsaketh his sins and cometh unto me, and calleth on my name, and obeyeth my voice, and keepeth my commandments, shall see my face and know that I am" (D&C 93:1).
>
> Now this testimony, my brethren and sisters, I bear unto you in the name of the Lord, Jesus Christ, and in the authority of the holy apostleship which I hold, and I tell you it will be binding upon you.[33]

In 1972 Marion was called by President Harold B. Lee into the First Presidency of the Church. He also served for many years as a counselor to President Spencer W. Kimball. In this position he was able to serve measurably well until the early 1980s when his eyesight began to fail him, as did his memory. These and other health issues hindered his service in his last years. In late 1985, with the death of President Kimball, he became President of the Quorum of the Twelve. He was unable to actively serve in that position. He died in 1988.

Notes

1. Marion G. Romney, "How to Gain a Testimony," *New Era*, May 1976.
2. Marion G. Romney, "To Him That Asketh in the Spirit" (October 18, 1974), 1–4; hardcopy in author's possession.
3. Ibid., 4.
4. Ibid.
5. Ibid.

6. As cited in the oral history of Marion G. Romney, 5–6, and quoted in an email from Glen L. Rudd to Dennis B. Horne, January 25, 2012. Another account of this experience is found in F. Burton Howard's *Marion G. Romney: His Life and Faith* (Salt Lake City: Bookcraft, 1988), 77–79.

   Elder Boyd K. Packer remembered hearing Elder Romney explain his Australian experience. "Some years ago, I was with President Marion G. Romney, meeting with mission presidents and their wives in Geneva, Switzerland. He told them that fifty years before, as a missionary boy in Australia, late one afternoon he had gone to a library to study. When he walked out, it was night. He looked up into the starry sky, and it happened. The Spirit touched him, and a certain witness was born in his soul. He told those mission presidents that he did not know any more surely then as a member of the First Presidency that God the Father lives; that Jesus is the Christ, the Son of God, the Only Begotten of the Father; and that the fulness of the gospel had been restored than he did as a missionary boy fifty years before in Australia. He said that his testimony had changed in that it was much easier to get an answer from the Lord. The Lord's presence was nearer, and he knew the Lord much better than he had fifty years before" (Boyd K. Packer, "The Weak and the Simple of the Church," *Ensign*, November 2007).

7. Romney, "To Him That Asketh in the Spirit," 5.

8. Ibid., 8–9.

9. As quoted in *Thoughts on Welfare from the Words of President Marion G. Romney*, comp., Glen L. Rudd (Salt Lake City: privately published, 2012), 51; quotations are extracts from Marion G. Romney's oral history as interviewed by James B. Allen, December 18, 1972, and January 4 and 10, 1973.

10. Howard, *Marion G. Romney: His Life and Faith*, 101–2.

11. Rudd, *Thoughts on Welfare from the Words of President Marion G. Romney*, 51.

12. Marion G. Romney, "How to Gain a Testimony," *New Era*, May 1976. (Original address given at Brigham Young University, June 15, 197; audio available at speeches.byu.edu.)

13. As summarized and quoted from Howard, *Marion G. Romney: His Life and Faith*, 161.

14. Ibid., 169–71.

15. Marion G. Romney, "A Testimony of the Redeemer," *Improvement Era*, December 1951, 892–93.

16. Marion G. Romney, in Conference Report, April 1953, 122–26.

   While not directly related to the focus of this book, the subject of evolution and pre-Adamites does bear on the doctrine of the Fall and therefore the Atonement. After giving this talk, Elder Romney stated, "Following this conference on April 13, 1953, President David O. McKay wrote me a letter in which he said, 'I have heard many express gratitude for your remarks, as well as for your fine spirit. I assure you I have agreed heartily in every instance.' I would assume that this statement of President McKay's did not repudiate what I had said about the origin of Adam." Elder Romney also wrote, "I don't suppose that any two minds in the world understand exactly alike any statement on any subject. The General Authorities of the Church are, of course, like all other men, different in their personalities. However, on the fundamentals they are in accord, and one of those fundamentals upon which they are in accord is that Adam is a son of God, that neither his spirit nor his body is a product of a biological evolution which went on for millions of years on this earth." And last, "If you will study these documents, I think you will be persuaded that they, with the written revelations which the Lord has given, teach rather clearly that the physical bodies created by God, not only for man but for the animals upon this earth, were created after the likeness of the pre-existent spirits which were to inhabit them. I think the scriptures are clear that animals, as well as man, were endowed by the Creator, in the day that they became mortal, with the power to bring forth young after their own kind, and not after some other kind" (correspondence, Marion G. Romney to Mr. Joseph T. Bentley, March 24, 1955, accompanying letter to unnamed recipient, February 18, 1955; copy in author's possession).

17. Ibid., 125.
18. Marion G. Romney, in Conference Report, October 1953, 34–37.
19. Ibid.
20. Marion G. Romney, in Conference Report, April 1955, 31–33.
21. Marion G. Romney, "Making Your Calling and Election Sure," in Conference Report, October 1965, 20–23; see also *Improvement Era*, December 1965, 1115–16.
22. Howard, *Marion G. Romney: His Life and Faith*, 136–42.
23. Ibid., 184.
24. Ibid., 222.
25. Romney, "How to Gain a Testimony."
26. Marion G. Romney, "Seek the Spirit," in Conference Report, September 1961, 57–61.
27. Howard, *Marion G. Romney: His Life and Faith*, 225–26.
28. Marion G. Romney, "Learn from the Standard Works" (address to Church Educational System religious educators, April 13, 1973), 4.
29. Marion G. Romney, "Prayer and Revelation," *Ensign*, May 1978.
30. Marion G. Romney, in Conference Report, April 1961, 116–20.
31. Marion G. Romney, in Conference Report, October 1964, 48–52.
32. Howard, *Marion G. Romney: His Life and Faith*, 230.
33. Marion G. Romney, in Conference Report, October 1967, 134–37.

8

ELDER DAVID B. HAIGHT'S
SPECIAL WITNESS OF JESUS CHRIST

"I was shown a panoramic view of His earthly ministry:
His baptism, His teaching, His healing the sick and lame, the
mock trial, His Crucifixion, His Resurrection and Ascension."

David B. Haight's commitment to the Lord was firmly established long before his call to full-time service as a General Authority of the Church. After being invited to the Church Administration Building to meet with the First Presidency, a new life's path was set. He said, "As President Tanner directed me by the arm down the long corridor to the First Presidency's office, there to look into the faces of our living prophet [President Joseph Fielding Smith] and President Lee and President Tanner, I knew in my soul that I was in the presence of the Lord's anointed. I knew not what may lie ahead, but one thing was certain: I was already committed in my heart to serve the Master, wherever and whenever called." Such are the thoughts he expressed to those assembled in general conference in his first address following his call. Then he added, "I know he lives, that he is real, that he stands at the head of this, His Church, the only true church on the face of the earth."[1] These early words of surety began to introduce him to the membership of the Church.

David was born in Oakley, Idaho, in 1906. He fell in love with his small hometown and would tell many stories about growing up there throughout his eventful life. It was there that tragedy struck, when, at the age of nine, he learned that his father had passed away. His father had been a beloved bishop and community leader. David attended Oakley High School, Albion State Normal School, and Utah State University in Logan, Utah.

FINDING HIS WIFE

Elder Haight loved to tell the story of first meeting his future wife, Ruby Olson, whom he married in 1930.

> I saw her first at a dance at the Old Mill in a canyon east of Salt Lake. I remember the dress she was wearing. I remember how much fun she was having with her date. I was sitting there with someone else. As I watched this girl dancing by, I asked my date, "Do you know her?" She said, "Yes." I recall saying, "Why don't you introduce me to her?" Now, that isn't the way you win friends and influence people!
>
> I remember how hard I worked to get a date with her. I would phone her. She would have a date, and I would say, "What time is he coming?" "Eight o'clock." "How about seeing me at six?" I was determined, because I had a deep impression that this was the girl I should marry. I wanted to marry the right person in the right place.[2]

LESSONS LEARNED FROM THE WAR

During World War II, David served as an officer involved with overseeing the coordination and distribution of supplies, helping to ensure that the military would have what they needed when they needed it. He often joked that during the war he commanded an "LOD"—short for "Large Oak Desk." Although he was not a front-line soldier, he still occasionally found himself in stressful situations, one of which was while trying to sleep in an airplane that had an engine spewing visible flames. Elder Haight related this experience:

> As I lay awake through the night, I prayed long, pouring out my heart to the Lord with a renewed commitment that if I got out of the war alive and back with my family, the Church would always be uppermost in my life. I shall always remember that long, sleepless night. Although I had had a testimony of the gospel all my life, and was currently serving as a counselor [in a bishopric], it seemed to me as I pondered that night that I hadn't given it my all. I didn't have my priorities in proper order. That night my whole life passed in review before

me. I reappraised my life and recommitted myself to the Lord, not only to serve but also to give my life gladly and do all in my power to build the kingdom.[3]

Business and Church Service

In business, David worked for various retail establishments, such as Montgomery Ward, where he rose to become one of the top officers in the company. His employment caused him to occasionally relocate, but he eventually settled in Palo Alto, California, and went into business for himself. He served as mayor of Palo Alto from 1959 until 1963, when he resigned at President David O. McKay's request in order to serve as the president of the Scottish Mission. He served as a stake president and a regional representative, and from 1970 to 1976, he served as an Assistant to the Quorum of the Twelve. He was later called as a member of the Quorum of the Twelve and served there until his death at age ninety-seven.

Called as a General Authority

Of his call as an Assistant to the Quorum of the Twelve in 1970, David related,

> I was called to the First Presidency's office to meet with President Joseph Fielding Smith. His name would be presented the next day for sustaining as the new President and Prophet of the Church, . . . Harold B. Lee was to be sustained as the first counselor, and N. Eldon Tanner as the second counselor. They spent a few moments with me extending the call, and then reminded me that the next morning my name would be read in the conference.
>
> After that call was extended to me, I walked down the granite steps of the Administration Building. I felt amazement and wonder. How could this happen? How could this come to me? As I walked around the block, I thought and wondered about the changes that would come into my life now. How would I ever measure up to the responsibility that would now rest upon me? How could I go out and represent this great and glorious organization out in the world?[4]

In entertaining these feelings of inadequacy, Elder Haight was no different than his associates in the leading councils of the Church. Virtually all had experienced them and had been tested by the adversary. In Elder Haight's case, a few years after his call, he would state with some gravity, "I bear witness this day that the devil is real. I have felt of his influence."[5] He had experienced the opposition in all things created by the devil's efforts to hinder or thwart the work of God's servants. However, he had also experienced the sublime joy of coming to know the

Savior. "The Jesus I know and believe in is Jesus the Christ, the Son of God. This witness has been revealed to me by the blessing and influence of the Holy Ghost. I know that he is the Author of the plan of salvation and exaltation, the Creator of the world and all that is in it, that he is our Savior who loves each of us and who died on the cross for us, who teaches us compassion and forgiveness, the friend of all, healer of the sick, the giver of peace to all who will listen and believe."[6]

As an Assistant to the Twelve, he did what General Authorities do. He organized stakes, called stake presidents, ordained and set apart local leaders, blessed the sick, prepared talks and spoke constantly to diverse audiences both large and small, sealed couples for time and eternity in the temples, directed various administrative affairs at Church headquarters, toured missions, and traveled constantly. In other words, he magnified his calling.

Becomes a Special Witness of Jesus Christ

The years passed with Elder Haight serving others in the ministry, until (in 1976) life changed markedly for him again when he was called to the Quorum of the Twelve Apostles to be a special witness of Jesus Christ. Elder Haight related some details of his call to BYU students.

President Kimball phoned me at my office and requested me to meet him in the Salt Lake Temple. It was about two o'clock. I walked to the Temple wondering what I had done wrong. Did he plan to change my assignments or my responsibilities? Perhaps I wasn't measuring up to my calling. As we met on the fourth floor in the Temple, he had his usual warm greeting, which was reassuring to me. President Tanner and President Romney and the eleven were meeting in another room. President Kimball invited me into an empty room there on the fourth floor where we were alone—alone in this beautiful room in the house of the Lord with the Lord's prophet. After some inquiry about my life, President Kimball took me by both of my hands and, looking deeply but kindly into my eyes (and, it seemed, right into my soul), he said he was calling me to fill the vacancy in the Quorum of the Twelve. I was overcome. I could hardly say a word. . . . There comes a swelling within that is indescribable. You think, "Me? Why is he calling me? How can I? There are so many that are more worthy. Such great men have been so honored."

With the two of us all alone, communicating with our hearts and our souls, the Lord's prophet calling me, I knew I was in the presence of the Lord's anointed. . . . The prophet invited me to meet the other Brethren. As we walked across the hall and into the room where they were waiting, they were all so warm and friendly. It helped my feet get back on the floor. . . . And then my Brethren, with their great warmth and understanding, assured me that they had all had the same experience. . . .

President Kimball, joined by all the Brethren of the First Presidency and the Quorum, placed his hands on my head. He ordained me to this calling with words I will always remember: "an apostle is entitled to the revelations of the Lord in very deed"; "we promise our lives, all of our efforts, our thoughts"; "keys, powers of the apostleship." I was reminded, "You are the eighty-second so chosen in this dispensation."[7]

The following year he shared further details of that event.

To you, my dear young friends, as one of those called to be a special witness to you and to all the world, I testify in all solemnity that I know that God lives, that he is real, that he is our Father. President Kimball and his counselors and all the Twelve ordained me an apostle in the temple a little over a year ago; they left me alone after this sacred occasion and I had the opportunity to be all alone in that upper room in the temple, to get on my knees and to pour out my heart and soul to my Heavenly Father. I had an event happen to me at that time that I may testify and witness to you that Jesus is the Christ, the Son of God, that he lives—*that he lives*—that he is real; that this is the church of Jesus Christ restored to the earth in these latter days; and that Spencer Woolley Kimball is a prophet of God, a living prophet here upon the earth now for you to see, to listen to, to read what he says, to follow the direction that he gives to you as the living prophet who understands your challenges. I bear my witness to you that these things are true, for the witness is mine.[8]

Elder Haight did not on that occasion explain further about what he meant by "an event." However, he did seem to offer some clarification in his first general conference talk after his call to the Quorum of the Twelve.

A few hours after [the meeting in which] President Kimball ordained and set me apart, I traveled to meetings in Norfolk, Virginia. My soul was still filled with wonderment. But as I entered the meeting room of a regional conference of Young Adults, they were singing "I Need Thee Every Hour." They had heard of my call. . . .

The weight of this new calling and the responsibility to which you have just sustained me would be overwhelming were it not for my knowledge of the Savior.

I have prayed daily for a deeper understanding of the Master as I prepare for this sacred responsibility of being a special witness to all the world. . . .

God bless us with faith in Christ—the faith Christ stressed when he appeared to the eleven. Thomas, you recall, wanted proof—wanted to personally see what had been described to him. The Savior said, "Thomas, because thou hast seen me, thou hast believed: blessed are they that have not seen, and yet have believed." (John 20:29.)

I have not seen, but I know. I have always known, but now I have received a greater assurance and pray that I will always know that this is the gospel of the Lord Jesus Christ, that it has been restored in our day, that God is a reality. I know that he lives, that man was created in his image and likeness. I know that Jesus of Nazareth, born of Mary, is the Christ, the Son of God, and that there is no other name under heaven by which man can be saved. I know that he lives now—today—and that salvation is only through him; that he will bring us back, if worthy, to the presence of God, our Eternal Father.[9]

In an address given at a temple dedication, wherein Elder Haight set aside his prepared remarks, he shared this much more about the experience of his call and the "event" he mentioned.

> I remained alone in the upper room—the sacred room where the affairs of the Church have been administered since the Salt Lake Temple was dedicated, and where hang portraits of all the prophets since Joseph Smith. In my state of amazement and wonderment at the call that had come to me, I pleaded with the Lord to bless me with an understanding of the call of an Apostle, that I might humbly qualify through my faith and desire to be a special witness of the name of Christ, and to grant me the courage and the spiritual direction to do what I had been asked to do.
>
> As I testify to you that I know God lives, that he is our Father, that he loves us, and that Jesus is the Christ, born of Mary, but the Son of God, and as I testify to you that the temple is the house of the Lord, I want you to know that I am a witness that these things are true. They are true by personal revelation.[10]

Bearing His Witness to the Church and the World

From that time forward, Elder David B. Haight began to share and bear his special witness with urgency and power, and with the kind of sure knowledge that he excelled at humbly describing. To an audience at BYU he testified, "Now as I leave you with my witness and my testimony and my blessings, I want all of you to know that I *know*—that I do not just hope or anticipate, but that sacred experiences have been mine, one only a few weeks ago in the temple—that God lives, that He is real, that He is our Father, that He loves us, and that Jesus Christ is His Son, the Only Begotten of the Father in the flesh. I know this to be true."[11]

To a like audience a couple of years later, he stated, "I share with you my witness—my personal, intimate witness—that Jesus is the Christ, the Only Begotten Son of our living God, our Savior, and our Redeemer, the only name under heaven whereby we might be saved. I testify that He lives. The accounts found in the Gospels are true. And, as promised by the 'two men . . . in white apparel' when He was 'taken up' in a cloud, He will 'come (again) in like manner.' (See Acts 1:10–11.)"[12]

When general conference came, he continued to testify. "I declare to you, my friends everywhere, my witness that God does live, that he made us in his own image, that he sent his divine Son, our Savior, to show us the way. I know that my Redeemer lives."[13]

Very often, as part of his special witness, Elder Haight included his testimony of the First Vision, when the Father and the Son appeared to a youthful Joseph Smith. As part of a lengthy discourse and explanation of that vision, he declared the following:

> I have been blessed, as the years have passed, with unusual experiences with people, places, and personal events of an intimate, spiritual nature, and, through the power of the Holy Ghost, I have received an ever-deepening witness and knowledge of this heaven-directed restoration of the Lord's plan of salvation. The events related by Joseph Smith of the Restoration are true. . . .
>
> The knowledge is mine that God did reveal himself unto Joseph—his witness of this final dispensation. . . .
>
> I leave each of you my love and testament that God, our Father, lives, that Jesus is the Christ, the Son of the Living God, crucified for the sins of the world "to cleanse it from all unrighteousness; that through him all might be saved" (D&C 76:41–42). He is our Redeemer, our Lord, our King. His kingdom is again established on the earth. In the year 1820, God, our Eternal Father, and his son, Jesus Christ, appeared to Joseph Smith, who was foreordained to be the instrument of the Restoration, which is The Church of Jesus Christ of Latter-day Saints. This Church, by divine direction, is preparing the world for his Second Coming—for he will come again.[14]

CONFIRMATION OF A PROPHET'S CALL

With the death of President Spencer W. Kimball in late 1985, Ezra Taft Benson became the senior Apostle of the Quorum of the Twelve, and its president. This became the first occasion for Elder Haight to participate in the selection and ordination of a new prophet, which he described in simple but moving terms as follows.

The calling of Ezra Taft Benson as the thirteenth President of the Church of Jesus Christ of Latter-day Saints will long be remembered, particularly by the seven newest members of the Quorum of the Twelve, who experienced for the first time the holy direction we received in the calling of a President of the Church. After much fasting and prayer, and the seeking of personal revelation to know the mind and will of God, it was confirmed to our souls who should be called—even Ezra Taft Benson. This I know! With that heavenly confirmation to each of those present, Ezra Taft Benson was ordained and set apart on Sunday, November 10, 1985, as prophet, seer, and revelator, and President of the Church of Jesus Christ of Latter-day Saints.[15]

Regarding sacred experiences such as this and many others, he noted, "In my lifetime I have been permitted to witness events, to see and feel divine influences of the Lord in his providence, revealing his gospel by the power of the Holy Ghost."[16] When he made that statement, he did not know that the most physically painful but spiritually powerful experience of his life yet awaited him and would come upon him in less than two years. In a way, this extended and trying experience constituted an answer to many earlier prayers that he would come to better know the Master.

Powerful Confirmation by Extended Vision

In early 1988, Elder Haight experienced a health crisis of such severity that he lost conscious track of the world of mortality. He found himself in communication with the next, and with the Divine. (We might perhaps liken his experience to that of Alma or King Lamoni in the Book of Mormon, where they fell to the earth unconscious, and their spirits were taught the sublime things of heaven in a special way.) As he later stated, after he lost consciousness, "The terrible pain and commotion of people ceased. I was now in a calm, peaceful setting. All was serene and quiet. I was conscious of two persons in the distance on a hillside, one standing on a higher level than the other. Detailed features were not discernible. The person on the higher level was pointing to something I could not see. I heard no voices but was conscious of being in a holy presence and atmosphere."[17]

It was then that he received divine manifestations and visions of "the eternal mission and exalted position of the Son of Man." He said, "I witness to you that He is Jesus the Christ, the Son of God, Savior to all, Redeemer of all mankind, Bestower of infinite love, mercy, and forgiveness, the Light and Life of the world. I knew this truth before—I had never doubted nor wondered. But now I knew, because of the impressions of the Spirit upon my heart and soul, these divine truths in a most unusual way."[18]

Elder Haight related what happened. "I was shown a panoramic view of His earthly ministry: His baptism, His teaching, His healing the sick and lame, the mock trial, His Crucifixion, His Resurrection and Ascension. There followed scenes of His earthly ministry to my mind in impressive detail, confirming scriptural eyewitness accounts. I was being taught, and the eyes of my understanding were opened by the Holy Spirit of God so as to behold many things."[19]

Elder Haight described seeing in vision Jesus and the Apostles in the upper chamber eating the Last Supper, the sacrament of the Lord's supper; his washing the feet of the Apostles, and Judas' departure to betray him. Also, the great intercessory prayer found in John 17 in the New Testament. Then he saw Jesus undergo the atoning sacrifice. "There, in the garden, in some manner beyond our comprehension, the Savior took upon Himself the burden of the sins of mankind from Adam to the end of the world. His agony in the garden, Luke tells us, was so intense 'his sweat was as . . . great drops of blood falling . . . to the ground.' (Luke 22:44.) He suffered an agony and a burden the like of which no human person would be able to bear. In that hour of anguish, our Savior overcame all the power of Satan."[20]

Elder Haight explained, "During those days of unconsciousness I was given, by the gift and power of the Holy Ghost, a more perfect knowledge of His mission. I was also given a more complete understanding of what it means to exercise, in His name, the authority to unlock the mysteries of the kingdom of heaven for the salvation of all who are faithful. My soul was taught over and over again the events of the betrayal, the mock trial, the scourging of the flesh of even one of the Godhead."[21]

He also declared, "I cannot begin to convey to you the deep impact that these scenes have confirmed upon my soul. I sense their eternal meaning and realize that 'nothing in the entire plan of salvation compares in any way in importance with that most transcendent of all events, the atoning sacrifice of our Lord. It is the most important single thing that has ever occurred in the entire history of created things; it is the rock foundation upon which the gospel and all other things rest,' as has been declared."[22]

This testimony and extended declaration of sacred spiritual experience and affirmed witness are some of the most unusual in detail ever uttered in a general conference. They obviously indicate that Elder Haight was given permission by the Lord to share some of his experience. His firm and measured words then were later added to by President Gordon B. Hinckley as part of his own address at Elder Haight's funeral. On that occasion, the Prophet added some further details and confirming witness from Elder Haight.

> On May 4, [1989,] he spoke to us at our meeting in the temple. I hope that I am not stepping beyond the bounds of propriety in repeating a few of his words as they were recorded on that occasion. Said he:
>
> I am here as a result of your faith and prayers in my behalf, and the blessing of the Lord. I am grateful for the blessing I received from President Hinckley. I did not know about it until later as I had lapsed into unconsciousness. I pleaded with our Heavenly Father, that if it be His will, my life be spared. I didn't see God or the Savior but I had the feeling of being in the presence of Holy Personages. I talked to them and pleaded with them. I was taught by vision or inspiration or revelation as a result of my pleadings. I was taught about the Savior, of John the Baptist, of the cries of repentance and of the need to be baptized. I was taught about the baptism of the Savior and of the Last Supper and the scene was clear—of the Savior washing the feet of the Twelve, of girding Himself and of administering the Sacrament and His suffering in the Garden of Gethsemane and of the trial. Of his beating by the soldiers and of his trying to carry the cross, and of the nails being driven into his wrists and his feet, and of the blood and suffering. The teaching that came to me was that I should teach repentance and baptism and of the Savior. I had marvelous manifestations regarding the Prophet Joseph Smith and of the Angel Moroni and of the prophets since Joseph Smith. This testimony filled my heart and soul during the hours of unconsciousness. There are things that happened to me that I am not able to reveal. I would not have words to express [them]. I knew I would survive the illness. I love this work. It is true. God is our Father. He loves us. We have a responsibility to carry out His teachings of the Savior.[23]

(One might wish President Hinckley had shared more of what Elder Haight said to his apostolic associates on that occasion.)

Afterward, having regained his health and renewed his ministry, Elder Haight bore his special witness to a student audience at Ricks College (now Brigham Young University—Idaho) in 1991, briefly referencing his sacred experience.

> God lives. I had a tender [spiritual] experience happen to me in the hospital. And when I tell you that I know that God lives, I tell you from the depths of my soul; and that Jesus is the Christ, the Son of God. He is the Christ. He is our Savior. He is our Redeemer. He atoned for our personal and our individual transgressions, our sins. If you had some little inkling, only, an inkling of what the Savior did for you personally. He who knows the names and the numbers of

all of the stars, knows you. . . . You are a son or daughter of God. They live. I am a witness to it—which I will bear all the days of my life, in hoping to thank them for what they have done for me. The gospel is true.[24]

Furthermore, he said, "I testify that the name of Jesus Christ is the only name under heaven whereby men may be saved and that all men, everywhere, must be brought to a knowledge of this truth if they are to receive the great, eternal exaltation provided by a gracious and loving Father."[25]

Lucille C. Tate, Elder Haight's biographer, shared with an audience a special experience she enjoyed as a result of working with the beloved Apostle as she wrote his life story. "I can tell this experience because he expanded upon it in general conference in 1989," she said. "I had interviewed him at his office, gathered my notes, and had my hand on the door to leave. Suddenly he stood, and with a faraway look, described the details of the Lord's supper as if he were there. When he finished, I slipped out, thinking, 'I have heard an Apostle of the Lord speak as in vision.' "[26]

In the April 1994 general conference, Elder Haight gave a message entitled, "Jesus of Nazareth," which reviewed much of the same scriptural truths as his earlier 1989 recitation of his visionary experience, although therein he acknowledged the influence and powerful language aiding him in his desire to express his testimony. He was grateful for "prophets—ancient and modern—especially . . . the Prophet Joseph Smith for his personal witness that God the Father and His Son live, and for his faithfully following divine instructions in bringing forth the fulness of the everlasting gospel as contained in the Book of Mormon and other latter-day scriptures; also to the apostolic writings of Elders James E. Talmage and Bruce R. McConkie; and to others, including theologian and believer Frederic Farrar." He then noted, "Our scriptures teach us gospel truths, and inspired writers add to our understanding."[27]

His Witness of the 1978 Revelation on the Priesthood

The April 1996 general conference audience witnessed a choice reminiscence from Elder Haight, who by then was too blind to read from the teleprompter or a printed text. So instead, he gave an extemporaneous address and touched on several subjects. One of them was the circumstance of his call as an Assistant to the Twelve, as related previously in this chapter. Another was his firsthand present-as-witness account of the 1978 revelation to President Kimball granting the priesthood and temple blessings to all men based solely on worthiness. With tender but emphatic emotion in his voice, he declared, "I was in the temple when President Spencer W. Kimball received the revelation regarding the priesthood.

I was the junior member of the Quorum of the Twelve. I was there. I was there with the outpouring of the Spirit in that room so strong that none of us could speak afterward. We just left quietly to go back to the office. No one could say anything because of the powerful outpouring of the heavenly spiritual experience."[28] Then he commented on his reaction to a newspaper editor's reaction to the announcement of the revelation.

> But just a few hours after the announcement was made to the press, I was assigned to attend a stake conference in Detroit, Michigan. When my plane landed in Chicago, I noticed an edition of the *Chicago Tribune* on the newsstand. The headline in the paper said, "Mormons Give Blacks Priesthood." And the subheading said, "President Kimball Claims to Have Received a Revelation." I bought a copy of the newspaper. I stared at one word in that subheading—*claims*. It stood out to me just like it was in red neon. As I walked along the hallway to make my plane connection, I thought, *Here I am now in Chicago walking through this busy airport, yet I was a witness to this revelation. I was there. I witnessed it. I felt that heavenly influence. I was part of it.* Little did the editor of that newspaper realize the truth of that revelation when he wrote, "Claims to Have Received a Revelation." Little did he know, or the printer, or the man who put the ink on the press, or the one who delivered the newspaper—little did any of them know that it was truly a revelation from God. Little did they know what I knew because I was a witness to it.[29]

He closed his extemporaneous message by again bearing his special witness. "God lives. He is our Father. We are His children. He loves us. Jesus is the Christ, the Only Begotten of the Father in the flesh. He is our Savior, our Redeemer. He is our advocate with the Father. He is the one who died and suffered great agony, great humiliation, and great pain for us."[30]

Some years earlier, he had shared a like testimony of the priesthood revelation with some college students. "Our Heavenly Father lives. Some of us are still around who were in the temple with President Kimball when he received the [1978] revelation regarding the priesthood. I was there. I was the junior member of the Quorum of the Twelve. I experienced, along with those that were senior to me, the pouring out of the Spirit of the Lord, in the upper room of the temple, when President Kimball was on his knees, pleading with the Lord to make His mind and will known to His servant Spencer W. Kimball. When he received a marvelous manifestation of the hand of the Lord, I was a witness to it. Someday we'll go into the details. But I am a witness of that event; it's true. Jesus is the Christ; I know."[31]

Bearing Witness to the End of His Days

His final years were filled with apostolic expressions of surety. "The gospel of our Lord and Savior has been restored to the earth. God lives. He is our Father. I know. Jesus is the Christ. I have heard His voice because I have felt of that Spirit as He explains to us, 'My voice is Spirit; my Spirit is truth' (D&C 88:66). I know that is true."[32]

Again, "I leave you my witness, my testimony, that the gospel is true, that God lives, that He is our Father, and that in some miraculous way, He reaches our hearts and our consciences regarding the truthfulness of this work. We sense it, we feel it, and we feel of His love and His mercy regarding all of us."[33]

And last, he proclaimed, "God lives. I know He's real, that He is our Father, and I know that He loves us. I know that. And I know that Jesus is the Christ, the Son of God. I have felt of that influence. I'm a witness to it. I know that the Prophet Joseph Smith and all of the historical accounts we have of what he did as the instrument of the Restoration are true and that the prophets down through the years and including President Hinckley are called of God. The work is true. I leave you my love, my witness, and my testimony that burns in my heart. All the days of my life I hope to be able to tell somebody and help somebody understand that this work is true."[34]

Elder Haight died in 2004, just ten days after his fellow Apostle and beloved associate Elder Neal A. Maxwell. Both will long be remembered.

Notes

1. David B. Haight, in Conference Report, October 3, 1970, 85–86.
2. David B. Haight, "Come, Listen to a Prophet's Voice" (Brigham Young University fireside, March 7, 1976), 3–4, speeches.byu.edu.
3. As quoted in Lucile C. Tate's *David B. Haight: The Life Story of a Disciple* (Salt Lake City: Bookcraft, 1987), 129–30.
4. David B. Haight, "This Work Is True," *Ensign*, May 1996.
5. David B. Haight, "The Power of Evil," April 1973 general conference; audio and text available at lds.org.
6. David B. Haight, "What Does Jesus Mean to Modern Man?" April 1974 general conference; audio and text available at lds.org.
7. Haight, "Come, Listen to a Prophet's Voice," 4.

8. David B. Haight, "Your Purpose and Responsibility" (Brigham Young University fireside, September 4, 1977), 7–8; italics in original; see speeches.byu.edu.

9. David B. Haight, "He Is the Son of God," April 1976 general conference; audio and text available at lds.org.

10. David B. Haight, the Papeete Tahiti Temple dedication address, October 27, 1983; as quoted in Tate's *David B. Haight: The Life Story of a Disciple,* 307.

11. David B. Haight, "The Uttermost Part of the Earth" (Brigham Young University fireside, November 5, 1978), 6, speeches.byu.edu.

12. David B. Haight, "By Their Fruits Ye Shall Know Them" (Brigham Young University fireside, December 7, 1980), 8, speeches.byu.edu.

13. David B. Haight, "He is Not Here, He is risen," *Ensign,* May 1980.

14. David B. Haight, "Joseph Smith: the Prophet" (Brigham Young University fireside, March 2, 1986), 1–2, 8; speeches.byu.edu.

15. David B. Haight, "A Prophet Chosen of the Lord," *Ensign,* May 1986.

16. David B. Haight, "The Streams of Your Life" (Brigham Young University devotional, November 24, 1987), 2, speeches.byu.edu.

17. David B. Haight, "The Sacrament—and the Sacrifice," *Ensign,* November 1989, 59–61.

18. Ibid.

19. Ibid.

20. Ibid.

21. Ibid.

22. Ibid.

23. Transcription made by the author of a portion of an audio recording of funeral remarks by President Gordon B. Hinckley, August 5, 2004.

24. David B. Haight, "Obedience Is the Key to Perfection" (Ricks College [now Brigham Young University–Idaho] devotional, February 19, 1991). Transcription made by the author of the conclusion of the remarks. For audio, listen at byui-media.ldscdn.org/byui_ft/devo_audio/1991_02_19_ADV_Haight.mp3.

25. David B. Haight, "Filling the Whole Earth," *Ensign,* May 1990.

26. Lucille C. Tate (Brigham Young University commencement address, August 2001). Transcription made by the author of a segment of the audio file available at speeches.byu.edu.

27. David B. Haight, "Jesus of Nazareth," *Ensign,* May 1994.

28. Haight, "This Work Is True."

29. Ibid.

30. Ibid.

31. David B. Haight, "Remember Who You Are" (Ricks College [now Brigham Young University–Idaho] devotional, March 14, 2000). Transcription made by the author

of the conclusion of the talk. For audio, listen at byui-media.ldscdn.org/byui_ft/
devo_audio/2000_03_14_ADV_Haight.mp3.

32. David B. Haight, "Live the Commandments," *Ensign*, May 1998.

33. David B. Haight, "Love and Service," *Ensign*, May 1999.

34. David B. Haight, "Faith of Our Prophets," *Ensign*, November 2001.

9

PRESIDENT JAMES E. FAUST'S
SPECIAL WITNESS OF JESUS CHRIST

"He lives. There is no question about that. I can testify with the same conviction and sureness as the brother of Jared."

"At times I have stumbled and been less than I should have been," stated President James E. Faust. "All of us experience those wrenching, defining, difficult decisions that move us to a higher level of spirituality. They are the Gethsemanes of our lives that bring with them great pain and anguish. Sometimes they are too sacred to be shared publicly. They are the watershed experiences that help purge us of our unrighteous desires for the things of the world."[1]

Such words spoke of life lessons learned and sacred spiritual experiences received by one who became a special witness of Jesus Christ.

EDUCATION, HARROWING MILITARY
EXPERIENCE, AND MARRIAGE

Jim Faust was born in 1920 in Delta, Utah. His teenage years were spent in Salt Lake City, where he went to school and then served a mission to Brazil (from 1939 to 1942). He studied law at the University of Utah and then went into private practice for two decades, earning a reputation for strict honesty and high ethics. Before receiving his law degree, he served in the military. He noted how that experience changed him spiritually when he said, "I served three long years in the military in World War II. One time when we were in peril of our ship capsizing in a horrendous storm in the Pacific, I put myself in the Lord's hands and fervently promised Him that if I survived I would try to serve Him all of the days of my life."[2] In 1943, during his military service, he married Ruth Wright, his high school sweetheart.

Throughout his lifetime, Jim served as a bishop, high counselor, stake president, regional representative, Assistant to the Quorum of the Twelve, member of the Presidency of the First Quorum of the Seventy, as an Apostle, and as a counselor in the First Presidency.

CALLED AS AN ASSISTANT TO THE QUORUM OF THE TWELVE APOSTLES

Jim Faust was thoroughly enmeshed in the practice of law and often served in various associated political and legal capacities where he could have an influence for good in the profession and with government. But one day, when the call came, his life's course was changed. During a tender moment, speaking before an audience of students at Ricks College, Elder Faust shared the story of his call as a General Authority.

> Because of the feeling [I have] of your [receptive] spirits, I would like to share with you something special in my life. A year ago last October, about three weeks before general conference, I left my office in the Kearns Building [in Salt Lake City] and got in my car and drove home . . . and approached the intersection of highland drive and thirty-ninth south. As the traffic light changed . . . I stopped in my car and in the process while the light was changing I received a very interesting message. The message was that at the next general conference I was going to be called as an Assistant to the Council of the Twelve. Now having received this message, I was shaken. I shed some tears; the light turned green and I drove on home. When I got home I went into my bedroom and my wife is a sensitive person and she came in and asked if anything was wrong. I said no.
>
> Three weeks later, I was with the other regional representatives and with my companion brother Neal A. Maxwell, when the President of the Church [Harold B. Lee] walked up the aisle in the 17th ward, the day before conference, and as he came up the aisle, I knew what he was going to tell me. He was going to tell me that he wanted to see me in the bishop's office. And so when he came up he

greeted brother Maxwell very warmly with a smile on his face; his face sobered when he looked at me; and he said Jim, "I want to see you in the bishop's office at the break." Well, he didn't wait for the break; he came down off the stand (he being the first speaker), he motioned with his eyes for me to follow and I followed. I went into the Bishop's office. I knew what he was going to tell me. He said, "The Lord has called you to be an Assistant to the Council of the Twelve. The Presidency and the Twelve approved of it yesterday." Then he shared some other circumstances with me—told me I had a good wife; commended me for some service in the Church—and then he put his arms around me and hugged me. He had tears, as did I. He told me that Brother McConkie was going to be called to the Twelve. Brother Rex D. Pinegar was going to be called to the First Council of the Seventy. He told me I could tell my wife; she was our stake relief society president over in a meeting in the tabernacle. And I found her and took her in the back room behind the great organ and told her what had happened. And she asked, "Did you know about this?" And I reached in my pocket and said, "Here are the notes I made three weeks ago."

I shared this experience with President Lee about three weeks later. He said, "That's interesting; it was about that time I was struggling to know the mind and will of the Lord." And he said, "Bruce" (meaning Elder McConkie) "had been over in the temple, before he was called, pleading for strength." The amazing thing about that was that the message that I received was not that I should be called to the Twelve or to the Seventy, but it was plain and definite that my calling was to be an Assistant. The interesting thing about that is nobody knows when new Assistants are going to be called. But on that day that was the message that I received.

Now this isn't the first time the Lord has spoken to me. He spoke to me as a humble missionary and He spoke to me as a bishop and stake president. All of those years. Since God is no respecter of persons, he'll speak to you to if you live so as to enjoy the companionship of His Spirit. I leave my testimony and witness with you as one of those called to bear witness in the name of the Lord Jesus Christ, that He lives.[3]

Having been called to serve the Lord full time, and coming to know something of the depth of the burden placed upon him, Elder Faust related his feelings and qualifications to a general conference audience as he contemplated his new responsibilities.

Since President Lee notified me of my call in the most moving and touching experience of my life last Thursday morning, there have come to me the most solemn broodings that can come to a human soul. I have asked myself a hundred times, Why me?—because it is beyond my understanding that I should be asked to join these great brethren of the General Authorities, all of whom I hold in such great esteem.

I pray that God will have mercy upon me because of my weakness and shortcomings. As long as I remember I have had a personal witness of the divinity of Jesus Christ and of his church, and it has always been easy for me to believe and to testify. I have concluded that if there is one amongst all the General Authorities who is the weakest and the least qualified, then I can fill that position.[4]

Before a group of LDS lawyers, he explained what happened to his legal practice entanglements as he transitioned from law to serving the Lord full time.

"Thirty years ago when I was first called as a General Authority of the Church, I had an office full of matters, some of which had been pending for some time. It took a few months to get them resolved. The remarkable thing that happened was that I never had to go back into court again on a contested matter. It was like the waters of the Red Sea had parted."[5]

CALLED TO THE PRESIDENCY OF THE FIRST QUORUM OF SEVENTY

In 1975 and 1976, President Spencer W. Kimball announced inspired revisions to the First Council of the Seventy. The calling of the Assistants to the Quorum of the Twelve was dissolved, and the First Quorum of the Seventy was reorganized so that it was presided over by the Presidency of the Seventy. (This new organization of the Seventy eventually became other Quorums of the Seventy, while local-level Seventies Quorums were also eventually dissolved.)[6] These changes affected Elder Faust personally since he was called to become a member of the Presidency of the First Quorum of the Seventy in October 1976. In his conference address, he took occasion to open his heart and speak deeply of his life, service, and struggles in coming to know the Lord. For those with ears to hear and hearts to understand, his message carried great meaning. Elder Faust had long been climbing the stretching path of the true disciple. He said,

> During the years of my life, and often in my present calling, and especially during a recent Gethsemane, I have gone to my knees with a humble spirit to the only place I could for help. I often went in agony of spirit, earnestly pleading with God to sustain me in the work I have come to appreciate more than life itself. I have, on occasion, felt the terrible aloneness of the wounds of the heart, of the sweet agony, the buffetings of Satan, and the encircling warm comfort of the Spirit of the Master.

I have also felt the crushing burden, the self-doubts of inadequacy and un-worthiness, the fleeting feeling of being forsaken, then of being reinforced an hundredfold. I have climbed a spiritual Mount Sinai dozens of times seeking to communicate and to receive instructions. It has been as though I have strug-gled up an almost real Mount of Transfiguration and upon occasion felt great strength and power in the presence of the Divine. A special sacred feeling has been a sustaining influence and often a close companion.

It is my testimony that we are facing difficult times. We must be coura-geously obedient. My witness is that we will be called upon to prove our spiritual stamina, for the days ahead will be filled with affliction and difficulty. But with the assuring comfort of a personal relationship with the Savior, we will be given a calming courage. From the Divine so near we will receive the quiet assurance,

"My son, peace be unto thy soul; thine adversity and thine afflictions shall be but a small moment;

"And then, if thou endure it well, God shall exalt thee on high; thou shalt triumph over all thy foes" (D&C 121:7–8).

As I come to a new calling, I recognize that I am a very ordinary man. Yet I gratefully acknowledge one special gift. I have a certain knowledge that Jesus of Nazareth is our Divine Savior. I know that He lives. From my earliest recol-lection I have had a sure perception of this. As long as I have lived, I have had a simple faith that has never doubted. I have not always understood, yet still I have known through a knowledge that is so sacred to me that I cannot give utterance to it.

I know and I testify with an absolute awareness in every fiber and innermost recess of my being that Jesus is the Christ, the Messiah, the Divine Redeemer, and the Son of God. May we be obedient to His wish, "Come unto me thy Sav-ior" (D&C 19:41), I pray humbly in His holy and sacred name. Amen.[7]

Having endured such experiences, Elder Faust was continually growing as a special witness. He only served in the Presidency of the Seventy for two years until 1978 when he was called to the Quorum of the Twelve to serve as an Apostle of the Lord. In his first conference talk as a special witness of Jesus, Elder Faust humbly stated,

No one has ever come to this calling with a greater sense of inadequacy than I do at this time. In the sweet agony of the pondering, in the long hours of the days and the nights since last Thursday, I have had the feeling of being complete-ly unworthy and unprepared.

I understand that a chief requirement for the holy apostleship is to be a personal witness of Jesus as the Christ and the Divine Redeemer. Perhaps on that basis alone, I can qualify. This truth has been made known to me by the unspeakable peace and power of the Spirit of God. . . .

. . . I know that Jesus is the Christ, the Son of God. I know that the Savior knows that I know that he lives. So I willingly accept the call, the keys, and the charge, and promise to do the best I know how.[8]

His Struggle to Obtain His Special Witness

In speaking to a large group of BYU students, Elder Faust shared his feelings regarding his new calling as a member of the Quorum of the Twelve, and in doing so, used some similar language to that used by him earlier, though he also mentioned other thoughts and feelings as well.

I can speak to you with some insight and feeling on this . . . for two reasons. First, I am the most newly called of the special witnesses. No one else in the world has more recently experienced the sacred happenings of coming to this sacred calling than I. . . . What I have to say to you, however, is more than feelings, but is rather fact and knowledge to me, the truth of which may be known to you by sacred whisperings. . . .

I now wish to set my seal and testimony upon these events, and upon the divine calling of Jesus as our Lord, Savior, and Redeemer, in my capacity as the newest special witness. In my journal for September 28, 1978, it is noted, "Today I was called as a member of the Council of the Twelve Apostles of The Church of Jesus Christ of Latter-day Saints. I have prayed to make myself somehow worthy in a small measure and to be qualified, and I hope that I come to this new calling with a pure heart and purged of all personal ambition." I will not chronicle further the details concerning this calling because they are so personal and so sacred that the smallest part which one feels cannot be said. I am certain that it is an experience like none other. It is a feeling of terrible aloneness, a feeling of wounds in the heart, a feeling of sweet agony. There are the buffetings of Satan, and the encircling warm comfort of the Spirit of the Master. There are the feelings of crushing burden, self-doubt, and unworthiness—the fleeting feeling of being alone, and then of being reinforced a hundredfold. This special sacred feeling is a sustaining influence, and often a very close companion. I have prayed to be sustained in a work that I have come to appreciate more than life itself. I testify that He lives, that He loves us, that this is His holy work. I testify that His are the words of eternal life. I testify that through this Church His work and His glory—to bring about the immortality and eternal life of the faithful and the obedient—is being accomplished.[9]

From considered and sensitive expressions used by Elder Faust in sharing various details of his growth in service as a General Authority and member of the Twelve, it is evident that he had been given many spiritual experiences that confirmed his special witness. To a good friend he explained, "I felt I became acquainted with the Savior before I came into the Council of the Twelve. A calling to the holy apostleship is a warm spiritual experience and assurance. I have never felt adequate in this assignment. I'm constantly challenged. But I enjoy a great brotherhood and a great association in the Quorum. My feelings for this work exceed life itself. There comes a time when testimony becomes more than belief; it becomes a part of your sure knowledge. The wonderful thing about it all is—it's true."[10]

Elder Faust served as a member of the Twelve until 1995, taking advantage of every opportunity to bear his special witness.

> My dear brothers, sisters, and friends. Sixteen years ago I was called to be a General Authority of this Church, and ten years ago at this conference I was sustained as a member of the Quorum of the Twelve Apostles. These years have been challenging and, in many ways, difficult, but they have also been fulfilling. My wife and I have been trying humbly to serve the Lord as best we know how. We have traveled over much of the earth in my ministry. This has afforded us opportunity to bear witness of the Savior in many countries.
>
> During those years, having worn as a spiritual cloak the knowledge that Jesus is the Christ, I feel led today to give my personal witness concerning Jesus of Nazareth and his mission. I wish to testify of the mediation, the Atonement, and the Resurrection of the Lord Jesus Christ. I speak of these transcendent events in light of my spiritual knowledge that Jesus is the Redeemer and the Son of God. I also testify of His divinity and of those events in the office, the priesthood, the calling, and the authority of the holy apostleship with which I and my Brethren are charged. . . .
>
> In conclusion, I wish to make a humble declaration and affirmation that Jesus is the Christ, our Redeemer, and the Savior of the world. I do this with all the solemnity of my soul. This testimony has come to me, not alone from a lifetime of study or from reason or logic, but more by personal revelation under the spirit of prophecy.[11]

THE SAME WITNESS AS THE BROTHER OF JARED

It becomes evident that Elder James E. Faust received a special manifestation from the Lord that, while he did not describe it in forthright terms, he did speak of it as comparable to the experience of the brother of Jared, the great Jaredite prophet of the Book of Mormon (see Ether chapter 3). One instance of Elder Faust's so speaking occurred with a group of Latter-day Saints as they traveled. Among those listening to Elder Faust's witness was Henry B. Eyring and his wife. In his journal, he recorded the instance, "Elder Faust bore testimony that he, like the brother of Jared, could say that he knew the Lord lived. When Kathy thanked him later for sharing something so sacred with us, he smiled and turned away without comment."[12] Another recorded instance took place over ten years later, while Elder Faust was traveling in a similar part of the world, accompanying the Tabernacle Choir on a tour. To them, during a sacrament meeting, he declared, "I would tell you of the divinity of the work we are all engaged in. My testimony is like that of the Brother of Jared, who saw the finger of God and believed no more, for he knew. It has been given to me to know, for I have become acquainted with the Savior."[13] Thirteen years later, President Faust again used this descriptive comparison to relate the extent of his special witness.

It is now my privilege and blessing to leave you my witness and blessing. I do so as one of the special witnesses, declaring to you with all of the conviction of my being and every cell of my body, from the crown of my head to the soles of my feet, that Jesus is the Christ and the Redeemer of the world and our Savior, the head of this Church. I know that He is close to the leadership of this Church. I know that His Spirit is available to all of us individually and in our callings. He lives. There is no question about that. I can testify with the same conviction and sureness as the brother of Jared. As he saw the finger of God, it is written, he believed no more, for he knew (see Ether 3:6, 19).

I know, and I testify in the words of Peter. When some of the Saints began to fall away and the Savior became discouraged and said to the Twelve, "Will ye also go away?" Peter replied, "To whom shall we go? thou hast the words of eternal life. And we believe and are sure that thou art that Christ, the Son of the living God" (John 6:67–69). By and through that same authority, I testify concerning His divinity and His being. I know this with a certainty that exceeds the knowledge that comes through our visual senses, for it is given to us by the Spirit to know with greater certainty than by our physical senses.[14]

DECLARING HIS SPECIAL WITNESS AS A COUNSELOR IN THE FIRST PRESIDENCY

Elder Faust was conscious of how often he was blessed by the Spirit to receive repeated confirmation of his special witness of Jesus Christ. He spoke of this to a group at Brigham Young University.

I close with my witness and my testimony to you. I have been a believer all of my life. I can't ever remember when I didn't have some growing testimony. Perhaps it is a spiritual inheritance that I have not earned, because of forebears who paid such a terrible price for their membership in the Church. But as the years have come and gone there have occurred in my life (as in yours) confirmations that come which we cannot deny, which strengthen us. They come now two and three and four times every day. And so I am able to witness to you, testify to you, from the depths of my soul and my being that Jesus is the Christ, the Savior and Redeemer of the world, the most profound feeling and knowledge which I have. And I have the witness and testimony of the work of the Prophet Joseph. Like perhaps many of you, my forebears were by his side and forfeited their lives along with his. That testimony and witness is precious, but I have acquired my own. For we must stand on our own spiritual footings. In my ministry I have become acquainted with the Savior, and the reality of His Being I witness and testify to you. [President Faust then invoked an apostolic blessing upon the audience.][15]

In an article published in the *Ensign* magazine, he again spoke of the many repeated confirmations he had received over his apostolic ministry.

As one of the special witnesses of the Lord, I desire to declare my testimony to you. I am grateful that I have always had a testimony of the gospel. I cannot remember when I did not believe. I have not always understood everything and do not claim to do so now, but through thousands and thousands of spiritual confirmations throughout my life, including my calling to the holy apostleship, I can declare my testimony to you that Jesus is the Christ. With every fiber and cell of my being, I know that He is our Savior and Redeemer. I testify that Joseph Smith was the greatest prophet who ever lived upon the earth and of great importance to the Savior in the work of God on the earth. I know this to be true.[16]

Further, in the *Ensign*, President Faust wrote,

I have lived a long time. As I look back over my life, I recognize one source of singular strength and blessing. It is my testimony and knowledge that Jesus is the Christ, the Savior and Redeemer of all mankind. I am profoundly grateful that all of my life I have had a simple faith that Jesus is the Christ. That witness has been confirmed to me hundreds of times. It is the crowning knowledge of my soul. It is the spiritual light of my being. It is the cornerstone of my life.

As one of the least among you but in my calling as one of His Apostles, I testify of the Christ as our Savior and the Redeemer of the world. Since this testimony has been forged by a lifetime of experiences, of necessity this requires my relating experiences which are very personal in nature. But this testimony is mine, and I feel that the Savior knows that I know that He lives. . . . I humbly acknowledge that these many experiences have nurtured a sure knowledge that Jesus is our Savior and Redeemer. I have heard His voice and felt His influence and presence.[17]

Also,

> The Lord has promised that "every soul who forsaketh his sins and cometh unto me, and calleth on my name, and obeyeth my voice, and keepeth my commandments, shall see my face and know that I am."
>
> When I was called to the holy apostleship many years ago, my sure witness prompted me to testify on that occasion in these words: "I understand that a chief requirement for the holy apostleship is to be a personal witness of Jesus as the Christ and the Divine Redeemer. Perhaps on that basis alone, I can qualify. This truth has been made known to me by the unspeakable peace and power of the Spirit of God."
>
> Since accepting that call many years ago, my certain witness has been greatly magnified. This is because of my undeniable testimony that Jesus is the Christ, the Son of God.[18]

As he grew older, and as a member of the First Presidency, President Faust was required to use a wheelchair for a time since back pain precluded him from walking. With a group of priesthood holders, he noted that his condition made it necessary for him to sit while speaking. "Brethren of the priesthood of God, I am again seated as I deliver my message this evening. As you are aware, I am working through a temporary back problem. Those of you who have had back trouble will understand. Those of you who haven't—just wait a while! Any other explanation of what ails me is not true!"[19] It seems the trials and tribulations of aging did not elude President Faust.

In March 2005, an article by President Faust appeared in the *Ensign* (which would have actually been written some nine to twelve months earlier) titled "The Testimony of Christ." Herein he described the major events of the last week of the life of Christ and His Resurrection, quoting from the New Testament accounts in some detail. He concluded, "In my capacity as a special witness, I set my seal and testimony upon these events and upon the divine calling of Jesus as our Lord, Savior, and Redeemer. I testify that He lives, that He loves us, and that this is His holy work. I testify that His are the words of eternal life. I testify that through this Church, His work and His glory—to bring about the immortality and eternal life of the faithful and the obedient—is being accomplished."[20]

Along with his special witness, President Faust evidently felt his insights into the future of the wicked world surrounding the Latter-day Saints should be known, since he twice publicly spoke of the following prophecy, once in general conference and again years later in an *Ensign* article. It applies more and better today than ever before. "I think we will witness increasing evidence of Satan's power as the kingdom of God grows stronger. I believe Satan's ever-expanding efforts are some proof of the truthfulness of this work. In the future the opposition will be both more subtle and more open. It will be masked in greater sophistication and cunning, but it will also be more blatant. We will need greater spirituality to perceive all of the forms of evil and greater strength to resist it. But the disappointments and setbacks to the work of God will be temporary, for the work will go forward."[21]

After suffering from some debilitating effects of aging, President Faust died in August 2005, having dutifully and gratefully declared his special witness for over thirty years with great fervency and power, sharing as much as the Spirit would allow of the details, but leaving no doubt as to the surety.

Notes

1. James E. Faust, "A Growing Testimony," *Ensign*, November 2000.
2. Ibid.
3. James E. Faust (Ricks College [now BYU–Idaho] devotional, March 26, 1974); transcription made by the author is of the last few minutes of an audio recording of President Faust's remarks to the students.
4. James E. Faust, "To Become One of the Fishers," *Ensign*, January 1973.
5. James E. Faust, "Be Healers" (J. Reuben Clark Law Society satellite fireside given at Brigham Young University on February 28, 2003); see also *Clark Memorandum*, 7. For a copy of this publication, which includes this article, see jrcls.org.
6. See L. Aldin Porter, "A History of the Latter-day Seventy," *Ensign*, August 2000.
7. James E. Faust, "A Personal Relationship with the Savior," *Ensign*, November 1976. President Faust repeated much of this talk word for word in a January 1999 *Ensign* message, "That We Might Know Thee."
8. James E. Faust, "Response to the Call," *Ensign*, November 1978.
9. James E. Faust, "A Testimony of Christ" (Brigham Young University devotional, March 13, 1979), 1, 8; see speeches.byu.edu.
10. As quoted in *The Collected Works of William Grant Bangerter: Speeches and Presentations Made as a General Authority of The Church of Jesus Christ of Latter-day Saints* (Alpine, Utah: privately published, 2008), 535.
11. James E. Faust, "The Supernal Gift of the Atonement," *Ensign*, November 1988.

12. Henry B. Eyring's journal, Sunday, October 17, 1982, when he was sailing from Florence to Cairo; as quoted in Robert I. Eaton and Henry J. Eyring's *I Will Lead You Along: The Life of Henry B. Eyring* (Salt Lake City: Deseret Book, 2013), 458.

13. James E. Faust, speaking at a sacrament meeting held in Tiberias, on the west shore of the Sea of Galilee, January 2, 1993; account written by Florence Bittner; hardcopy in possession of the author.

14. James E. Faust, "Beginnings" (Church Educational System fireside for young adults given at the University of Utah Institute of Religion, May 7, 2006), 4; video presentation available at broadcasts.lds.org.

15. James E. Faust, "Enhancing Secular Knowledge Through Spiritual Knowledge and Faith" (Brigham Young University's annual university conference, August 23, 1994). Transcribed by author from audio recording found at speeches.byu.edu.

16. James E. Faust, "The Importance of Bearing Testimony," *Ensign*, March 1997.

17. Faust, "A Growing Testimony."

18. Ibid.

19. James E. Faust, "The Key of the Knowledge of God," *Ensign*, November 2004.

20. Faust, "A Testimony of Christ."

21. James E. Faust, "The Forces That Will Save Us," *Ensign*, January 2007.

10

PRESIDENT JOSEPH FIELDING SMITH'S
SPECIAL WITNESS OF JESUS CHRIST

*"I have felt His presence. I know that the Holy Spirit has
enlightened my mind and revealed Him unto me."*

"I recall a conversation I had with Elder [Matthew] Cowley" remembered Elder
Glen L. Rudd, "when we were discussing the Brethren's kindness. He told me
that the kindest, most understanding Apostle of all was President Joseph Fielding
Smith. To the general Church membership, he was known to be a little sharp and
direct at the pulpit, but they didn't know the 'real' President Smith.

"I had asked Brother Cowley, 'What about President so-and-so? He's thought
of as the kindest man in the Church.' And he replied, 'I don't want to argue. I just
want to tell you that Joseph Fielding is the one man I would want to be my judge
if I should get into any kind of trouble. He would be the most understanding,
lenient, and merciful. I would choose him above all the others.' "[1]

Elder Marion G. Romney shared Elder Cowley's feelings, declaring, "I love
Brother Smith, President Joseph Fielding Smith. He has been most kind and
thoughtful of me. I thought he treated me especially good until I got talking to the
other brethren about him and found out that he treated them all the same."[2] These
opinions about President Smith, shared by those who knew him best, would likely

come as a surprise to many of the older generation today, who only remember his formal presence at the pulpit, or who have read his direct and uncompromising doctrinal writings.

Childhood Struggles and Joys

Joseph Fielding Smith Jr. was born in 1876 in Salt Lake City, Utah. He was a favored son of President Joseph F. Smith, the sixth President of the Church (after whom he was named). His childhood and earlier years were a mixture of happiness and stress because of anti-Mormon antagonism directed at his father. Joseph F. was away from home off and on during many of those years. On those occasions when he was able to be with his father, he was taught the gospel. "Among my fondest memories," he stated, "are the hours I have spent by his side discussing principles of the gospel and receiving instruction as only he could give it. In this way the foundation for my own knowledge was laid in truth."[3]

Young Joseph was able to obtain the equivalent of a good high school education. He also had to work part time as a teenager to help the large Smith family economically. In 1898, after a long courtship, he married Louie Shurtliff, and the next year left for a mission to Great Britain, returning in 1901.

Employed in the Church Historian's Office

Once home, his first item of business was to find a job. After looking around for a while, he was offered a job working for the government at a favorable salary. The job was to act as inspector and tax collector at various business establishments, such as houses of ill repute, pool halls, saloons, and such places. He decided to obtain the counsel of his father, who then served as first counselor to President Lorenzo Snow but would become the President of the Church in a few weeks. "Remember this, son," his father said, "the best company is none too good for you." Joseph decided not to take the job, and, as fortune would have it, a few days later he was offered employment working on the staff of the Church Historian's Office. Because of the timing of the offer and his father's position in the First Presidency, it seems evident that well-placed influence may have brought the son his good fortune. Joseph Jr. went to work in the Historian's office on October 1, and Joseph Sr. became President of the Church approximately three weeks later. Joseph Jr. would be closely associated with the Historian's office in one way or another for most of the rest of his life, until he became President of the Church himself.

TRAGEDY STRIKES WITH THE DEATH OF HIS FIRST WIFE

Joseph Fielding immediately started working toward a home and family. As the years passed, he was advanced from an office clerk to an Assistant Church Historian (in 1906), and then Church Historian. After having two children, his wife Louie died in 1908 of severe complications of pregnancy, throwing Joseph into deep grief. On the counsel of his father, he soon married again, this time to a nineteen-year-old secretary named Ethel Reynolds, who also worked in the Church Historian's Office. Happiness and companionship returned to Joseph Jr.'s life, and his small children had a new mother they loved.

CALLED TO THE QUORUM OF THE TWELVE APOSTLES

At the April 1910 general conference, Joseph Fielding would get the shock of his life. His biographers shared Joseph's story:

> As I was going to the tabernacle to attend meeting . . . Ben E. Rich, who was the president of the mission in the Southern States, met me as I crossed the street. He put his arm on my shoulders. . . . He said to me as we went to cross the street to the tabernacle, "Are you going to take your place up on the stand as one of the Council of the Twelve today?" I said, "Brother Rich, I have a brother in that council. There is no reason for you or anybody to think that I would be called into that council. I am not looking for it or anything of that kind."[4]

Joseph's son-in-law, Elder Bruce R. McConkie, finished the story:

> I have heard Brother Smith say several times that when he was called to the Twelve he had no prior notice; that he walked through the gate of the Tabernacle grounds and one of the gate keepers said to him, "Well, who is going to be called to fill the vacancy in the Council of the Twelve today?" He replied, "I do not know, but there is one thing I do know—it won't be you and it won't be me." He then went to the meeting and sat down. When the time came for the reading of the Brethren for a sustaining vote, this proceeded according to pattern. About thirty seconds before they got to the point where they would read the [name] of the new apostle, he suddenly knew that the name they would read was his.[5]

Joseph Fielding was flabbergasted. He said, "The reading of my own name as an Apostle to fill the vacancy caused by the removal of Elder John Henry Smith from the Quorum of the Twelve and his promotion to the First Presidency came to me, as to the entire assembly, as a most sudden and, to me, unexpected shock that left me in complete bewilderment from which I have not in days recovered. I feel extremely weak and pray to my heavenly Father for strength and guidance in my great responsibility that I shall not falter nor fail to perform all that is required of me."[6]

Then came his ordination on April 7. "This morning I met in the temple with the First Presidency and was ordained an Apostle, to be an especial witness for the Redeemer of the world, my father being mouth."[7] Joseph then began serving as an Apostle, but also continued as an Assistant Church Historian. These activities and home life occupied the next three decades, keeping him very busy.

Knowing Death and Doctrine Well

Death would again intrude into his life when his older brother, Apostle Hyrum M. Smith, and his father, Joseph F. Smith, both died in 1918. Shortly before his father died, he dictated to Joseph Fielding his vision of the redemption of the dead, now known as section 138 of the Doctrine and Covenants. Joseph Fielding had been acting as a personal secretary and close companion to his father for some years and was often with him during his last months and weeks. Joseph Fielding read the vision that he had written at his father's dictation to the First Presidency and Quorum of the Twelve, who accepted it, sustained it, and directed its publication in the Church periodicals of the time.

As the decades passed, Joseph Fielding would write a number of doctrinal volumes, as well as carry on a question and answer column in the *Improvement Era*. These writings contributed to his earning a reputation as a gospel scholar almost without peer in the Church. Today his best remembered works would probably be *Doctrines of Salvation*, a three-volume set compiled and edited by his son-in-law, Elder Bruce R. McConkie. Elder McConkie expressed his opinion that the subject most often referenced by President Smith related to the spirit of Elijah, temples, and family history work. At the end of 1938, President Heber J. Grant wrote Joseph Fielding a personal letter in which he said, "I don't want to flatter you, Joseph, but I want you to know that I consider you the best posted man on the scriptures of the General Authorities of the Church that we have."[8]

Sharing His Testimony with the World

The April 1930 general conference is considered one of Elder Joseph Fielding Smith's more well-known and historic addresses, especially as it relates to his special witness.

I have no set theme to present to you, but if I may be led by the spirit of truth, I desire to bear witness of the truth and reaffirm before you my faith.

I believe in God the Father and in his Son Jesus Christ and in the Holy Ghost. I believe, without any reservation, that Jesus Christ is the Son of God and the Redeemer of the world. I believe that through the shedding of his blood he brought redemption to this earth and to all things upon its face, and, through obedience to the gospel, he has given unto all men the privilege of the remission of their sins; for he has suffered for all, that they might not suffer if they will repent. I believe that through obedience to the gospel, all who believe on his name and endure in faith to the end shall be saved in the celestial kingdom in the presence of the Father and the Son. I believe it is the purpose of the Father to bring to pass the redemption of all men from death and from hell, except those who turn away from the light and the truth after having received it, thus becoming sons of perdition. I believe that our Father has prepared a place for every man according to his works and worthiness, but only through obedience to his laws in their fulness will men come back into the presence of the Father and the Son to receive an exaltation as sons [and daughters] and joint heirs with Jesus Christ.

I believe sincerely and absolutely in the mission of the Prophet Joseph Smith. I have faith, yes, the knowledge, that he was called of God and is a prophet and that he stands at the head of this great dispensation of the fulness of times. I believe he was chosen to this mission before the foundation of the world was laid, and that he filled it acceptably before the Lord, in diligence and faith, in the midst of constant persecution. He was called to give to the world the light and fulness of the gospel that through it men might be saved and come back into the kingdom of God.

I am very grateful for the First Vision, in which the Father and the Son appeared to the youthful prophet and again restored to man the true knowledge of God. I am grateful for the coming of Moroni, revealing the everlasting gospel, and making known again to the world the fact that God is the same yesterday, today and forever; that the heavens are not sealed and God will and does inspire men in this age and generation as well as he did in times of old. I believe that the people upon the earth today are just as precious in the sight of the Lord as were the people who lived anciently, and just as much entitled to guidance as they who lived in former times, when the Lord revealed himself to them in person and through his prophets. I believe that the reason the Lord has not revealed himself to man in the ages that are past, when the gospel was not on the earth, is that man rejected him and refused to be guided by his divine truth.

I am grateful for the coming of Peter, James, and John, and, preceding them, John the Baptist, to restore the priesthood of God, that authority might be on the earth through which men receive remission of their sins and may come back into the kingdom through their faithfulness. I am exceedingly thankful for the Church and that again the Lord has established in the earth the same organization which existed primitively and which was taken from the earth because of the wickedness of men, and not, as I have said, because God willed it; not because he has shown favoritism, but because the people themselves refused to hear the prophets and turned from the truth.

I am very grateful for the coming of Moses, Elias, and Elijah, restoring further keys, and in fact for the coming of all the prophets from the days of Adam to the time of Peter, James, and John. For by these prophets the keys of all the dispensations past have been restored in this dispensation of the fulness of times, that the work of the Lord might be made complete according to the promises made by our Lord and by his servants. Paul has said the Lord purposed in himself "that in the dispensation of the fulness of times he might gather together in one all things in Christ, both which are in heaven, and which are on earth."

I am very grateful for the temples; for the sealing power which Elijah restored to Joseph Smith, which made it possible for the family to be preserved as a unit forever, husbands and wives having claim upon each other, and children having claim on their parents, through obedience to the ordinances of the temple of the Lord. I am grateful that the knowledge has been revealed and the authority given for the redemption of the dead who have died without a knowledge of the gospel, but who would have received it had that opportunity come; in fact, for all the ordinances of the house of the Lord by which the fulness of salvation comes.

I am thankful for the great volume of scripture which has been revealed, restoring to the Hebrew scriptures many of the most plain and precious parts that were taken away through the wickedness and unbelief of the world. I am thankful for the witnesses the Lord raised up who have testified in this dispensation that God lives, for they saw him and conversed with him and with his holy angels. Above all, I am most grateful for the testimony of the truth which I have received myself that all these things are true.[9]

THE DEATH OF HIS SECOND WIFE

It seems Joseph Fielding's life would never be free of the grief associated with the death of close loved ones. After nearly thirty years, his second wife, Ethel, having been plagued with severe headaches, depression, and other unknown medical disorders, died in 1937 at age forty-seven of a cerebral hemorrhage. Thus Joseph Fielding again endured the miserable grief of the death of a beloved wife. He again found solace in the scriptures and the comfort of the Holy Spirit. In 1938 he married his third wife, Jessie Evans, who was thirty-six years old. This last marriage again changed his grief to joy.

THE LOVE OF AN APOSTLE FOR THE SAVIOR

In a letter to a son serving a mission, he wrote, "Let me say that I KNOW that Joseph Smith spoke the truth. It is not a question of guessing or belief, just as you know that 2 added to 2 will equal 4. I know that Jesus Christ is the Only Begotten Son of God, and the Redeemer of the world. What a glorious thing it is to know this! How soul satisfying it is! What peace and comfort it brings to me!"[10] And he needed that peace and comfort. His love of Jesus meant everything to him. He said, "I try to love Him, our Redeemer, above everything else. It is my duty to. I travel up and down in this country as one of His special witnesses. I couldn't be a special witness of Jesus Christ if I didn't have the absolute and positive knowledge that He is the Son of God and Redeemer of the world." Another son remembered, "As children so frequently we would hear him say, 'If only the people in the world would understand the trials, the tribulations, the sins our Lord took upon himself for our benefit.' Whenever he would refer to this, tears would come into his eyes.

"[Once] as I sat alone with my father in his study, I observed that he had been in deep meditation. I hesitated to break the silence, but finally he spoke. 'Oh, my son, I wish you could have been with me last Thursday as I met with my Brethren in the temple. Oh, if you could have heard them testify of their love for their Lord and Savior, Jesus Christ!' And then he lowered his head, and tears streamed from his face and dropped to his shirt. Then, after many seconds, without as much as raising his head, but moving his head back and forth, he said, 'Oh, how I love my Lord and Savior Jesus Christ!' "[11]

THOUGHTS ON NOT HAVING SEEN THE SAVIOR

As thoroughly explained by President Joseph Fielding Smith (in chapter 3, "Teachings about Whether a Modern Apostle Must See the Savior"), he did not believe that one had to see the resurrected Lord in order to be an Apostle and special witness. He felt that the overwhelming witness of the Holy Spirit of God was enough and all that was necessary. On two known occasions he indicated that he had not, at least at the time he made those expressions, seen Jesus by vision or personal appearance—yet he still knew himself to be fully qualified to act in his apostolic office and bear testimony as a special witness. One of the explanations (in 1948) was to sons then serving missions. Joseph Fielding was about seventy-two years old.

I had a noble father, and grandfather, and great-grandfather, and I must not fail them. I am duty bound, for their sakes, as well as for my own, to be faithful and true to the Church, the mission of the Prophet Joseph Smith and above all, to our Redeemer.

I sit and reflect at times, and in my reading of the scriptures, I think of the mission of our Lord, what he did for me, and when these feelings come upon me I say to myself, I cannot be untrue to him. He loved me with a perfect love, as he has done for all men, especially those who serve him, and I must love him with all the love I can, even if it is imperfect, which it should not be. It is wonderful. I did not live in the days of our Savior; he has not come to me in person. I have not beheld him. His Father and he have not felt it necessary to grant me such a great blessing as this. But it is not necessary. I have felt his presence. I know that the Holy Spirit has enlightened my mind and revealed him unto me, so that I do love my Redeemer, I hope, and feel it is true, better than everything else in this life. I would not have it otherwise. I want to be true to him. I know he died for me, for you and all mankind that we might live again through the Resurrection. I know that he died that I might be forgiven my follies, my sins, and be cleansed from them. How wonderful is this love. How can I, knowing this, do anything else but love him, my Redeemer. I want my boys in the mission fields to feel this same way. I want my children and my grandchildren to feel that way, and never stray from the path of truth and righteousness.

I know the truth! I am not deceived, and I know if I continue in faithfulness to the end, keeping the covenants which I have made, and the commandments the Lord has given, that I will be worthy of a place in the celestial kingdom.[12]

A second occasion on which it is known that President Smith talked about not having seen the Savior at that time, is not dated, but probably occurred some years after the above recitation. His daughter Amelia remembered,

After my siblings were all married and had homes of their own, we continued to get together with Dad for family nights. One memorable family night still stands out in my mind. As usual when we met, dad taught us something from the scriptures, . . .

As he always did when he finished teaching us, he bore his testimony. As he spoke of his love for the Savior and His teachings and the great love he felt for Christ, I began to wonder, "How can he say the things he is saying, in the way he is speaking, and with such power unless he has actually seen the Savior?"

So I asked him, "Have you ever seen the Lord?"

His answer taught us all a very vital principle. "No," he said, "but I have felt His Spirit and that is more important."[13]

Having considered these expressions of testimony and sureness from President Smith, we still cannot discount the possibility that at a later time, of which he said nothing, he may have received such a blessing. Again, we do not know and cannot say.

BECOMES THE PRESIDENT OF THE CHURCH

In 1951, with the death of President George Albert Smith, David O. McKay became the President of the Church and Elder Smith became President of the Quorum of the Twelve. Nineteen years later, President McKay died in January 1970, and at ninety-three, Joseph Fielding Smith was ordained the President of the Church.

After thirty-three years married to his third wife, Jessie, she died at sixty-eight, and he knew for the third time the keen grief of the loss of a spouse. At her death, he moved in with his daughter and son-in-law's family, Bruce and Amelia McConkie, where he lived out the rest of his days. He served as President of the Church for two and a half years.

His last years were mixed. He was both mentally and physically active and sharp on some occasions, but less so on others. President Harold B. Lee described the first months of President Smith's tenure as the Church's President.

Now we have a President of the Church who has grown to great years. Since he was installed as President six months ago, he has been down in Mexico with Sister Smith. He has been to the Arizona Temple, where he gave the sealing keys to a new temple presidency. He has been in the Hawaiian Islands, where he participated in an anniversary of the Church College of Hawaii, and some of the early events in the history of that place.

In connection with this conference, there has been an intense assignment to the President of the Church.

A week ago Thursday, all the General Authorities met in an upper room of the temple fasting and praying, trying to prepare themselves spiritually for this conference. I believe we witnessed the outpouring of the Spirit, which is an evidence of the Lord's answer to the prayers that were offered at that time. President Smith addressed the General Authorities. He participated in the Relief Society conference and spoke to the sisters. He spoke at the Sunday School conference. He addressed this conference in the first session. He addressed the priesthood session, and he will address this session.

As I thought of the role of President Tanner and myself as his counselors, I thought of a circumstance in the life of Moses, when the enemies of the Church in that day were just as they are in this day. They were threatening to overcome and tear down and to stop the work of the Church. As Moses sat upon a hill and raised the rod of his authority, or the keys of his priesthood, Israel prevailed over their enemies; but as the day wore on, his hands became heavy and began to droop at his side.

And so they held up his hands so they would not be weakened and the rod would not be lowered. He would be sustained so that the enemies of the Church would not prevail over the Saints of the Most High God. (See Exod. 17:8–12.)

I think that is the role that President Tanner and I have to fulfill. The hands of President Smith may grow weary. They may tend to droop at times because of his heavy responsibilities; but as we uphold his hands, and as we lead under his direction, by his side, the gates of hell will not prevail against you and against Israel. Your safety and ours depends upon whether or not we follow the ones whom the Lord has placed to preside over his Church. He knows whom he wants to preside over this Church, and he will make no mistake. The Lord doesn't do things by accident. He has never done anything accidentally.[14]

THE SPECIAL WITNESS OF A PROPHET OF GOD

The further he progressed into his presidency, the less he was able to do, but he was always able to speak, even if it meant simply reading his text. In one address he reviewed his life, testimony, and teachings.

> For more than sixty years I have preached the gospel in the stakes and missions of the Church—pleading with the Saints to keep the commandments, inviting our Father's other children to accept the truth of salvation, which has come to us by revelation in this present dispensation.
>
> All my days I have studied the scriptures and have sought the guidance of the Spirit of the Lord in coming to an understanding of their true meaning. The Lord has been good to me, and I rejoice in the knowledge he has given me and in the privilege that has been and is mine to teach his saving principles.
>
> As I ponder the principles of the gospel, I am struck forcibly by the uniform manner in which I and all the Brethren have taught them over the years. The truths of the gospel are everlastingly the same. Like God himself, they are the same yesterday, today, and forever. What I have taught and written in the past I would teach and write again under the same circumstances.[15]

As part of his talks, he would bear his witness. "And now to all men—in and out of the Church—I bear my testimony to the truth and divinity of this great latter-day work. I know that God lives and that Jesus Christ is his Son. I have a perfect knowledge that the Father and the Son appeared to Joseph Smith in the spring of 1820 and gave him commandments to usher in the dispensation of the fulness of times."[16]

Sharing his special witness became the concluding component of his addresses. "Now, as one among you who has come to know, by the power of the Holy Ghost, that the Lord has restored his gospel and set up his kingdom again on the earth for the last time, I bear my testimony to the truth of these things. I know that God lives; I know that Jesus Christ is the Only Begotten of the Father; and I know that Joseph Smith and his successors have been the instruments in the Lord's hands of making the blessings of heaven available to men on earth in this present day."[17]

On each occasion that he spoke in general conference, he declared his witness. "All my life I have studied and pondered the principles of the gospel and sought to live the laws of the Lord. As a result there has come into my heart a great love for him and for his work and for all those who seek to further his purposes in the earth. I know that he lives, that he rules in the heavens above and in the earth beneath, and that his purposes shall prevail. He is our Lord and our God."[18] As with other Apostles before him, as he approached his last months on earth, he felt the compelling need to ensure all who could had heard his witness, and that he would then be able to stand before his Maker having filled the scriptural mandate of his office as Apostle and President.

> As I stand now, in what I might call the twilight of life, with the realization that in a not-far-distant day I shall be called upon to give an account of my mortal stewardship, I bear testimony again of the truth and divinity of this great work.
>
> I know that God lives and that he sent his beloved Son into the world to atone for our sins.
>
> I know that the Father and the Son appeared to the Prophet Joseph Smith to usher in this final gospel dispensation.
>
> I know that Joseph Smith was and is a prophet; moreover, that this is the Lord's Church, and that the gospel cause shall roll forward until the knowledge of the Lord covers the earth as the waters cover the sea.
>
> I am sure that we all love the Lord. I know that he lives, and I look forward to that day when I shall see his face, and I hope to hear his voice say unto me: "Come, ye blessed of my Father, inherit the kingdom prepared for you from the foundation of the world" (Matt. 25:34).[19]

And last,

May I conclude by bearing personal testimony of the truth and divinity of the Lord's work on earth and of the eternal verity of those doctrines he has revealed through Joseph Smith and his associates.

I know by the revelations of the Holy Ghost to my soul that God our Heavenly Father lives; that he sent his Only Begotten Son into the world to work out the infinite and eternal Atonement; and that he has restored in these last days the fullness of his everlasting gospel.

I know and testify that the Lord's purposes on earth shall prevail. The Church of Jesus Christ of Latter-day Saints is here to stay. The Lord's work shall triumph. No power on earth can prevent the spread of truth and the preaching of the gospel in every nation.[20]

NOTES

1. As quoted in Glen L. Rudd's "More Stories about Matthew Cowley" (Salt Lake City: privately printed, 1997), 23.
2. Marion G. Romney, "A Testimony of the Redeemer," *Improvement Era*, December 1951, 893.
3. Joseph Fielding Smith Jr. and John J. Stewart, *Life of Joseph Fielding Smith* (Salt Lake City: Deseret Book, 1972), 40.
4. Ibid., 175.
5. *Amelia Smith McConkie: Remembrances for Her Family*, comp. Mary McConkie Donoho (privately published, 2007), 490.
6. Joseph Fielding Smith journal, April 6, 1910; quoted in Smith and Stewart's *Life of Joseph Fielding Smith*, 178.
7. Ibid., 179.
8. Ibid., 213.
9. Joseph Fielding Smith, in Conference Report, April 1930, 89–94.
10. Smith and Stewart, *Life of Joseph Fielding Smith*, 303.
11. *Teachings of Presidents of the Church: Joseph Fielding Smith* (Salt Lake City: The Church of Jesus Christ of Latter-day Saints, 2013), 48–57.
12. Smith and Stewart, *Life of Joseph Fielding Smith*, 387.
13. *Amelia Smith McConkie*, 133–34.
14. Harold B. Lee, in Conference Report, October 1970, 152–53.
15. Joseph Field Smith, in Conference Report, October 1970, 5–8.
16. Ibid., 8.
17. Joseph Fielding Smith, "Out of the Darkness," *Ensign*, June 1971.

18. Joseph Fielding Smith, "I Know That My Redeemer Liveth," *Ensign*, December 1971.
19. Joseph Fielding Smith, "Let the Spirit of Oneness Prevail," *Ensign*, December 1971.
20. Joseph Fielding Smith, "Counsel to the Saints and to the World," *Ensign*, July 1972.

II

ELDER MATTHEW COWLEY'S
SPECIAL WITNESS OF JESUS CHRIST

"I know that God lives; I know that Jesus is the Christ.
No one can take that witness from me."

After Elder Matthew Cowley died, Glen L. Rudd spent considerable time and energy striving to perpetuate the memory of his mission president and Apostle-mentor.[1] He assisted with the writing and publication of two books by and about Elder Cowley, gave many talks about him, and recorded personal reminiscences for perusal by associates, friends, and family.[2] Another Apostle-mentor Harold B. Lee warned him that people forget quickly. Elder Rudd said, "Brother Lee once told me that 'in twenty-five years, no one gives a darn.' Then he said, 'Twenty years ago, the most electrifying and most interesting man in the Quorum of the Twelve was Melvin J. Ballard. People used to travel miles just to go and hear him at a stake conference. People just flocked to hear him. Hardly anyone knows who he is now.' Brother Lee told me that when we were putting out the book on Brother Cowley, *Matthew Cowley Speaks*. He said, 'Get it out fast, because it won't be long.'"[3]

Enough time has passed that Elder Cowley, as well as many others of his generation, are now little remembered by the membership of the Church at large. Yet

Elder Cowley's life and faith can still be accessed to tell a remarkable story and bear a powerful witness of faith in Jesus Christ.

FORETOLD TO BECOME A PROPHET

At Elder Cowley's funeral, Bishop Glen L. Rudd related that "When his father and mother built a home in Preston, Idaho, they asked one of the Brethren of the Council of the Twelve to dedicate that home, and he did so in a lovely prayer. During the course of that prayer, he paused and he prophesied that within those walls would be born a prophet, seer, and revelator, and then he concluded the dedicatory prayer of the home."[4]

Matthew Cowley was born August 2, 1897, in Preston, Idaho, but soon thereafter, his family moved to Salt Lake City at the time that his father, Matthias Cowley, was called to the Quorum of the Twelve Apostles. Young Matt was raised in a home on what was then nicknamed "Apostle's row" on West Temple near Temple Square. Most of his friends were sons of Apostles.

At about five years old, he received his patriarchal blessing, an excerpt of which read, "Thou shalt live to be a mighty man in Israel, for thou art of royal seed, the seed of Jacob through Joseph. Thou shalt become a great and a mighty man in the eyes of the Lord and become an ambassador of Christ to the uttermost bounds of the earth. Your understanding shall become great and your wisdom reach to heaven. . . . The Lord will give you mighty faith of the brother of Jared, for thou shalt know that He lives and that the gospel of Jesus Christ is true even in your youth."[5] Such remarkable portents if he lived faithfully bespoke much of future possibilities.

DEVELOPS MIGHTY FAITH AS A MISSIONARY

As a young man, he worked as a stagehand in the old Salt Lake Theater, where he met a number of famous actors of the day when they performed in the theater. He was called to New Zealand on his first mission, where he became something akin to what an assistant to the mission president would be today. While there, he became ill for some months, and things looked worrisome for him. Matthew remembered,

> There were sixty-five of us [missionaries] there then . . . the grand old mission president put his chair down in the center of the hall and he motioned for me to come and sit in it. I walked over and sat in that chair. I could hardly make it I was so weak. I sat down there and sixty-five of my brethren put their hands on me . . . and the mission president blessed me.

His name was William Gardner, a man seventy-three years of age. . . . He hadn't been to school, but he was full of common sense and the Spirit of God. He put his hands on my head. It is the shortest blessing I believe I ever received. He said, "In the name of Jesus Christ and by virtue and authority of the Holy Melchizedek Priesthood, we command you to be made well immediately." That was all. I stood up out of the chair perfectly well. The old strength came right back through me from head to foot just as if it were being poured into me, and it was, by the gift and power of God.[6]

Elder Cowley enjoyed a number of special experiences while serving, especially in blessing and coming to love the Maori people. He said,

I am grateful that I learned to pray in my infancy because I had only passed from infancy when I was called as a missionary to the uttermost bounds of the earth; I had just turned seventeen. I was called to faraway New Zealand, and in that mission I was assigned, without a companion, to one of the most humble places I have ever seen in all my life, one of the most poverty-stricken places, and in that little village, I had to pray. I was there but a few days when a woman came rushing to my room, and I have a picture of that room—no floor, just the ground with a woven mat and a blanket or two. She came rushing to that room and asked me to arise from my bed and hurry to her little hut, and when I arrived there, I found her companion lying on the ground, being consumed by the fire of typhoid fever. All I could do was pray; and I knelt beside that suffering native and I prayed to God, and opened up my heart to him; and I believe the channel was open; and then I placed my hands upon that good brother; and with the authority of the priesthood which I as a young boy held, I blessed him to be restored to health. The next morning the wife came again to my room and said, "If you have anywhere you desire to go, you are now free to go; my husband is up."

I remember that on another occasion I rode horse back all day long and far into the night to arrive at a native village on the seacoast of New Zealand, and when I arrived at a bay dividing the place where I had to stop and that little village, I made a fire so that the people across in the village would send a rowboat to get me, and when that boat arrived, I was taken across the bay, and I walked through that village, and in every home there were cases of typhoid fever. But I walked fearlessly, with my head erect, impelled by the priesthood of God which I held, and in each of those homes I left the blessings of heaven, and I laid my hands upon the sick. And then I had to go across the bay again and get on my horse and ride all night long to arrive at another native village where there was sickness.[7]

Another of the miracles he received was the gift to learn the Maori language. He said, "I studied eleven hours every day for several weeks. I read the Book of

Mormon in Maori, and my studies were punctuated with fasting and with prayer; and on my twelfth Sunday I delivered my first sermon in the Maori language. They do speak with new tongues, those who accept the call to the ministry of our Lord and Savior Jesus Christ."[8] At the conclusion of his mission, young Matthew was assigned to retranslate the Book of Mormon and to translate the Doctrine and Covenants and the Pearl of Great Price into Maori. In a letter to his sister, he wrote of this experience.

> After the Book of Mormon was completed, two native brethren and I were set apart by the president to translate the Doctrine and Covenants and Pearl of Great Price. The three of us would read a verse in English, then each of us would make our own translation into Maori. We would then read the three translations and select the best. We continued this method for two or three weeks, and then, because my translation was the one invariably that was chosen, my two friends left me to it, and I spent two years translating these two books.
>
> The work was extremely interesting and comparatively easy when I had the spirit of it. At intervals, however, I would lose the spirit, and this would cause me to spend hours over one short verse. Sometimes I could not work at all. When I found myself in this predicament I would lock myself in my room, fast and pray, until I felt the urge to continue.
>
> I can say in all sincerity that I experienced, during this work, the feeling of a helping power outside and beyond my own. Now when I read these books, I marvel that I was the one who was supposed to have done the translating. The language surpasses my own individual knowledge of it. This was the great experience of my life and it will always remind me that God can and will accomplish his purposes through the human mind.[9]

Also to his advantage was his superb memory, which would serve him well throughout his life.

Exercises Powerful Faith as a Mission President

On returning from his mission, Matthew went to law school and then worked as a private lawyer and a county attorney for approximately twelve years. Then, from 1938 to 1945, he returned to New Zealand, this time as the mission president.

> In early 1938, Matthew Cowley—a practicing attorney in Salt Lake— was walking down Main Street . . . where he bumped into President David O. McKay, then a counselor in the presidency of the Church. President McKay said to him, "Matt, how would you like to be the president of the New Zealand

Mission?" Brother Cowley said, "I wouldn't like it, but if I was called properly, I would be glad to go." That was the end of their conversation.

The very next day, Brother Cowley's phone rang and it was President David O. McKay. He said, "Brother Cowley, this is David O. McKay, and this is your official call to preside over the New Zealand Mission. We need you there in about six weeks."

He and his wife had very little time to get ready, but they made it and got to New Zealand sometime during February 1938. They stayed for almost seven and a half years.[10]

It was while again faithfully serving among the Maori people that he was involved with many mighty priesthood blessings, such as that in the following narration, among others.

> I was called to a home in a little village in New Zealand one day. There the Relief Society sisters were preparing the body of one of our Saints. They had placed his body in front of the big house, as they call it, the house where the people come to wail and weep and mourn over the dead, when in rushed the dead man's brother. He said, "Administer to him."
>
> And the young [Maoris] said, "Why, you shouldn't do that; he's dead."
>
> "You do it!"
>
> This same old man that I had with me when his niece was so ill was there. The [dead man's brother] got down on his knees, and he anointed this man. Then this great old sage got down and blessed him and commanded him to rise. You should have seen the Relief Society sisters scatter. He sat up and said, "Send for the elders; I don't feel very well."
>
> Of course, all of that was just psychological effect on that dead man. Wonderful, isn't it—this psychological effect business? We told him he had just been administered to, and he said, "Oh, that was it." He said, "I was dead. I could feel life coming back into me just like a blanket unrolling."
>
> He outlived the brother that came in and told us to administer to him.[11]

President Cowley was not a planner or organizer, but instead simply allowed himself to be led by the Spirit of the Lord through prayer as he ministered among the native people. He was greatly beloved by the Latter-day Saints in New Zealand.

CALLED AS A SPECIAL WITNESS

On President Cowley's return from his service as mission president, a further call from the Lord awaited him. Glen Rudd told the story.

When Brother Cowley returned home in September 1945, he didn't own a car—didn't own a home—didn't have any insurance—didn't have any money, everything had been spent during his years in New Zealand. He was looking for a job. He had two or three opportunities, but didn't like them. Only three weeks after he got home, he went to October conference. The night before, President George Albert Smith called him and told him to sit on the front row in the Tabernacle and in the event that they had five minutes, they would call on him to give his testimony. If they didn't have five minutes, they were going to call on him to offer a prayer.

I went with him to the Tabernacle. I was a bishop and had a pass, but because he didn't have a pass, we were given quite an argument getting him in. We talked him in and he sat on the front row. After the opening prayer, President J. Reuben Clark Jr. read off the names of all of the General Authorities. There were then only eleven members of the Twelve. President George Albert Smith had just been made President of the Church, which created a vacancy. When President Clark read off the eleven names, he paused, and then announced the twelfth Apostle—Matthew Cowley. That was the first Brother Cowley knew about it. He had not been told, and it was a surprise to him and all of the rest of us. His wife was home doing some work when the phone began to ring with people calling congratulating her. She was upset because she hadn't been to conference. President George Albert Smith didn't tell the Twelve until only just a few minutes before the beginning of that general conference.[12]

During his first address as an Apostle in the Salt Lake Tabernacle, Elder Cowley declared his witness. "I bear my testimony to you that God lives, that Jesus is the Christ, that Joseph Smith was and is a prophet of God, that these men who have been called to build upon the foundation of him who stood at the opening of the dispensation of the fulness of times have built well upon that foundation and are, therefore, worthy to be sustained as prophets, seers, and revelators of the Most High."[13]

HEALS THE SICK AND AFFLICTED BY FAITH

Thus began Elder Matthew Cowley's formal service as an Apostle and special witness of Jesus Christ. Having served for so many years among the natives of New Zealand, he had developed a more laid-back, easy-going style, and he came to dislike the many business meetings he was expected to attend. He preferred to visit the sick and afflicted in the area hospitals and give priesthood blessings to anyone who needed or desired one. Glen Rudd was often his companion in blessing the sick. He remembered,

There were many miracles. I was blessed to be a part of some of them. It got to be where he could hardly go anywhere to bless the people without me or one of the other missionaries. He would come to my office, my poultry business where I was always busy trying to get orders out, and wait an hour or an hour and a half till I could clean up and go with him to the hospital or to wherever someone was waiting for a priesthood blessing. It was wonderful to know how he loved to bless people.

The phone used to ring on some of those occasions. It would be the secretary to President George Albert Smith. She'd say, "Brother Rudd, President Smith's trying to find Brother Cowley. Have you got him down there?"

And I'd say, "Yeah, he's sitting right here."

"Well, tell him that President wants him right now."

You know, Brother Cowley was not lazy, but he didn't want to stay in his office. He just had to get out of the Church Office Building because he knew of half a dozen people who needed blessings. So, he played hooky a lot from work. He would come and wait and President Smith would know how to find him. It was wonderful what teamwork it took to get Brother Cowley back uptown where President Smith could use him.

This is a day of miracles and it was in his lifetime. He was a man of great faith, a man who had the ability to bless people. He had the ability to call down from heaven those blessings. It was marvelous to be at his side on a dozen, a hundred, two hundred—at least, maybe more—occasions where we blessed the people.[14]

One of the people they blessed was a child named Joe. Elder Cowley shared with a general conference audience what happened.

I am going to talk about my little friend, Joe, who is in the polio ward of the county hospital.

A few weeks ago I went with a young bishop to visit Joe. I did not know how old he was, I could not see how large he was, all I could see was his head protruding from an iron lung. He was unconscious. He was afflicted with polio and double pneumonia. When we went in, the nurse placed robes on us, and we had to put masks over our faces. We prayed over little Joe. Two weeks later we called again at the hospital and asked if we could see the little lad. The nurse said, "Yes," and when she called him, he came running up the hall to meet us.

I said, "Do you know who I am?"

He replied, "Are you Brother Cowley?"

I said, "Yes."

He then said, "I was unconscious when you came before, wasn't I?"

"You certainly were," I said, and then he replied, "No wonder I don't recognize you."

He took us into his room, and lying in an adjoining bed to his was another young chap, twice the age of Joe. And after visiting for a while, we were about to go when little Joe said, "Wait a minute, don't forget my partner."

I said, "What do you mean?"

And he said, "You pray over my partner, and then he can thank you for a prayer the same as I did."

And so we turned to his companion, a young lad sixteen years of age, stricken with polio, and he said, "I would like a blessing. I am a teacher in the Aaronic Priesthood in my ward." And so we blessed Joe's partner. Two weeks later we called back again. On this visit little Joe was rather sad, and we asked him what was the matter. He said, "I am lonely. Maybe I shouldn't have asked you to bless my partner. He got well too soon and has gone home."

Well, little Joe is probably listening in, and maybe he can see me on television as I speak, so I want to say to you, little Joe, we are thinking about you. We are praying for you. We have been told here by the great leaders of this Church that we should have a simple faith. Christ himself says that we should have faith like yours, the faith of a little child, and unless we have your faith, we cannot enter the kingdom of heaven (Matt. 18:3). Joe, you are of the kingdom of heaven because yours is a faith which has not been tarnished by learning, by the wisdom of men. It is simple.[15]

Then there is the remarkable story of the healing of a little blind boy.

I've told the story about the little baby nine months old who was born blind. The father came up with him one Sunday and said, "Brother Cowley, our baby hasn't been blessed yet. We'd like you to bless him."

I said, "Why have you waited so long?"

"Oh, we just didn't get around to it."

I said, "All right, what's the name?"

So he told me the name, and I was just going to start when he said, "By the way, give him his vision when you give him a name. He was born blind."

It shocked me, but then said to myself, why not? Christ said to his disciples when he left them, "Greater things than I have done shall you do." (See John 14:12.) I had faith in that father's faith.

After I gave that child its name, I finally got around to giving it its vision. That boy is about twelve years old now. The last time I was back there I was afraid to inquire about him. I was sure he had gone blind again. That's the way my faith works sometimes. So I asked the branch president about him. And he said, "Brother Cowley, the worst thing you ever did was to bless that child to receive his vision. He's the meanest kid in this neighborhood; always getting into mischief." Boy I was thrilled about that kid getting into mischief![16]

A Trial of Health

Elder Cowley blessed many people who needed him, and often the results were miraculous, but on occasion he needed the power of faith and the priesthood in his own behalf. Glen Rudd recorded the following.

Matthew Cowley had a serious heart attack about one year after he became one of the Twelve. He was rushed home from BYU where he had been speaking and was taken directly to his home. He refused to go to the hospital. As soon as he arrived home, his wife called me and said, "Get Dave and come up quick." So I picked up Dave Evans in my old delivery truck and we raced up to the place where President and Sister Cowley were living in the Royal Arms Apartments on North and West Temple. We immediately went in and he said, "Hurry, Elders! Give me a blessing!" He was in terrible pain. So we administered to him. The pain left immediately.

Not many minutes later, the front doorbell rang. I went to the door and it was President George Albert Smith. He loved Brother Cowley, loved him with all his heart. He had called him to be an Apostle. He had helped raise him as a young boy. He went with him to New Zealand when President Cowley went to be the mission president. President Smith said, "I have come to see Brother Cowley." I took him into the bedroom where President Cowley was.

It was a lovely thing to see the Prophet of the Lord as he knelt down close to Brother Cowley. You could feel that great feeling between the President and the Apostle. He said, "Matt, I have come to give you a blessing." Brother Cowley said, "Well, my missionaries just gave me a blessing." And then the President of the Church said, "But, don't you think it would be okay if the President of the Church could give you a blessing too?" The President smiled, and then he said to Dave and me, "Come on brethren." And then he gave Brother Cowley a blessing, just as a father would to his tender son.[17]

Elder Cowley's life was filled with miracles.

A little over a year ago a couple came into my office carrying a little boy. The father said to me, "My wife and I have been fasting for two days, and we've brought our little boy up for a blessing. You are the one we've been sent to." I said, "What's the matter with him?" They said he was born blind, deaf, and dumb, no coordination of his muscles, couldn't even crawl at the age of five years. I said to myself,

"This is it. This kind cometh not out save by fasting and by prayer." I had implicit faith in the fasting and the prayers of those parents. I blessed that child, and a few weeks later I received a letter. "Brother Cowley, we wish you could see our little boy now. He's crawling. When we throw a ball across the floor he races after it on his hands and knees. He can see. When we clap our hands over his head he jumps. He can hear." Medical science had laid the burden down. God had taken over. The little boy was rapidly recovering or really getting what he'd never had.[18]

A Sacred Manifestation in the Last Days of a Special Witness

Elder Cowley's speeches and conference addresses are bursting with such miraculous accounts from his eventful life, which was shorter than many of his Brethren. Elder Cowley did not want to grow old and suffer the pain and infirmities of age as he observed them in some of the senior Brethren. This caused him to go to the Lord in mighty prayer and faith over the matter. Glen Rudd has preserved the story.

> [On December 6, 1990,] all of the General Authorities were in the temple. President Benson was able to come for a while. President Hinckley called on me to talk and bear my testimony. With his approval, I spoke about Matthew Cowley and his last days of life after he realized he was not going to live very long. I shared Elder Cowley's testimony that life is eternal and that he knew he would soon pass away. I discovered that most of the Brethren had never heard about his last few days and were interested.[19]

This account follows:

"For fifteen years I had the privilege and opportunity of being extremely close to President Matthew Cowley. I first met him in 1938 when I arrived in the New Zealand Mission. He always had a positive and happy disposition. He rarely got angry. He had the ability to accept life and to adjust to all situations. He had the greatest sense of humor of any person I ever met. I think the most important part of his personality was his great ability to see interesting, exciting, humorous aspects of every occurrence of his life. He did not have the ability to allow himself to get depressed. However, in the last two or three months of his life, I saw a great change come over him. He always joked and pointed out to me and others the humor in normal events that took place in our lives.

"Even with his great call to the apostleship, he continued to carry the heavy loads of the Church, but never to feel weighed down with the problems of the whole Church. He still worried about individual people and their concerns in life. He would rather bless the sick sister than solve some of the pressing problems that weighed heavily upon the Brethren. He had respect for other men's ability and earnestly worked toward helping individuals solve some of their personal problems.

"Up until October conference of 1953 he lived in his rather normal, happy fashion, but something happened to President Cowley during the conference. He had a rather light-hearted spirit about him and had humorously talked about two or three different subjects he might speak about during conference. He had always wanted to give a talk on baptism. He evidently had some great thoughts that had never been expressed about the principle of baptism. As conference approached, he told me two or three times, 'I believe I'll say what I want to say about baptism this time.' And so, I was somewhat surprised when he delivered a different talk. It was his old theme song, and as I read it now, I think it was a farewell address. When the conference was over, he still had his sense of humor, but there had been a decided change in him. He told me he didn't think he'd live long and we had quite a number of discussions about life and how long men ought to really live.

"In the next two months, that is through the balance of October and all of November, on almost every occasion that we were together, he talked about not living to be an old man. He told me many times that he had never had a desire to be an old man. I think one reason he blessed the old people so much was he had a great sympathy for them and their struggles. I know President [J. Reuben] Clark's advanced age with its many problems seemed to worry President Cowley. We went many times to visit Brother Albert E. Bowen as he slowly died by inches. Sometimes, late at night after we had been places, he would say, 'Let's go into the hospital.' We would go up to the room where Brother Bowen was and stand by his side and comfort him. When we came out, Brother Cowley was always touched by the difficulties men [and women] had to grow old and die.

"As we talked and went about our usual visits together, he began to tell me things he had never told me before. During November he had a little kidney problem and missed a [stake] conference or two, but on Thanksgiving he told me that [the doctor] told him he was in real good shape. He said the doctor had given him an examination and told him he had no problems. He said to me, 'But there are some things that he doesn't know.' As he recovered from his little kidney problem, I sensed a sadness that I had never seen before and yet it was a kind of happy sadness. He was anything but depressed, and as we talked he told me that he didn't think he would live very long.

"He had to go to Logan to appear on a panel discussion at the University. I was extremely busy in my business. It was turkey time and during November and

December we were tied to the business. However, I didn't want him to go to Logan alone, and so on the third of December, I took the day off and drove him to Logan. As we drove up, he told me about his boyhood and lots of experiences he had as a youngster. We talked a lot about our friends in New Zealand who had passed away and others that we had known who had gone to the other side. He told me very bluntly, very openly, that he and the Lord had arrived at a decision about his future and that he would not be living much longer. I argued with him and told him he was maybe a little tired and needed to rest, but he said he wasn't tired and he didn't need to rest.

"He said he wanted to tell me something that was very sacred and once or twice he started to tell me. Each time . . . he changed his mind and said, 'Oh, I better not.' I had a feeling that he knew something or had had some kind of a manifestation or a great spiritual experience, but because of the sacredness of it he declined to tell me the whole story.

"I am thoroughly convinced that sometime during the October conference he had a special spiritual experience where his future was made known. He was totally at ease when he talked about passing away and going to the other side.

"As we returned from Logan, we talked all the way about taking care of last minute things for him. As we got to Salt Lake he said, 'Let's not go home, let's go get a bowl of soup.' So we went to a Chinese restaurant and sat in the back booth. There were hardly any people in the restaurant that night. We stayed and stayed for at least three hours. About 11:30 the manager came and asked us if he could do anything for us and let us know that he wanted to close up, then in a nice way he asked us if we could leave. It was almost midnight when I took him home. He told me that night he knew that he was going to die and he convinced me that he knew what he was talking about. Up to that day, I had been arguing with him and telling him he wasn't going to [die], but there were so many details of things he wanted me to know that he thoroughly convinced me. He said to me, 'When I go to bed now, I know that I'm going to die one of these mornings soon. I'm not going to die until after I have had a good night's sleep.' He said, 'I'm not going to the other side all tired out. When I go to bed at night now, I look around the house, take one good look, give my wife a little extra kiss, say my prayers, and get into bed and then go to sleep.' He said, 'I know the exact time that I will pass away.'

"I said to him, 'Tumuaki [President], if I knew I was going to die some night, I don't believe I could go to sleep.'

"Then he said, 'Oh, yes you would. You know as well as I do that life is eternal. If I go to bed and go to sleep and pass away in my sleep, then when I wake up on the other side, I'll do what whomever is in charge tells me to do. If I wake up and I'm still here, then I'll do what President McKay tells me to do here, so what difference does it make? Life is eternal.'

"He emphasized the fact that I knew it as well as he knew it and that there was nothing to be nervous about. I told him how nervous I would be and he said, 'Well, if you knew what I know you wouldn't be nervous. It's fine with me. I'm happy. I think this is the way it ought to be.'

"He then told me he had one or two regrets and the biggest of all was that he didn't have a lot of money to leave his family and that he didn't make enough to help [his daughter] get a house. He had been greatly concerned about her and the struggles of married people. I told him, 'Tumauki [President], it will do her [and her husband] a lot of good to get their own house, so don't worry about it.' He agreed that that was true.

"He had had one severe critic who very unjustly said things about him. This had bothered me much more than him. On two or three occasions, I had asked permission to straighten this person out, but he never would allow that. However, on this last day that we were together for such a long time, he said, 'When I'm gone, if you ever hear any more criticism from this individual, you go ahead and straighten it out.' Fortunately, I never heard any more and that problem just dissolved.

"President Cowley told me that he did not know which morning, the exact day, that he would die on, but he said to me, 'You know what time I wake up every day.'

"I said, 'Yes.'

"'Well,' he said, 'that's when I will pass away or that's when I'll go. . . .' He said, 'I'm going to get a good sleep and then at the time I generally wake up I will wake up and then I will take a great big deep breath and turn over and just quietly drift away. There won't be any pain or suffering or any difficulty and that's just the way I've always wanted it. It's all arranged and I'm looking forward to it.' And that's exactly the way he died.

"Most all of the General Authorities went to Los Angeles for the laying of the temple cornerstone. He had had a great time going down and they had had a lovely experience on the Saturday morning of that big event. That night he was in the hotel in Los Angeles and had a good night's sleep. At the usual wakeup time, he turned over and took a big deep breath and then never breathed again.

"He said to me, 'One of these mornings she will call you (meaning Sister Cowley), and will tell you that it's happened.' He said, 'Now don't get all upset and go to pieces; it's just the way it ought to be.' He told me very bluntly that he and the Lord had arrived at the decision, which he felt calm and good about. On Sunday morning, December 13, just ten days after he had been very specific and given very many details about his passing, it all came true. He went to the other side without any great distress or suffering. Somehow or other, as I have looked back on it over these many, many years, I have wished he had told me about the special spiritual experience, but I presume it was better that he had not.

"The one thing above everything else was his testimony of the fact that life goes on and that we serve here and there and it doesn't make much difference which side we are on, there's plenty to do and there's someone in charge, and that he was thoroughly at ease in following the direction of whomever was in charge of him and his activities.

"President Cowley didn't want his wife to know that he knew how he was going to pass away. He was certain in his mind that he did not want to distress her, but he went out of his way to tell me enough things so that I was thoroughly convinced that it was going to happen sometime. I guess my great desire to see him live on and on kept me from getting too excited. When the moment came for him to leave, I was not surprised, but then I realized more than ever before of the closeness that he had reached with the Lord and how true it is that the Lord lives and is in control of everything that goes on in our lives.

"During the fifteen years we were really close friends, he was constantly strengthening my testimony. I think one of the greatest testimonies of my entire life is the one that came as a result of his being warned or being prepared to die, knowing that it was just the way he really wanted it.

"On the day that he and Sister Cowley left to go to California on his last trip, he called me and wanted me to come and see him. I was extremely busy that day and told him I could get off work in time to take him to the train, which I most generally did. He said, 'No, I don't want you to take me to the train today.' I said, 'Well, you've got to go and I can come and get you, but I can't come and spend much time.' He then told me that [his daughter] was going to come and take him to the train, but that he had to see me. He almost insisted that I leave work. It was a strange kind of request. He generally could wait and understand my business in my work. I talked to him a couple of times during the morning and finally went up to the apartment where we talked for a couple of hours.

"He was all packed and ready to go and about one hour before [his daughter] was to come, he got more nervous than I had seen him for a long time. He kept wondering where she was and why she didn't come. I told him, 'Don't worry about it if she doesn't come, I can run you to the train.' But he didn't want that and kept looking out the front window. He asked me at least a half dozen times to be sure and be at the train depot when he got home. I told him I would do that. This was not unusual, because I had been in the habit of meeting him during the past few weeks as he traveled as one of the Twelve. In fact, it became our usual pattern that when he came home on the train, I almost always met him and we then went to breakfast.

"On this last day he had nervousness, an anxiety that I didn't understand until three days later. He wanted to spend as much time with me as possible. There were a few final things to talk about. . . .

"Over the years, I have reviewed in my mind many, many times little things he mentioned and said, and I have thought what a great experience it was for me to be close to such a great man who lived so close to the Lord that he and the Lord were able to arrive at a calm agreement when he would conclude his life's activities. Few men have had that privilege."[20]

LIVING BY THE SPIRIT

Elder Rudd also noted, "After he died, some people asked me to explain Matthew Cowley to them. One man in a high position said, 'I just can't understand how he did all the things he did.' The real answer was that he went directly to the Lord, told the Lord what he wanted, and received the answer. There wasn't anything hard about that. He just did it. . . . Brother Cowley never planned anything. He just lived by the Spirit of the Lord."[21] Elder Rudd received the following special dream of his dear friend.

On 18 March 1986, while serving as president of the New Zealand Temple, I dreamed a very unusual dream.

In my dream, I was at a stake conference, sitting in the rear of a building. As the meeting broke up and only a few people were left standing in the corner of the chapel overflow, a man quickly approached me. It was President Matthew Cowley, my old mission president, exactly as I knew him years ago. He wore a beautiful, double-breasted, jet black suit which seemed to sparkle.

He took hold of me, turned me away from the people, and began talking to me. Without a special greeting or small talk of any kind, he informed me that my life would be changing dramatically within a short time. He gave me a real vote of confidence; and although he didn't smile or laugh, he made me feel at ease. Then he left as quickly as he came.[22]

(The next year, 1987, Elder Rudd was called from his position as a temple president to become a General Authority.)

In one of his last, if not his last, major public addresses, Elder Cowley stated, "I leave my witness with you. I know that God lives; I know that Jesus is the Christ. No one can take that witness from me. Science cannot take it from me. Because I have had the witness, I know that Joseph Smith was a prophet of the living God; that every prophecy which he uttered which has not been fulfilled will be fulfilled in God's due and appointed time."[23]

Notes

1. Glen L. Rudd served as a missionary in New Zealand under President Matthew Cowley, working as a mission office secretary and traveling companion. Later, while serving as a ward bishop, Glen accompanied Elder Cowley on numerous occasions as they visited hospitals, giving priesthood blessings to hundreds of ill people. Many of them were healed.

2. Glen Rudd served as the manager of Welfare Square in Salt Lake City, Utah, for many years, but eventually also served as a mission president, temple president, and member of the First and Second Quorums of the Seventy. He assisted with arranging for the publication of *Matthew Cowley: Man of Faith* (issued by Bookcraft), and *Matthew Cowley Speaks* (by Deseret Book). Elder Rudd has given many talks over the decades about Elder Cowley, striving to keep his memory alive and thereby enrich and strengthen the faith of others. When Glen Rudd died at ninety-eight near the end of 2016, he was the last remaining missionary of Elder Cowley's.

3. Email, Glen L. Rudd to Dennis Horne, July 13, 2012. In his capacity as a member of the General Welfare Committee of the Church, and also as a General Authority, Elder Rudd traveled with and became friends with many senior Church leaders. Elder Harold B. Lee became one of Elder Rudd's closest friends and mentors, almost a father figure. For further information about Elder Melvin J. Ballard (the grandfather of Elder M. Russell Ballard), see chapter 13 on Elder Melvin J. Ballard's special witness. See also Bryant S. Hinckley's *Sermons and Missionary Services of Melvin Joseph Ballard* (Salt Lake City: Deseret Book, 1949) and *Melvin J. Ballard: Crusader for Righteousness* (Salt Lake City: Bookcraft, 1966).

4. Glen L. Rudd, *Tender Moments: Life Experiences with Elder Matthew Cowley* (Salt Lake City: privately published, 2007), 87.

5. Ibid., 3.

6. Ibid., 5.

7. Matthew Cowley, in Conference Report, October 1953, 106–9.

8. Matthew Cowley, in Conference Report, October 1948, 155–62.
   This conference report of Elder Cowley's addresses is filled with examples of healings by the power of the priesthood among the Polynesians. Of Elder Cowley's stories, Glen Rudd said, "President Cowley was a great storyteller. Everything that happened to him was interesting. He could take any little event and make it into a fine story. However, he never exaggerated. He just told excellent details about every wonderful thing that happened, and everything in his life was exciting" (*Kia Ngawari: Life of Glen L. Rudd* [Salt Lake City: privately published, 2002], 104).

9. Glen L. Rudd, *The Gift of Service: From the Life of Elder Matthew Cowley* (Salt Lake City: privately published, 2014), 6–7.

10. Rudd, *Tender Moments*, 39.

11. Matthew Cowley, "Miracles," *Ensign*, October 2004.

12. Rudd, *Tender Moments*, 39–40.

13. Matthew Cowley, in Conference Report, October 1945, 49–51.

14. Ibid., 45–46.

15. Matthew Cowley, "The Faith of a Child," in Conference Report, April 1953, 93–95.

16. Cowley, "Miracles."

17. Rudd, *Tender Moments*, 46–47.

18. Cowley, "Miracles."

19. Glen L. Rudd, *Kia Ngawari: Life of Glen L. Rudd* (Salt Lake City: privately published, 2002), 494.

20. Rudd, *Tender Moments*, 84–90.

21. Glen L. Rudd, "Keeping the Gospel Simple," *Ensign*, January 1989. (From a devotional originally given at Brigham Young University, February 16, 1988; see speeches.byu.edu.)

22. Rudd, *Tender Moments*, 94.

23. Matthew Cowley, "Put Your Hand into the Hand of God" (Brigham Young University address, October 20, 1953; testimony at conclusion); audio version available at speeches.byu.edu.

12

Elder James E. Talmage's
SPECIAL WITNESS OF JESUS CHRIST

"I am thankful in my heart that we have an iron rod to which we can cling—the rod of certainty, the rod of revealed truth."

Elder James E. Talmage would probably be little remembered today if it were not for his authorship of two fine books, *Articles of Faith* and *Jesus the Christ*, that were long found on the list of approved works for missionaries. These doctrinal-literary efforts and others that he wrote have helped keep the memory of him alive and situated him as almost a legendary apostolic figure among the older generation.

James Talmage was one of the earlier Latter-day Saints to be academically oriented and pursue and obtain advanced education and degrees. As the decades passed, he became an indispensable asset to the First Presidency and the Twelve until he eventually became one of them. They made frequent use of his scientific knowledge, his sharp and well-informed mind, his writing skills, and his public speaking ability. Because these qualities were combined with profound spiritual strength and depth, he became a powerful advocate and defender of the gospel and an ambassador for the Church throughout his life.

Early Years: Testimony and Education

In an autobiographical sketch of his early life, Elder James E. Talmage reviewed and reflected on some of his educational and spiritual attainments, including his testing of the truth of the restored gospel and obtaining his testimony. He wrote,

"I have often been asked how, when, and where I received a testimony as to this Church being what its name proclaims—'a testimony of the gospel,' as generally worded. I have had to answer that I know not. I believe I was born with a testimony—like Paul, freeborn. This is natural, in that I belong to the third generation of Talmages in the Church. . . .

"I was baptized and confirmed by my father on June 15, 1873, at Hunger ford, Berkshire, England. . . .

"I was ordained a deacon in England, August 18, 1873, and have been ordained successively as teacher, elder, high priest, and apostle—the last named ordination on December 8, 1911, under the hands of President Joseph F. Smith, assisted by his counselors and members of the Council of the Twelve.

"I came with the family to Utah in 1876, where we located in Provo, and in the autumn of that year entered the Brigham Young Academy (now University). . . .

"Though as stated above I seem to have been born with a testimony, yet in my early years of adolescence I was led to question and wonder as to whether that testimony was my own or merely an expression of tendency derived through heredity. I set about investigating the claims of the Church, and pursued that investigation—by prayer, fasting and research—with all the ardor of an investigator on the outside [of the Church]. While such a one investigates with a view of coming into the Church if its claims can be verified, I was seeking a way out if by any chance the claims should prove to me to be unsound. After months of such inquiry I found myself in possession of an assurance beyond all question that I was in solemn fact a member of the Church of Jesus Christ; and since that time I have never wasted an hour in doubt or further questioning. I was convinced once for all, and this knowledge is so fully an integral part of my being that without it I would not be myself.

"After being graduated from the Brigham Young Academy, Normal Course, I was offered a position in the public school service, Provo—a position known now as that of the city superintendent of schools but which in that day was not so well defined. This would have brought me what was then considered a very high salary—$85 per month—but as I was about to accept the offer, I was literally called by the presidency of Utah Stake to enter the Brigham Young Academy as a teacher, to have especial charge of the scientific courses. The incident was to me a real test. I had not intended following teaching as a vocation and yet had desired to have the experience of a few years in that field. I was entirely without money and knew well that I could reasonably expect but little from the Brigham Young Academy, which was then regarded as a missionary institution, and this idea was impressed upon the teachers. When nearly a quarter of the school year had passed, my salary was fixed at $3.00 per week for the school year of forty weeks. The position in the public schools had not been permanently filled and was still open to me. I went to the Lord with my question as to what was his will in the matter. I received my answer in the form of a convincing impression that I should go on with my work in the Academy. Many of my friends called me a fool for so doing, but that interesting sobriquet has been applied to me many times for following what to me was a line of duty instead of taking the course that promised material gain. I thank the Lord that I was such a fool then and afterward, and that I have remained so until this day.

"It having been thus settled in my mind that I was to labor in the educational field, I laid plans for taking a college course. Against this many of my brethren to whom I looked for counsel in the institution and in the stake advised and warned. I was told that to go away from home to college would jeopardize my faith and that I was well enough educated as it was for the work I had to do.

"With a boldness that may have appeared as presumption, I went direct to President John Taylor, asking his counsel with the voluntary assurance that whatever it was I would endeavor to follow it. I have often marveled at the kindness and condescension of President Taylor in spending nearly two hours in conversation with me, in the course of which he inquired into many aspects of my work and plans. He then advised me strongly to enter a university in the East; and to my grateful surprise he laid his hands upon my head and blessed me for the undertaking. The blessing thus invoked and pronounced has been realized richly in both spirit and letter.

"I entered Lehigh University, Bethlehem, Pennsylvania, as a special student in 1882. My purpose in registering as a 'special' was to secure a measure of freedom in the selection of my subjects of study, for at that time the courses laid out for regular students were very rigidly prescribed. I registered for the courses which, as I thought, I most needed, and passed examinations in the prerequisites.

"After a year and a half at Lehigh, I felt that I should go to another institution and thus broaden my experience. Then came another great test. Strict economy had been necessary to my school work. I was offered a position as laboratory assistant, which carried a salary sufficient to meet all my needs for the next year. But I remembered the injunction laid upon me by President John Taylor—not to stay at any institution longer than was necessary to procure what I sought, with which was associated the promise that if I would follow that counsel I should receive academic recognition even beyond my expectations. So I declined the offer—and was roundly denounced by the professor-in-charge as a fool! Later I completed all the courses required for graduation at Lehigh and received my degree.

"I went to Johns Hopkins University, Baltimore, where I specialized particularly in chemistry and geology.

"The buildings of the Brigham Young Academy, Provo, had been destroyed by fire in the spring of 1884 and I was called home to resume work in that institution. Again I was called a fool for breaking away from the enticing prospects at Johns Hopkins, where a fellowship seemed to be within my reach; but I responded to the call. It was a great disappointment to find that the fire was cited as a sufficient reason for paying only very small salaries to the teachers. My remuneration was fixed at $750.00 for the year—a smaller sum than would have been paid in the ordinary course had I remained at the institution instead of going to college—and at that juncture a tempting offer came to me from other sources. But I followed the counsel of my presiding officers and resumed work at the old institution. Again the title which I had won by so many disappointments was applied to me—fool, fool, fool! That seems to have been my most distinguishing title.

"Experience has bred in me the conviction that priesthood is conferred upon man for service and not as a means of honor to the individual. When I was ordained a deacon in Ramsbury, England, I was sent immediately from the chair in which I had sat for the ordination to act as sentinel at the door of the cottage in which the meeting was in progress. We had reason to expect interference, and possibly mobbing. In the very hour in which I was ordained a teacher, I was sent out with a more experienced brother to make the rounds of visitation to the homes of the people. In the very hour of my ordination to the office of elder, I was sent with another to administer to the afflicted. I was ordained a high priest at a meeting of the high council of Utah Stake, and at the same time was set apart as an alternate member of that council and was appointed then and there to a place in the council which was sitting as a tribunal [Church disciplinary Council]. On the day of my ordination to the apostleship, I was assigned to special and immediate work pertaining to that calling. Every call I have received to office in the priesthood has come to me because someone was needed to fill a particular place, and in no sense a matter of advancement or honor to myself as an individual.[1]"

EARLY TRAGIC EXPERIENCES

Elder Talmage's life was filled with trials, tribulations, and learning experiences both difficult and sublime, many of which he noted in his journal. One of the most emotionally trying for him, and one which stayed with him for the rest of his life, was a horrific accident that occurred between him and his little brother.

James recorded,

> On October 10, 1873, while working after nightfall—a very dark night, a fearful accident occurred. My brother Albert, then about six years of age, came quietly toward me as I was still working with a [pitch] fork in my hands. He gave me no notice of his approach, and until he screamed, I had not an idea he was near me; then to my horror I discovered that while in the act of pitching with the fork I had struck him with the tool, one tine piercing the ball of his left eye. This organ was finally entirely removed, though not before the right had become sympathetically affected and he was almost absolutely blind, being only enabled to distinguish very bright colors and then only when within a few inches of the eye. True, evils must come; but woe unto them by whom they come. I need say nothing in regard to my feelings and reflections at this mishap; but that my relief lies in the promise pronounced on him by the priesthood of God that he shall recover.[2]

Less than a year after the traumatic accident with the pitchfork, James lost his grandfather to illness, a man that he loved deeply and that he had become very close to.

> Soon after . . . my grandfather was attacked by sickness. I remained with him at his home in Ramsbury [England] during his illness, which lasted about four weeks. His death occurred July 16, 1874. Having been very closely attached to him, his death affected me severely; and the more so as I had never before lost a near relative to my knowledge. I began to reflect seriously on his actions, as brought up by memory to note them very closely, and at length to meditate on his present lot; fully knowing he died in the possession of the priesthood and a firm belief and faith in The Church of Jesus Christ of Latter-day Saints. One night while meditating in this manner, I received a very curious dream concerning him (the details are probably immaterial) which had the effect of so firmly imprinting on my mind the conviction that his lot was "alright," that not the slightest doubt in that respect has ever been entertained.[3]

Then, several years later, death again invaded his family circle when James' sister Martha passed away. As he described her frail condition, she had been plagued by ill-health for years, only receiving temporary relief from her condition by frequent priesthood administrations. On one occasion, her illness became so severe that she lapsed into unconsciousness. After being blessed by a family friend, she revived, and "on regaining consciousness astonished all by relating, in her childlike manner, what she had witnessed during her suspension of consciousness. She said that while hands were being laid on her by Elder [Karl G.] Maeser, she had seen God; and described him as being a person who looked as if covered with lamp oil and set on fire (that probably being the nearest comparison she was capable of drawing [to heavenly glory]). She went on to say that he had spoken to her and . . . had told her that she would recover her health, but furthermore promised her that 'he would call for her again.'"[4] She spent a year in excellent health, but then became seriously ill and passed away in January 1879.

Such experiences served to deepen the young man's spiritual growth. The years passed, and in 1887, James was called to serve on his stake's high council. As noted above, his first assignment thereon was to sit among his brethren in judgment on one who had erred. This experience taught him much about the Lord's intervention in the affairs of men.

> Attended a trial meeting of the high council. . . . I was appointed to fill the place of an absent regular [high] councilor, and it fell to the turn of the number which I held to be speaker on the side of justice. The trial [disciplinary council] lasted during the afternoon and evening and the outcome again demonstrated strongly that justice is only to be secured through inspiration. As I arose according to the revealed order of procedure to offer a summing-up address, a curtain seemed to be withdrawn from my eyes, and a feeling scarce to be described, of an understanding of circumstances beyond the evidence fell upon me; and in direct opposition to the intention nearest my mind on arising, I spoke contrary to the desires of the brother on whose side I was speaker. This opinion was held by the [stake] president in his decision and unanimously sustained by the council.[5]

Severe Trials of Accident and Illness

Several months later, while working in his scientific laboratory at the Church academy (or high school) where he then taught, James would undergo one of the most painful and challenging experiences of his life, wherein his faith and spiritual mettle was tested to the fullest extent. Regarding February 20, 1888, he wrote that,

> Today, a painful accident befell me. While pouring molten slag from an assay crucible into the mould, or rather after such had been poured, an explosion occurred, by which some of the fused material was thrown into my left eye. My first impression was that the eye was entirely ruined; the pain of course was intense. I called for assistance; and asked that the teachers of the Academy administer to me. They did so; and I received another manifestation of the power of the priesthood; for the pain immediately eased. It returned later but in the

interval I revived from the effects. [Doctors] came as soon as they heard of my condition and examined the eye. They announced severe burning of the lids and a gash on the ball of the eye about half an inch in length. I was told to keep away from the light, and not try to use the other eye. The pain continued intense during the day. . . .

The next few days were "excruciating."

Last night was a very miserable one; constant pain; and today was spent in the same condition. I remained in my private office at the Academy all day, entirely unable to attend to work of any sort. The eye is very inflamed and the only relief I experienced from the excruciating pain was by anointing and administration of the priesthood; and that *never failed*!

The ordeal lasted for days, with Talmage receiving many priesthood blessings, commenting that, "on each separate occasion [the pain] was eased for a time. The priesthood promised me recovery, and also that the sight should be preserved; and I felt faith in the assurances."

On February 23, he wrote,

This day was the most severe of the whole experience. Of course I was still kept in darkness; and, both eyes tightly bandaged. Oh! What must darkness forever be! How I can sympathetically feel for the blind—and my brother Albert especially. He has been blind now over fourteen years; and yet he has learned the lesson of contentment and resignation. This night was worst—the eyeball throbbing so violently as to be observed in motion through thick bandages; and it bled profusely. I had been compelled to remain in an upright condition since the accident; lying down always increased the pain. The physicians have dosed me heavily with morphine. Still the promise of the priesthood is recognized. . . .

Of the next day he wrote,

Pain less severe than yesterday; still unable to lie down; or to sleep without opiates [morphine]. My friends are all expressing great sympathy; though by the physicians orders they cannot see me. I feel the effect of their prayers. . . . Each night some kind and sympathetic student comes to the house and stays with me.

Some days passed and Talmage began to notice some improvement.

Still better; able to eat with relish today. The doctors pronounce the improvement almost miraculous. I feel it so. I am a believer in faith; but I think it should be accompanied by works also. For this reason I submit to the treatment of medical view of skill. My eye had to be freed from the foreign bodies—and this required works. I believe in doing all I can to help myself, by my own labors as well as by the aid of others; and they ask the Lord to accept of and recognize the endeavor.

The month of March began and improvement continued. By the fifth, he was feeling good enough to attempt some work.

Went to the laboratory; strength seemed to come to me as the classes followed each other; and although I intended but to take a few I succeeded in conducting the whole line of classes. At night I felt only naturally tired in consequence. It was a healthful fatigue—this night I slept well without opiates for the first time. But my greatest thanks are due for the clear way in which the benefit of this accident has been shown me. I cannot describe in detail even here in my private journal; but I have been made to know that if this mishap had not befallen me, a more terrible thing might have happened. Someday I may explain it further. The priesthood has repeatedly promised me that the accident and the suffering following it were for my good; and that declaration is understood and realized by me.

By March 10, Elder Talmage had pronounced himself healed and his eye "nearing perfect recovery." He gave the credit to his surviving the crisis with sight to administrations from the priesthood, "who have been untiring in my behalf."[6]

Brother Talmage had survived a great personal trial, but there were others to endure. Only two years later, in the summer of 1890, he again experienced a severe bout of ill health, this time almost losing his life. He had been working too hard in a laboratory filled with chemicals and poor ventilation. These elements combined to make him very ill.

He wrote, "This evening, after quitting my office, I found myself scarcely able to stand, intense pains in the head soon manifested themselves, associated with nausea and extreme lassitude; and I was soon convinced that I had poisoned myself with foul air. My body, I believe, was rendered especially susceptible to such ill influences through over-work. . . ."

He continued, "The night proved one of great suffering to me. I scarcely slept at all, pains in head and bowels were intense. I recognized all the symptoms of a severe case of Typhoid Fever." The next day, miserable as he was, he summoned the strength to fulfill a field appointment for his consulting business. On returning home, he called for the elders and was blessed, but noted, "I experienced some relief, but passed a very restless night suffering greatly. The fever is asserting itself rapidly. I have little faith in the doctors of today, and feel to rely upon the administration of the elders."

The days passed, the fever became worse, and he continued to receive priesthood administrations. "All the brethren who have thus far officiated in the ordinances of the Church upon me have exercised great faith, and have promised me great blessings. I feel great faith too, indeed, the administrations of the priesthood are all in which I have confidence and faith; yet, after an administration, however strong and acceptable it may have seemed, I do not feel at present that answering confidence which tells me that I shall soon recover. The will of the Lord be done," he concluded.

A number of other administrations followed, including one from President George Q. Cannon, about whose blessing James wrote, "The President's administration and blessing were strong ones, and, as in almost every instance of the ordinance being performed upon me, I experienced great satisfaction and temporary relief, yet without any conviction that I would soon recover."

Depression and pain were getting the best of him. He explained, "It would perhaps be well to describe my own state of mind at the time. A deep, unmistakable conviction has settled upon my mind that I am smitten unto death. I do not feel that I shall ever rise from this bed."

In his journal, Talmage mused about his feelings at the time, thinking perhaps an evil influence sought to take his life, and worrying about his condition before God and also his financial condition for his family. He concluded such thoughts by writing, "My prayers are earnest and sincere that the Lord will spare my life yet to do a good work in Zion."

Along with the typhoid fever, he endured severe constipation, resulting in even more severe hemorrhoids, or "piles" as he referred to them. The agony of the treatments and the intensity of the fever caused him to temporarily want to expire rather than be cured, and he endured bouts of delirium.

Talmage suffered through several days of high fever. He took chloroform to endure at least four separate operations on his hemorrhoids and pain he had never before known. Delirious day and night, the pain became unbearable. Over two weeks of agony passed, with James receiving many priesthood blessings or administrations.

But the beginning of the end of his ordeal was at hand. On July 15, the journal states that he "Passed a day of great pain and suffering. In the evening Bishop Hardy called and administered to me alone. After the ordinance he sat by the bed, fanning me in silence for ten minutes, then he arose and somewhat abruptly administered to me again and left the house. I was deeply impressed with his administration, and soon fell into a calm sleep, from which I awakened with a conviction deep and not to be doubted that I shall recover from this illness and shall live. I know that the Lord has been moved by the faith of my friend and perhaps by my own feeble prayers, for I have felt to pray sincerely. My gratitude knows no bounds. This feeling within my heart is so convincing as to admit of no shadow of doubt. I am sure that the Lord will permit me to rise from this bed and resume my work among His people."

Even with this conviction, the trial continued. "The pain of the piles is not decreased. The Lord seems to intend that I shall run the entire course. There is to be no miraculous and instantaneous healing, yet His power is none the less apparent. I shall be well again, though the road to recovery may lie through a sea of pain. Perhaps my Father [in heaven] desires to test my faith under a long siege, perhaps to make this great lesson in my life the more impressive." By later that July, the worst of the fever had passed. The hemorrhoids were still present but feeling better, his pain had greatly diminished, and he was able to sit up and begin learning to walk again. Another operation for the piles was ineffective, with Talmage commenting on his decision to not use chloroform. "Such pain, however, I have seldom, if ever, before endured."

When the doctors briefly proposed a more radical surgery for the hemorrhoids, President Wilford Woodruff heard about it and sent a messenger to the doctors to recommend that they not do it. "Pres. Woodruff says he is opposed to Bro. Talmage's being dissected." That settled the matter, and the decision was made to let nature follow its course. By the end of the month this had occurred, and he was well again, ready to get back to work. In his journal Brother Talmage gave the credit for his recovery to God and the continual exercise of His priesthood, but was also appreciative of the doctors help.[7]

This traumatic ordeal became a refining experience that strengthened him in a later hardship that he willingly endured. The situation involved an epidemic of diphtheria as it ravaged various families in the area in the spring of 1892. James recorded,

> About 1 pm today, just as I returned home from calling on a sick person, I was informed of a terrible case of suffering and of destitution in an immediate neighborhood—a family being stricken by that dread disease, diphtheria, and they being without help. The officers of the Relief Society of our ward report that they can find no one who is willing to go to the pest [disease]-stricken house, most of the people having children for whose safety they fear and others being afraid for themselves.

I hastily changed my clothing and went to the house, and there I found to exist a pitiful state of affairs. One child, 2 1/2 years old, lay dead on a bed—having been dead about 4 hours, and still unwashed; two other children, one a boy of 10, the other a girl of 5, lay writhing in the agonies of the disease; a girl of 13 years is still feeble from a recent attack of diphtheria; and the 6-month-old baby seems to be sickening with the disorder. The father Mr. Abe Martin and the mother Marsha Martin are dazed with grief and fatigue; and the only other occupant of the house, a man named Kelly—a border in the family, is so ill and weak as hardly to be able to move about.

The siege has been so long about this afflicted family that all household affairs are in a state of utter neglect; the floors and furniture are unclean. The beds and the sick occupants are unwashed; to say nothing of the sickening aspect of the blood and mucus-covered corpse. Though the family are not members of our Church, the parents requested me to administer to the children, which I did. A lady hired for the occasion by the Relief Society came in; and we set to work together. First we washed and laid out the corpse; then the carpets were torn up, the room swept; filthy rags burned, and soiled clothes carried out; the sick children were washed and their clothes changed; food was sent for the parents, and burial clothes arranged for. While these operations were in progress a woman came to the house, saying she had heard of the sad bereavement, and afflictions, and desired to offer her aid, provided the people would agree to pay her $5.00 a day. When she was told of the families destitution, she lowered her price to $4.50 a day. Such a state of womankind filled me with disgust. I told her to go; and not stay in the house of poverty, suffering, and death to act the vulture; and I assured the people they should not be left without help; that I would stay with them myself until other aid arrived. I sent for . . . disinfectants. In the evening Bishop Hardy came, and together we administered to the sick several times. At night a Miss Sorenson from the 8th ward was secured as help, and Bro. Earnest Bassett of our own ward came as night watch. I disinfected myself; changed clothing, and went home, keeping in my own rooms, from which others of the family were excluded.

[The next day] Returned to the home of the afflicted Martin family at an early hour this morning. Found that the boy 10 years old had died during the night. The little girl was still suffering terribly. She clung to my neck, often times coughing bloody mucus upon my face and clothing; and her throat had about it the stench of putrification, yet I could not put her from me. During the half hour immediately preceding her death, I walked the floor with the little creature in my arms. She died in agony at 10:10 am.

So, the three children have departed, all within the space of 24 hours. Bro. Earnest Bassett and I washed the corpse of the child; then we carried out the bedding and useless furniture, and swept the rooms. Soon the coffins came, and with the aid of the undertaker's men, we put the bodies in neatly attired. At 2:30 the hearses arrived, and the sad ride to the cemetery was begun. The malignant nature of the disease forbade the holding of public service except at the grave. There, by request I delivered a short discourse, and Bishop Hardy offered the dedicatory prayer. The grief of the parents and little sister was indeed pitiable to behold. The coffins were placed in a single grave. After these sad rites were over, we made arrangements for cleaning the house, and furnishing the family with good bedding and food; then, by the Bishop's advice, I went home. I disrobed and bathed . . . and placed all clothing worn at the house, in a strong hot zinc solution. I confined myself to my own rooms, from which the rest of the family kept away.

[The next day] Confined to the house the entire day through illness—fever, lassitude, and pains in head. All temporary I hope—simply the effects of over exertion and nervous strain I think.[8]

The disease did not afflict Brother Talmage, and within a few days he had fully and gratefully recovered from his exertions. Such a deed as this one, freely risking his own health and life to help others in such great need, in part qualified James E. Talmage to one day be called as an Apostle of the Lord.

TEACHING AND WRITING DOCTRINE

In the 1890s, Brother Talmage received an assignment from the First Presidency of the Church to teach a class on theology, which would eventually become a book. These lectures began in October 1893 and ended in April 1894, with attendance increasing from several hundred to well over a thousand interested learners. Where there was the possibility of question concerning some points of doctrine that he was teaching, a committee was formed by the First Presidency to read the lectures in advance and ensure doctrinal correctness. Sometimes the First Presidency and certain members of the Twelve themselves became involved. Elder Abraham H. Cannon, a member of the Twelve assigned to work with Brother Talmage, recorded developments in his journal.

I went to the President's office with Bro. James E. Talmage in the forenoon to get some doctrinal points answered by the Brethren concerning a change in the articles of faith and about the subject of baptism. An answer will be given after these matters have been submitted to the Quorum meeting this afternoon. About the sons of perdition it was said we can scarcely tell who will be consigned to this doom. That there will also be daughters of perdition there is no doubt in the minds of the brethren. It was explained that only such can become sons of perdition who receive a testimony of the gospel—who receive the Holy Ghost, and the highest blessings of the Church, and then willfully deny the light they have obtained. Murderers who crucify Christ anew, or consent to His death, in that they shed innocent blood knowing at the time that they are thereby preventing the spread of the truth, will be subject to this penalty. The murderers of the Savior are not sons of perdition, for they did not know what they were doing, as Jesus said in His prayer while on the cross.[9]

The reason the theology class was suspended in April was because James was being considered for the position of president of the University of Utah, and the First Presidency didn't want the theology class to provide the local bitter anti-Mormons with the excuse of a conflict of interest to argue against his appointment.

The anti-Mormons were unsuccessful, and on April 9, 1894, James Talmage became the president of the University of Utah and also held a chair in the Department of Geology. He served as president until 1897, when anti-Mormon opposition increased, and he resigned and remained only as a professor of geology. In 1898 he was requested by the First Presidency to finish writing the lectures for the class that had been suspended, and by April 1899, the book *The Articles of Faith* was published.

In the succeeding years, including the first decade of the 1900s, James would immerse himself in his geology classes at the University of Utah, and he also formed a private mineral consulting practice, putting his knowledge of geology to practical use throughout Utah mining communities and other locations. He was given the assignment by the First Presidency to review the Pearl of Great Price and divide it into verses for better use by Church members. He also wrote lessons on the apostasy of the early Christian church that were eventually published in the book *The Great Apostasy*.

CALL TO THE QUORUM OF THE TWELVE APOSTLES

The year 1911 was a banner year for Talmage. In September, the anti-Mormon *Salt Lake Tribune* published an account of a blackmail plot against the Church. As the details eventually came out, it was discovered that a gardener working on Temple Square, with some petty grudge against the Church, had managed to let someone into the temple during its summer cleaning time, and this person had taken pictures of some rooms in the interior of the temple. This man then hired an agent to negotiate in his behalf. Unless the Church paid them one hundred thousand dollars they threatened to sell the pictures to movie houses and yellow journalism sheets in the East. President Joseph F. Smith quickly let it be known that the Church would have nothing to do with thieves or those who dealt in stolen goods.

Brother Talmage suggested to the First Presidency that a high-quality book with sharp photographs be published as one means of quashing the sensational plot. Thereupon he himself was assigned to do the work of writing the book, and a local Mormon photographer, Ralph Savage, was assigned to take the pictures of the interior of the temple. James went to work on the project, which was finished and became the book *The House of the Lord*, but in the midst of the project his life changed. He described his experience in his journal.

> Shortly after 4 o'clock this afternoon, I learned of a call for me which must mark a great change in my work. This is no less than a call to the holy apostleship. Action was taken at this day's council meeting of the First Presidency and Twelve, whereby Apostle Charles W. Penrose was sustained as second counselor in the First Presidency to succeed the late President John Henry Smith. I believe that all Israel will feel as I do—that this call is from the Lord. The Presidency, thus completed, will have my fervent support and prayerful service. The selection creates a present vacancy in the Council or Quorum of the Twelve, and to this exalted and special office I am called. The announcement of my having been chosen came as a wholly unheralded action. I was with President Joseph F. Smith until a late hour yesterday, but by no word, act, or intimation was such action suggested to my mind. I knew not that the President had then considered it. Were such an office offered me as a position in secular life I might be tendered, I feel that I would shrink from the responsibility and hesitate even if I did not actually decline, but I hold myself ready to respond to any call made upon me by and in the priesthood.
>
> Apostle Anthony W. Ivins called upon me about 4 p.m. on a matter of business and there told me with evidences of affection and emotion of the action taken by the Council. He testified to me that the call was from the Lord. Even at this time the announcement had been printed in the *Deseret News*, and within a few minutes I had many calls by phone from brethren who assured me of their support. May the Lord grant me His, and enable me to be a true witness of Him.
>
> Within half an hour after the news had reached me, May, my wife, came to my office and assured me of her loving support. She had learned of the call while she was attending a meeting of the general board of the Young Ladies Mutual Improvement Association. I feel that I need the help of my wife and family. I have looked upon myself as a lay member in the Church though I know that a patriarch, Jesse Martin of Provo [Utah], gave me to understand that I would be called and ordained one of the Twelve Apostles.[10]

Elder Talmage entered into his apostolic duties with zeal and carried on with many assignments. He wrote articles for Church magazines, represented the Church at various public venues, spoke before countless congregations, both Mormon and otherwise, and did his share of work in the stakes of Zion.

A Deepening Witness

Another major literary project came in September 1914, when he was assigned by the First Presidency to assemble and revise some earlier lectures he had given on Jesus the Christ, and prepare a formal book to be known by the same title. Because of the many pressures on his time and distractions that his calling brought upon him, he was given a special room in the Salt Lake Temple in which to do the actual writing of the book. During the seven months it took to write *Jesus the Christ*, Elder Talmage was relieved of most stake conference assignments so he could devote most of his time to preparing the manuscript. He often spent most of his days in the temple, returning home at night for needed sleep and food. When able, he worked six days a week on the manuscript, only resting on Sunday. On April 19, 1915, he recorded in his journal that he had finally completed the first draft. He then edited it, read it to another committee on criticism, seeking to ensure the doctrinal accuracy of the work, and also oversaw publication. Thus concluded one of the more famous assignments given Elder Talmage, still appreciated by informed Church members today.

This written work, which has been printed in many hundreds of thousands of copies and read by hundreds of thousands of missionaries and members, constitutes Elder James E. Talmage's greatest statement and witness as to the divinity and mission of Jesus the Christ. In a way, he was privileged to bear testimony of Jesus Christ for and in behalf of the Church, to the world.

> The Church of Jesus Christ of Latter-day Saints affirms her possession of divine authority for the use of the sacred name, Jesus Christ, as the essential part of her distinctive designation. In view of this exalted claim, it is pertinent to inquire as to what special or particular message the Church has to give to the world concerning the Redeemer and Savior of the race, and as to what she has to say in justification of her solemn affirmation, or in vindication of her exclusive name and title. As we proceed with our study, we shall find that among the specific teachings of the Church respecting the Christ are these:
>
> (1) The unity and continuity of His mission in all ages—this of necessity involving the verity of His preexistence and foreordination. (2) The fact of His antemortal Godship. (3) The actuality of His birth in the flesh as the natural

issue of divine and mortal parentage. (4) The reality of His death and physical resurrection, as a result of which the power of death shall be eventually overcome. (5) The literalness of the Atonement wrought by Him, including the absolute requirement of individual compliance with the laws and ordinances of His gospel as the means by which salvation may be attained. (6) The restoration of His priesthood and the reestablishment of His Church in the current age, which is verily the dispensation of the fulness of times. (7) The certainty of His return to earth in the near future, with power and great glory, to reign in Person and bodily presence as Lord and King.[11]

Encounters with the Adversary

It seems that Elder Talmage on occasion had to deal with the presence of evil. In September 1890, not long after his own severe illness recounted above, Elder Talmage's dear wife, May, was visited by three lying spirits who convinced her that her husband was cheating on her and had been excommunicated in a public scandal. At the time they exercised this sickly influence over her, she was enduring her own severe bout of typhoid fever. Elder Talmage was able to reassure her, and after blessing her, she was freed from the feverish hallucinations and delusions impressed upon her by the evil spirits.

Three decades later, in the spring of 1921, Elder Talmage found himself investigating a situation where some Church members living near a mining district had, through a combination of immoral activity and unworthily seeking for dreams and signs and wonders, been misled by evil spirits, leading to some excommunications and other disciplinary measures. These difficulties brought him into contact with a woman in a miserable condition, both physically and spiritually. He wrote,

> I then went to the home of Mrs. Crandall, to meet her daughter, Mrs. Erma Gudmundson, who appears to have been a victim of many painful conditions arising from [immorality]. . . . She has been harassed by occasional visits and more frequent messages from her husband; the nature of some of which was disclosed. Thus, he told her that should she say a word or do a thing against the interests of the people accused of wrongdoing . . . she would be the cause of his death, as it had been shown to him in vision that such action on her part would bring about his murder, and that calamity after calamity would be visited upon herself and her children. In her impressionable state, such messages as these threaten her sanity and even her life. She was really in the grip of an evil power; and I have seldom experienced a meeting with such a potent adversary as the evil spirit by which she was possessed. She seemed to crave my aid, and yet she

persistently refused to look me in the face, saying that my face and eyes were so bright as to terrify her. I was not conscious of any unusual condition of this sort, but she turned her head and shaded her eyes whenever for the moment I caught her gaze. I proceeded to administer to her, and rebuked the evil power, conscious all the while of a real struggle and conflict. Immediately after the administration she turned her eyes upon me and smiled, and was not disturbed by my gaze, but kept her eyes directed toward me. When I left her she was holding her baby and was in a state of comparative peace. I confess, however, that because of her weakened condition and of her state of nervous disturbance, I have not full faith that she will not suffer a relapse.[12]

DECLARING HIS SPECIAL WITNESS

From 1924 to 1928, Elder Talmage served as president of the European Mission of the Church, then headquartered in Liverpool, England. During this time he used his influence as a member of some prestigious English scientific societies to help quell the growing anti-Mormon yellow journalism common in the British press. His efforts often proved successful, as newspaper editors who would not give time to a lowly Mormon missionary would often open their office doors to him. Then he could often convince them to let him write a rebuttal for them to publish. On his return from Europe, he continued in his apostolic duties.

Elder Harold B. Lee shared a story involving Elder Talmage that is undated but probably took place sometime between 1915 and 1917, and which would have occurred not long after the writing of *Jesus the Christ*.

[Mission] President Melvin J. Ballard told me as we rode over the country in the early days of the Welfare Program of an experience at conference time. All the mission presidents would have a day with the Council of the Twelve in the temple where it was a time of report and testimony bearing. In that meeting one of the presidents presumed to explain philosophically how the Savior was able to atone for the sins of the world. He thought he had given a masterful talk that would teach the General Authorities. Dr. James E. Talmage immediately rose to denounce the ideas advanced by the mission president. Elder Ballard commented, "If I ever heard a man get a lashing from a scriptural standpoint, it came to this mission president who had the temerity to put aside all the scriptures that taught the true doctrine and presume to philosophize as to how the Savior could atone for the sins of mankind."[13]

This Apostle, Elder James E. Talmage, had over his lifetime come to a sure and certain witness that Jesus was the Christ, the son of God, and he would not be led astray by the theories of men, no matter where they originated. In a general conference address he declared,

> When I see how often the theories and conceptions of men have gone astray, have fallen short of the truth, yea, have even contradicted the truth directly, I am thankful in my heart that we have an iron rod to which we can cling—the rod of certainty, the rod of revealed truth. The Church of Jesus Christ of Latter-day Saints welcomes all truth, but it distinguishes most carefully between fact and fancy, between truth; and theory, between premises and deductions; and it is willing to leave some questions in abeyance until the Lord in his wisdom shall see fit to speak more plainly. As the result of the combined labors of wise men I learn that man is but the developed offspring of the beast; and yet I read that God created man in his own image, after his likeness; and again, I stand on the word of God, though it be in contradiction to the theories of men.[14]

Elder Talmage died at the age of seventy in 1933, having shared his special witness in many ways with all who would listen.

Notes

1. Excerpts quoted from James Edward Talmage's autobiographical sketch found in Brigham Young University's archives, 1–4. (See James Edward Talmage, "Papers, 1876–1933," MSS 229, L. Tom Perry Special Collections, Harold B. Lee Library, Brigham Young University.)
2. James Edward Talmage journal, 1876. Hardcopies of excerpts in author's possession. Original diaries located at Brigham Young University, L. Tom Perry Special Collections, James Edward Talmage. (See lib.byu.edu/collections.)
   Albert remained blind the rest of his life, at the same time faithfully living the gospel. James took him to the Salt Lake Temple to be blessed by President Lorenzo Snow.
3. Talmage journal, 1876.
4. Ibid., January 1880.
5. Ibid., November 4, 1887.
6. These summaries and the preceding six quotations are from the Talmage journal, February 20 through March 10, 1888.
7. Summaries and quotations of the experience are found in the Talmage journal, June 30 to July 30, 1890.
8. Talmage journal, May 30–June 1, 1892. See also John R. Talmage, *The Talmage Story: Life of James E. Talmage, Educator, Scientist, Apostle* (Salt Lake City: Bookcraft, 1972), 112–14.

9. As quoted in Dennis B. Horne's *An Apostle's Record: The Journals of Abraham H. Cannon* (Clearfield, Utah: Gnolaumbooks, 2004), 291–92 (November 29, 1893).

10. Talmage journal, December 7, 1911.

11. As quoted in the introduction of The Church of Jesus Christ of Latter-day Saint's online edition of Talmage's *Jesus the Christ* (see lds.org). The first edition of this book was published in September 1915 in Salt Lake City by The Church of Jesus Christ of Latter-day Saints.

12. Talmage journal, March 15, 1921.

13. Harold B. Lee, "Viewpoint of a Giant" (address given to Church Educational System religious educators at Brigham Young University, July 18, 1968), 3.

14. James E. Talmage, in Conference Report, October 1916, 73–76.

13

ELDER MELVIN J. BALLARD'S

SPECIAL WITNESS OF JESUS CHRIST

"I know as well as the doubting Thomas knew—when
he had handled Christ and felt the prints of the nails
in His hands and in His feet, all doubt was gone—
I know, as well as he knew, that Jesus is the Christ."

Elder Harold B. Lee once told a friend that "Twenty years ago, the most electrifying and most interesting man in the Quorum of the Twelve was Melvin J. Ballard. People used to travel miles just to go and hear him at a stake conference. People just flocked to hear him. Hardly anyone knows who he is now."[1] It is also true that comparatively few now know of his special witness of Jesus Christ. We might perhaps also conclude that Brother Ballard was given greater latitude by the Holy Spirit to share more detail about how he gained his special witness than many of his associates in the Twelve.

Melvin Ballard was born in 1873. Because his mother, Margaret McNeil Ballard, had lost other children and was in poor health while she carried him, she begged the Lord for His blessing on her unborn son, and promised him to the Lord if He would bless them. After pouring her heart out in prayer, she received an answer: "Be of good cheer. Your life is acceptable, and you will bear a son who will become an Apostle of the Lord, Jesus Christ."[2]

Prepared by Long and Inspired Missionary Service

Melvin grew up in Logan, Utah, where he was educated and cultivated a natural talent for singing. He used that gift to bless and entertain others for the rest of his life, in and out of Church settings. He married Martha Jones and then served a special mission in the Midwest and Eastern United States where he developed his public speaking skills and refined them under the tutelage of Elder B. H. Roberts of the First Council of the Seventy.

On his return, he spent ten years earning a living for his family, until 1909 when he was called as the president of the Northwestern States Mission. Brother Ballard served as the mission president for almost ten years. During this time, he recorded an occasion in which he received the gift of healing. "I was called in to administer to a child dying with pneumonia. It was in convulsions, and the doctor said that it could not live thirty minutes. The parents said, 'you have come in time to save the lost.' Fifteen minutes after administering to the child, it was at ease; and the next day it was well on the road to recovery."[3] Such miracles followed President Ballard throughout his ministry. On one occasion, while serving as the mission president, an inspired dream helped him seek to reactivate some spiritually wandering young men.

> On Wednesday, March 4, 1917, on his way to Helena, President Ballard had a most impressive dream. He dreamed that he was crossing a great desert, when he came upon the remains of a pony express rider. As he looked around, he discovered some leather pouches, kicked them, and they broke open and out fell nuggets of tarnished gold. He picked some of them up and rubbed them together with his hands until they became brilliant.
>
> During that year he discovered more than one hundred of our fine boys who had drifted away. As he talked to them, they became interested, so he hired a hall and began to round them up. He visited them often, and at the close of the year he had established strong branches of the Church. One of these boys later became a president of the Northwestern States Mission.[4]

It was also around this time that President Ballard noted a marvelous manifestation that presaged events to come. In his journal he wrote,

> May 14, 1917: Met with our branch at Wolfepoint among the Indians in Montana. We had some difficulty in satisfying some of these Indians. They all

wanted to be ordained priests. We had to ordain some of them deacons, some teachers, and some priests. Many problems arose and caused us great anxiety. We sought the Lord earnestly that we might have wisdom and light to know what to do concerning these problems. It was this night that I received a very unusual manifestation. In the dream or vision of the night I was carried to the Salt Lake Temple where I had a glorious manifestation of the Savior. I referred to this in some of my public talks.[5]

Prophetic Revelation Given

In late 1918, President Joseph F. Smith passed away, and Heber J. Grant became the President of the Church. These events left a vacancy open in the Quorum of the Twelve. President Grant had a close friend, Richard W. Young, whom he felt worthy in every way to become an Apostle of the Lord, and therefore he planned to present Young's name to the Twelve for their sustaining vote as the newest member of the Quorum. President Hugh B. Brown related the Prophet's experience in calling the new Apostle.

> President Heber J. Grant once gave me a fine example of how inspiration sometimes prevails over personal judgment. He said that when he was a member of the Twelve and a vacancy would arise, he would write down the name of a particular boyhood friend [Richard W. Young]. They had gone to school together. President Grant explained, "I knew him to be an exemplary and fine man in every respect, and I decided if I ever became President of the Church he would be the first man I would appoint to the Twelve."
>
> After he became Church President and a vacancy arose in the Twelve, he wrote down the name of his friend on a slip of paper and put it into his pocket. "I went into the elevator and rode up to the fourth floor of the temple. On the way up I heard three times, as clearly as I ever heard any voice in my life, the name Melvin J. Ballard. I only knew Brother Ballard in passing, that he was at the time president of the Northwestern States Mission. But I couldn't get away from that statement and didn't give it its proper interpretation until I got into the room where the Twelve were, when I said, 'Brethren, I have decided to recommend to you a certain man to be a member of the Council of the Twelve. The man's name is . . . Melvin J. Ballard.' I know that that was inspired of the Lord," President Grant concluded.[6]

In confirmation, President Grant recorded the substance of a conversation he had shortly after presenting Melvin J. Ballard's name to the Twelve for their sustaining vote.

I prayed about it and I was impressed to name Melvin J. Ballard, and I followed my impression, although Richard was at the time my nearest and dearest friend. . . .

I was delighted, shortly afterward—a few minutes only—when Joseph Fielding Smith said to me: "Brother Grant, at the time that Richard R. Lyman was nominated to be an Apostle by father, he said to me: 'My son, I cannot make up my mind which of two young men, both worthy to be members of the Council of the Twelve, to name—Richard R. Lyman or Melvin J. Ballard.' Now you have named the other one."

This filled my heart with joy . . . for me to have chosen the man that he felt was worthy filled my heart with joy.[7]

BECOMES A SPECIAL WITNESS

President Grant notified the currently serving mission president Ballard that his presence was requested. "January 5th, received a telegram from President Grant to come to Salt Lake on the first train. Left for Salt Lake at 11:00 p.m. and arrived at 9:30 a.m. January the seventh." Then, "Met President Grant, who told me that the Lord and the Brethren wanted me to devote the balance of my life to his work as an Apostle of the Lord Jesus Christ. At 10:30 a.m. I was ordained in the temple by President Heber J. Grant and all members of the Quorum."[8] In formally accepting his calling and ordination as an Apostle, and on being asked to share the feelings of his heart with the First Presidency and the Twelve, Elder Melvin J. Ballard related the following remarkable experience that qualified him to act as a special witness of Jesus Christ.

> President Grant and brethren. With feelings of great timidity, and yet with deep thankfulness and gratitude to the Lord, for His favor, and your love and confidence, I stand before you to say that nothing in this world has ever given me such pleasure, such happiness, as to work in the ministry of the Master. While I feel myself unworthy to stand here as one of His special witnesses, if I can be worthy it will be the highest ambition of my life to be one of His representatives, one of the special witnesses of the Lord Jesus; and with all my heart and soul— not with ambition but with pleasure, with deep joy—I shall give to this service all there is in me and all that the Lord will make it possible for me to do.
>
> I have not aspired, nor coveted a position of this character; but from my childhood I have desired to work in the service of the Lord, and have not waited for place or position to give my services. I am just as willing, today, to labor as

an elder, in a branch or a ward, as to any other calling, if that is where the Lord wants me; and if He wants me here, I am willing to say, as I have often sung— "I'll go where you want me to go," and "I'll be what the Lord wants me to be."

I know, as I know that I live, that this is God's work and that you are His servants. I have no more doubt about it than I have that I exist. I remember one little testimony, among the many testimonies which I have received. You will pardon me for referring to it. Two years ago, about this time, I had been on the Fort Peck Indian reservation, for several days, with the brethren, solving the problems connected with our work among the Lamanites. Many questions arose, that we had to settle. There was no precedent for us to follow, and we just had to go to the Lord and tell him our troubles, and get inspiration and help from Him. On this occasion I had sought the Lord, under such circumstances, and that night I received a wonderful manifestation and an impression which has never left me. I was carried to this place [the Salt Lake Temple]—into this room [the Council room of the First Presidency and the Twelve]. I saw myself here with you brethren, and I was happy joining in a prayer circle with you. I was told there was one other privilege that was mine; and I was led into a room where I was informed I was to meet someone. As I entered the room [the Holy of Holies] I saw, seated on a raised platform, the most glorious being I have ever conceived of, and was taken forward to be introduced to him. As I approached He smiled, called my name, and stretched out His hands towards me. If I live to be a million years old, I shall never forget that smile. He put His arms around me and kissed me, as He took me into His bosom, and He blest me until my whole being was thrilled. As He finished I fell at His feet, and there saw the marks of the nails; and as I kissed them, with deep joy swelling through my whole being, I felt that I was in Heaven indeed. The feeling that came to my heart then was, "Oh! If I could live worthy, though it would require four score years, so that in the end, when I have finished, I could go into His presence and receive the feeling that I then had in His presence, I could give everything that I am and ever hope to be!"

I know—as I know that I live—that He lives. That is my testimony; and having that kind of feeling and testimony, I accept with humility, and yet with deep thankfulness and gratitude to God, this honor; for I esteem it the highest honor that could be given to a man, to be a special witness of the Lord Jesus Christ. I hope you will be patient with me, and I shall do my best to come up to all the requirements the Lord will make at my hands.[9]

In all LDS Church literature, with the exception of the scriptural narrations given by the Prophet Joseph Smith, there are probably no other published accounts of an Apostle receiving his special witness that are as openly descriptive as this one. The following June, at a conference of the Mutual Improvement Association, Elder Ballard again shared his sacred experience.

I bear witness to you that I know that the Lord lives. I know that he has made this sacrifice and this atonement. He has given me a foretaste of these things.

I recall an experience which I had two years ago, bearing witness to my soul of the reality of his death, of his Crucifixion, and his Resurrection, that I shall never forget. I bear it to you . . . not with a spirit to glory over it, but with a grateful heart and with thanksgiving in my soul. I know that he lives, and I know that through him men must find their salvation, and that we cannot ignore this blessed offering that he has given us as the means of our spiritual growth to prepare us to come to him and be justified.

Away on the Fort Peck Reservation where I was doing missionary work with some of our brethren, laboring among the Indians, seeking the Lord for light to decide certain matters pertaining to our work there, and receiving a witness from him that we were doing things according to his will, I found myself one evening in the dreams of the night in that sacred building, the temple. After a season of prayer and rejoicing I was informed that I should have the privilege of entering into one of the those rooms, to meet a glorious Personage, and, as I entered the door, I saw, seated on a raised platform, the most glorious Being my eyes have ever beheld or that I ever conceived existed in all the eternal worlds. As I approached to be introduced, he arose and stepped towards me with extended arms, and he smiled as he softly spoke my name. If I shall live to be a million years old, I shall never forget that smile. He took me into his arms and kissed me, pressed me to his bosom, and blessed me, until the marrow of my bones seemed to melt! When he had finished, I fell at his feet, and, as I bathed them with my tears and kisses, saw the prints of the nails in the feet of the Redeemer of the world. The feeling that I had in the presence of him who hath all things in his hands, to have his love, his affection, and his blessing was such that if I ever can receive that of which I had but a foretaste, I would give all that I am, all that I ever hope to be, to feel what I then felt.[10]

Such is the experience that began Elder Ballard's apostolic ministry as a special witness.

Continuously Declares His Special Witness

At the April 1920 general conference, Elder Ballard restated his testimony in these forceful terms:

Therefore, we rejoice in the witness we have that Jesus told the truth, that the testimony of his disciples concerning his Resurrection is the truth, and we also know that the testimony of Joseph Smith and his brethren, who looked upon the face of the Redeemer, is true. I bear witness that I know what they have said is the truth. I know, as well as I know that I live and look into your faces, that Jesus Christ lives, and he is the Redeemer of the world, that he arose from the dead with a tangible body, and still has that real body which Thomas touched when he thrust his hands into his side and felt the wound of the spear, and also the prints of the nails in his hands. I know by the witness and the revelations of God to me that Thomas told the truth. I know that Joseph Smith told the truth, for mine eyes have seen. For in the visions of the Lord to my soul, I have seen Christ's face, I have heard his voice. I know that he lives, that he is the Redeemer of the world, and that as he arose from the dead, a tangible and real individual, so shall all men arise in the Resurrection from the dead.[11]

As the years passed, Elder Ballard became known as one of the greatest doctrinal speakers in the Church. His discourse on section 76 of the Doctrine and Covenants, the vision of the three degrees of glory, is still considered a classic and is sometimes quoted by present-day General Authorities. In that seminal talk, delivered in September 1922 at the Ogden Utah Tabernacle, amidst many other insights, he stated, "I cannot begin this night to tell you what that means—to enjoy the blessings and privileges of dwelling in Christ's presence forever and ever. I know how the soul is thrilled; I know the feeling that comes by being in his presence for but a moment. I would give all that I am, all that I hope to be, to have the joy of his presence, to dwell in his love and his affection and to be in favor with the Master of all things forever and ever."[12] Having been in His presence, Elder Ballard knew whereof he spoke and tried to convey that feeling to others.

The author of a history of the Logan Temple, the temple of Elder Ballard's hometown, shared an undated experience from temple records.

> Probably one of the mightiest preachers the Mormon Church ever had was Apostle Melvin J. Ballard. He had had Heavenly Manifestations, and did not hesitate to declare the Word of the Lord, and with power.
>
> Elder Ballard sat at our baptismal font one Saturday while nearly a thousand baptisms were performed for the dead. As he sat there, he contemplated on how great the temple ceremonies were, and how we are bringing special blessings to the living and the dead. His thoughts turned to the spirit world, and he wondered if the people there would accept the work we were doing for them.
>
> Brother Ballard said, "All at once a vision opened to me and I beheld a great congregation of people gathered in the east end of the font room. One by one, as each name was baptized for, one of these people climbed a stairway over the font to the west end of the room. Not one soul was missing, but there was a person for every one of the thousand names during that day."

Brother Ballard said that he had never seen such happy people in all his life, and the whole congregation rejoiced in what was being done for them.[13]

As Elder Ballard spoke to various groups as his ministry required, he declared his special witness. Before one gathering, he stated,

I know that my Redeemer lives as well as I know that I live. . . . The tangible evidences are so great that I know that God lives as well as I know that I see you and that you have an existence. I know that he is the Father of the spirits of all flesh. I know that his son Jesus Christ, our Savior, the Mighty Master of the elements, who has promised to bring us forth from the grave and give us immortal life, lives as well as I know that I live and exist. When the time shall come, and like Thomas of old, I shall feel the prints of the nails and the spear, I shall not know better that he is the Redeemer of man, than I do this day.[14]

In 1923, in a discourse given in the Salt Lake Tabernacle, he testified,

Only a few, not the multitude, saw him ascend, and a few have seen him return. In the Sacred Grove, Joseph Smith saw him, and Oliver and Joseph saw him in the Kirtland Temple, and upon other occasions a few have seen him already come. So in part at least that return has been fulfilled. The Latter-day Saints have a different conception from others with reference to his return. It is not a return for all the world to know. No, the few should see him return. In part that also has been fulfilled when Joseph Smith and Oliver Cowdery in the Kirtland Temple saw a wonderful vision of him. . . .

The Redeemer shall come to live upon the earth and reign with men for a thousand years; and we know it. I bear witness of it, with a heart full of gratitude that I have this knowledge and testimony, for I know that he lives. The testimony of the ancient prophets and apostles, as I observed, may be questioned by the world, but Joseph Smith and his associates have re-established the knowledge that Jesus Christ is a reality, the very Son of God, a tangible being having power such as the former witness testified concerning him. We rejoice in this knowledge. We have that witness because we have enjoyed the gift and power of the Holy Ghost, that by and through it we may attain the testimony that Jesus Christ lives, and that he is the Son of God. I know it as I know that I live. I know it as well as I know that I see you. I know it better than I know anything else in all this world—that Jesus Christ lives, and that he is the son of God, and that he did visit the Prophet Joseph Smith.[15]

In an address on the subject of the Resurrection of Jesus, Elder Ballard referred to his witness of the tangible body of the Savior.

On this Easter day, we rejoice therefore not only in the testimony of those who saw and bore witness of the Resurrection of Christ, but also that he still lives, the same resurrected being; and is the Savior of the world, that he still is planning for man's eternal salvation and redemption, that he has visited the earth in this age, and that he is presently to come again, to dwell upon it with men for a thousand years.

I know as well as the doubting Thomas knew—when he had handled Christ and felt the prints of the nails in his hands and in his feet, all doubt was gone—I know, as well as he knew, that Jesus is the Christ; that he is a reality; that he did visit Joseph Smith; that he did establish his work again a hundred years ago upon the earth; and that it shall be triumphant; that God is moving even among the nations of the earth today, preparing for the coming of his Son gloriously, in his resurrected state, to dwell upon the earth with men a thousand years.[16]

In late 1925, Elder Ballard and a few others were called by President Grant to go to South America and dedicate the land for the spreading of the gospel and to open the Church's first mission there. The task seemed overwhelmingly difficult, with virtually no member presence there, except some few who had emigrated from other lands. During a meeting with some of those Latter-day Saints in attendance, one of the missionaries present recorded Elder Ballard's comments about the future of that land to those assembled.

At a testimony meeting of the German Saints held in Buenos Aires, Argentina, July 4, 1926, Elder Ballard said, "The work of the Lord will grow slowly for a time here just as an oak grows slowly from an acorn. It will not shoot up in a day as does the sunflower that grows quickly and then dies. But thousands will join the Church here. It will be divided into more than one mission and will be one of the strongest in the Church. The work here is the smallest that it will ever be. The day will come when the Lamanites in this land will be given a chance. The South American Mission will be a power in the Church."

He said that he had seen the Lord Jesus and knew that he lives; and that the Lord had revealed to him (Brother Ballard), things that were to happen in the future. And they have happened. He said he had also healed the sick in cases too numerous to mention—bringing them, as it were, from the very jaws of death.[17]

Although Elder Ballard could not speak Spanish, he was still able to begin missionary work in what has become one of the fastest growing and strongest parts of the Church, with many missions and a number of temples located there today. After about ten months organizing the mission, Elder Ballard returned home and resumed his regular work in the ministry for another thirteen years. Then, in 1939, while holding meetings in the Eastern United States, he became ill. He died of leukemia on July 31, 1939.

The Passing and Influence of a Mighty Apostle

Elder Ballard's grandson, Elder M. Russell Ballard, described what he had learned of the passing of his grandfather.

> In my office I have a little plaque that reads, "Above all else, brethren, let us think straight." These were the last words in mortality spoken by my grandfather Melvin J. Ballard. As I understand the circumstance, Grandfather, after the very grueling experience of preaching the gospel all through the eastern part of the United States, drove his car from New York to Salt Lake City. When he came into the driveway of his home . . . in Salt Lake City, he collapsed. He was rushed to the LDS hospital, where he was found to have acute leukemia. He never came out of the hospital. He went in and out of a coma. As I have had it told to me by my father, who was there, Grandfather pushed himself up in bed, looked into his hospital room as though he were addressing a congregation or a group, and said clearly, "And above all else, brethren, let us think straight." Then he died. I don't go into my office any day of the week that I don't see those words, and I find that they help me a great deal.[18]

Elder Melvin J. Ballard's passing was not the end of his influence on the Church. It seems that he, with others on the other side of the veil, had something to do with the call of his grandson, Elder M. Russell Ballard, to the Quorum of the Twelve. The Apostle's grandson explained,

> I thought that you might be interested in some of the things that have happened in my life in the last few months. On Thursday morning, October 10, 1985, in the fourth-floor council room of the Salt Lake Temple, I was invited to sit on a small stool placed at the feet of President Spencer W. Kimball, who sat in a chair. With President Kimball's hands on my head, and surrounded in a circle by President Hinckley and all the members of the Council of the Twelve, I was ordained an Apostle of the Lord Jesus Christ and set apart as a member of the Council of the Twelve. President Hinckley was voice. I was given a blessing that is a great source of comfort and strength to me. To say the least, my brothers and sisters, I was then and still am now overwhelmed with this calling to serve as a special witness of the Lord and to serve you, the members of the Church. . . .
>
> I have, during the past three months, come to the comforting knowledge that the Lord and my Brethren see in me something I can do to help the work of the Lord continue to move forward. In my specific case I am also aware that the dedicated service of many of my forefathers could well have influenced my call to the Council of the Twelve. Since the very beginnings of the Restoration of the Church they gave all that they had, even their lives, for this great work. Family

members of the Prophet Joseph Smith and his brother Hyrum have served in the Council of the Twelve since the organization of the Council of the Twelve in 1835.

I count it a blessing to be a representative now of the family of Joseph and Hyrum, and acknowledge publicly that to follow my great-grandfather, Joseph F. Smith, and both of my grandfathers, Hyrum Mack Smith and Melvin J. Ballard, into the Council of the Twelve Apostles is a great honor and responsibility. I will do my very best to be the kind of a servant that is worthy of such a birthright.

On several occasions I have been assured by my Brethren that they felt my forefathers must have sustained my call in the councils on the other side as well as the First Presidency and the Council of the Twelve on this side of the veil.[19]

NOTES

1. Email from Glen L. Rudd to Dennis Horne, July 13, 2012.
2. Quotation from item about Elder Melvin J. Ballard as found in Bryant S. Hinckley's *Sermons and Missionary Services of Melvin Joseph Ballard* (Salt Lake City: Deseret Book, 1949), 23.

   From this work by Bryant Hinckley it becomes apparent that Melvin's mother received impressions on more than one occasion that he would eventually become a great leader in the Church. His patriarchal blessing also so stated.
3. Ibid., 67.
4. Ibid., 66.
5. Melvin J. Ballard journal, as quoted in Hinckley's *Sermons and Missionary Services,* 66–67.
6. As quoted in Hugh B. Brown's *An Abundant Life: the Memoirs of Hugh B. Brown,* ed., Edwin B. Firmage (Salt Lake City: Signature Books, 1988), 128–29.

   The following is recorded in President Heber J. Grant's journal: "Had a long chat today with Charles A. Callis, telling him of my having nominated Richard W. Young a number of times to be an Apostle, the first time way back when M. W. Merrill, Anthon H. Lund, and Abram H. Cannon were chosen, at the organization of the Presidency with Wilford Woodruff as President. The three names that I sent on that occasion were Anthon H. Lund, Richard W. Young, and Abram H. Cannon. I also nominated Richard W. Young a time or two more when there was a vacancy, but when I became the President and it was up to me to nominate someone to the Council of the Twelve, I told the Lord in prayer that he knew who I wanted for an Apostle, namely, Richard W. Young, but that I wanted the impression of the Spirit as to whom he wanted, and I finally nominated Melvin J. Ballard" (February 20, 1935). See *The Diaries of Heber J. Grant, 1880–1945* (privately printed, 2010). An account of this is also found in Francis M. Gibbons' *Heber J. Grant: Man of Steel, Prophet of God* (Salt Lake City: Deseret Book, 1979), 174–76.

7. *The Diaries of Heber J. Grant*, April 7, 1937.

8. Melvin J. Ballard journal, quoted in Hinckley's *Sermons and Missionary Services*, 68.

9. Melvin J. Ballard, January 7, 1919 (talk given to the First Presidency and the Twelve, LDS Church Archives, four typescript pages). Also quoted in Ballard's *Melvin J. Ballard: Crusader for Righteousness* (Salt Lake City: Bookcraft, 1966), 65–66.

10. Melvin J. Ballard, "The Sacramental Covenant," June Mutual Improvement Association conference address, in *Hinckley, Sermons and Missionary Services*, 155–56; also found in Ballard's *Melvin J. Ballard: Crusader for Righteousness*, 138–39.

11. Melvin J. Ballard, in Conference Report, April 1920, 40–41. See also Roy W. Doxey, comp., *Latter-day Prophets and the Doctrine and Covenants* [Salt Lake City: Deseret Book, 1978], 2:357).

12. Melvin J. Ballard, "The Three Degrees of Glory," delivered at the Ogden Utah Tabernacle, as quoted in Hinckley's *Sermons and Missionary Services*, 245.

13. Nolan P. Olson, *Logan Temple: The First One Hundred Years* (Logan, Utah: Keith W. Watkins & Sons, 1978), 170.
This history of the Logan Temple contains few references for sources, including none for this quotation regarding Elder Ballard's vision, although the introduction does indicate a number of sources the author consulted.

14. Hinckley, *Sermons and Missionary Services*, 138.

15. Ibid., 172–74.

16. Ibid., 187–88.

17. Taken from Vernon Sharp's journal, as quoted in Hinckley, *Sermons and Missionary Services*, 100.

18. M. Russell Ballard, "Let Us Think Straight" (Brigham Young University devotional, November 29, 1983), speeches.byu.edu.

19. M. Russell Ballard, "Choose to Serve" (Brigham Young University fireside, January 5, 1986), speeches.byu.edu.

14

PRESIDENT GEORGE F. RICHARDS'
SPECIAL WITNESS OF JESUS CHRIST

"I dreamed of seeing the Savior and embracing
Him. The feeling I cannot describe."

While mostly forgotten by the general membership of the Church today, George F. Richards might well be compared to someone like President Boyd K. Packer—a man of marvelous spirituality and closeness to the Lord. George was the son of Elder Franklin D. Richards, an early Apostle best known from Mormon history as the original compiler of the Pearl of Great Price while he served as European Mission president in the 1850s. Franklin D. Richards was called to the apostleship by President Brigham Young and died in 1899 during the administration of President Lorenzo Snow.

AN EARLY EXPERIENCE WITH THE PRIESTHOOD

Young George Richards spent most of his early years in the small Utah town of Tooele, where he worked at farming and attended school. An early formative experience helped teach him the reality of the power of the priesthood. A biographer shared this account:

His mother suffered from an extended illness and received some relief through several priesthood blessings at the hands of the ward bishop. On one occasion, however, her symptoms were particularly distressing and the bishop's blessing brought no relief. After the bishop departed, George's mother asked him to perform the healing ordinance in her behalf. Concerned and worried about her suffering as well as the prospect of performing the ordinance for the first time, George retired to another room to pray and regain his composure. He then returned to the sick room and "in a humble way and with a very few simple words," he performed the sacred ordinance. He later recalled that he "had the satisfaction of witnessing the power of the Lord therein, for my mother ceased her groaning and received relief from her suffering while my hands were still on her head." He believed God had withheld the healing blessing given by the bishop in order to teach the youthful elder one of the most impressive lessons of his life. George declared that even though the bishop was perfectly worthy to perform the ordinance, "the blessing was reserved to be given in answer to the prayer and administration of a boy who had been honored to bear the priest-hood, to teach that boy the lesson that the priesthood in the boy is just as sacred and potent as in the man, when that boy lives as he should and exercises the same in righteousness."[1]

In 1890 George was sustained as a counselor in the Tooele, Utah, stake presi-dency, and this position enabled him to attend special meetings with leaders of the Church at the dedication of the Salt Lake Temple in 1893. Some of these meetings were held on April 19 and 20 and included much prayer and testimony sharing among Church leaders. George wrote that "A glorious time we had indeed, and a spirit prevailed such as I never before witnessed."[2] A few months later, George was also sustained as the Tooele Stake patriarch.

BECOMING A SPECIAL WITNESS

In September 1900, George recorded a sacred dream that presaged events to occur six years later. He wrote, "I had a most pleasant night's sleep and rest, and during the night dreamed that I was ordained an Apostle under the hands of Prest. Lorenzo Snow and was told by him that there were other blessings for me which he had not the authority to give, greater than these."[3]

By 1906 three vacancies in the Quorum of the Twelve needed to be filled. As the April general conference of the Church approached, George F. Richards experienced another dream from the Lord, this one being more impressive and meaningful to him than all others.

On March 22 he recorded in his journal, "I dreamed I saw and embraced the

Savior."[4] In a letter to his son LeGrand (who was then serving a mission) he shared further details. "I had a remarkable dream last night. I dreamed of seeing the Savior and embracing him. The feeling I cannot describe, but I think it was a touch of Heaven. I never expect anything better hereafter. The love of man for woman cannot compare with it. May we be faithful and make every sacrifice necessary to obtain that blessing—to live in His presence forever."[5]

LeGrand commented, "On April 6, 1906, that same year, he was called to the Quorum of the Twelve. . . . I always figured this dream was given to Father to let him know he was the Savior's choice to fill the vacancy in the Quorum."[6]

Called to the Quorum of the Twelve

George described the events of his call thusly:

> Attended forenoon meeting, and at close of the meeting when President Joseph F. Smith concluded making announcements, President Francis M. Lyman requested him to announce that President H. S. Gowans and counselors were wanted at the stand after close of that meeting which announcement was made. We met President Lyman who requested me to meet him in about 30 minutes at the Historian's office. This I did and there met Elders John Henry Smith, George Albert Smith with President Lyman also Bishop Orson F. Whitney and David O. McKay. Then President Lyman made known the intended action of the conference to release from the Quorum of Apostles John W. Taylor and Matthias F. Cowley which with the vacancy occasioned by the death of Apostle Marriner W. Merrill would leave 3 vacancies which would have to be filled and we were asked as to the manner of our living and our faith in all the principles of the gospel, etc. President Lyman said the Spirit had indicated that we were the men—Each of us expressed our feelings and faith. I first then Brother Whitney and then Brother McKay after which we separated. I attended the general priesthood meeting in the evening.
>
> In the afternoon I was in a good seat in the Tabernacle and about 3:45 p.m. President Lyman, after talking for about twenty minutes, commenced to tell that John W. Taylor and Matthias F. Cowley had handed in their resignations because they were out of harmony with the Presidency of the Church and their Quorum [regarding plural marriage]. These resignations were presented October 28, 1905, and accepted by the Presidency and Apostles. President Lyman then presented the General Authorities. He presented the Presidency, then the old [current] members of the Quorum, after which President Lyman deliberately read my name off and called a vote. There were no opposing votes. Then Orson F. Whitney's name followed with the same result, and then Brother David O. McKay's with the same result.

After the meeting, many friends shook my hand and offered congratulations and expressions of pleasure at my appointment. Many said they thought I would be the man to fill the vacancy caused by the death of Apostle Merrill. Lorin J. Robinson saw it in a dream. President Lyman saw my father in Council, which he felt meant something. My dream of March 22, wherein I saw the Savior, seemed to have prepared me, in a measure, for this call. I received many letters of congratulations.[7]

In another journal entry, Elder Richards wrote,

At a special priesthood meeting at 10:00 a.m. President Smith introduced me and, by request, I stood up and made a few remarks after which President Smith said, "He has never been asked to do anything but what he has done it cheerfully." At the conclusion of the meeting, the Presidency and Apostles retired to the Temple, where we received valuable instructions from President Joseph F. Smith, after which the new members were ordained and set apart as members of the Quorum by President Joseph F. Smith as follows: George F. Richards, Orson F. Whitney, David O. McKay. All the members of the Twelve were present except George Teasdale, Heber J. Grant, and Reed Smoot. We had a regular Pentecost and brethren wept in one another's embrace.[8]

On a side note, the notice of the absence of Elder Grant from this meeting and the conference is because he was then serving as the president of the European Mission and George's son LeGrand was serving as a secretary for one of the missions. LeGrand remembered,

There were three men appointed in that same conference, in this order: George F. Richards (my father), Orson F. Whitney, and David O. McKay. I was at that time serving as the secretary of the Netherlands Mission, and just a few days before that conference was held, I received a letter from my father that read like this: "My son, I had a remarkable dream last night. I dreamed that the Savior came and took me in his arms, and as I found me in my Master's embrace, the love that filled my heart can't be compared with the love that a man feels for a woman. I feel the meaning of the words of the song, 'I Need Thee Every Hour.'"

Then, just two or three days after I received that letter, a cablegram came to our office, the mission headquarters. It was addressed to President Grant, who was then president of the European Mission, and he was up in Berlin. We used to open the telegrams to see if they were important enough to try to relay. As for this telegram, I can quote you the exact words. It read this way: "Cowley and Taylor deposed. Richards, Whitney, and McKay appointed."

When I read that, I figured that the dream my father had just had, of which I had just received word in that letter, was to let him know that he was being called by revelation. President Grant was due in Rotterdam the next morning so I went to the station to meet him. I handed him the telegram—I had sealed it up again—and he opened and read it, and he said, "Well, well. Cowley and Taylor deposed. Richards, Whitney, and McKay appointed." [He said, "This man Taylor's had more visions than all the rest of us put together."] Then he said, "I wonder who this Richards could be?" I could have told him but I waited for him to tell me. "There's your father, your uncle Charlie, your uncle Franklin"—and then he said, "I guess it's your daddy; Brother Lyman thinks he's the salt of the earth."[9]

Elder George F. Richards recorded counsel given him and the other Twelve by President Joseph F. Smith a year after his call to the Twelve. He wrote, "The Twelve are the Special Witnesses of Jesus Christ and should be able to testify that He lives as if He had been seen by them."[10]

Work in the Ministry

Years passed as Elder Richards began earnestly serving as a special witness. One issue that presented itself to him was the division of the Tooele Utah Stake where he himself had served as a counselor in the stake presidency. After waking up in the middle of the night while seeking an answer to prayer, he recorded, "A solution of a difficult problem was revealed to me. I made it known [to the stake president] and he said he thought it the most feasible way of division."[11]

After serving for some years in the apostleship, Elder Richards introspectively wrote in his journal, "I have served in this position with profit to myself and with, I trust, a little benefit to the cause of God. I desire to be humble, willing, and obedient, to be industrious and devoted." And, "I do love the Lord. He is my strength, and my refuge. He has brought me through the valley of the shadows of death and hath delivered me from the bondage of sin and hath given me peace, liberty, and freedom, and has made it easy and natural to trust in him."[12]

President Richards' work in the Quorum of the Twelve involved him with matters relating to formulation and determination of doctrine, issues, and policy related to temple work, stopping the unauthorized practice of plural marriage as the apostate fundamentalist movement began coalescing, dealing with the theory of evolution strongly promoted by certain misled Brigham Young University professors, implementing stricter observance of the Word of Wisdom among the Church membership, and many other matters of importance in the Church. In 1943,

Elder Richards had the heart-rending and sad duty of sitting with his Quorum members on a disciplinary council to excommunicate Elder Richard R. Lyman, an Apostle and the son of President Richards' close friend Elder Francis M. Lyman. This event emotionally devastated him.

From 1916 to 1919, Elder Richards served as president of the European Mission, which meant he had to do his best to keep things working during World War I, at a time when missionary calls and service were drastically curtailed by the Church. In response, he implemented policies and programs that more heavily involved service by local members and women.

From 1921 until 1937, Elder Richards served as president of the Salt Lake Temple, a position which, along with his status of being an Apostle, made him the de facto leader of all temple work done in the Church under the direction of the First Presidency. In this capacity he was responsible for implementing a number of refinements meant to streamline and improve temple work. His son LeGrand noted that he was told by President Heber J. Grant that one reason his father was called as the Temple president was because he felt him to be "the most spiritual member of all the Twelve."[13]

In 1937 Elder George F. Richards was released from his service as president of the Salt Lake Temple and called as "Supervisor of Church Temples," a position no longer in existence and now provided for by the Church Temple Department. This move simply officially confirmed his position as overseer of all temple work in the Church under the First Presidency. At this same time, he was also called as the Acting Patriarch to the Church, a position he held for several years.

In May 1945, with the death of President Heber J. Grant, George Albert Smith became the President of the Church, and George F. Richards, next in seniority among the Twelve, became the President of the Quorum of the Twelve Apostles. He was then eighty-four years old. At this time, during a couple of days while President Smith was returning home from the east because of the death of President Grant, George F. Richards took care of important Church business, including the planning of the President's funeral and calling a meeting of the Twelve.

President Richards' wife, Alice, died in 1946, and the next year he married Bessie Hollings, a woman he had been acquainted with while serving as president of the Salt Lake Temple.

THE SPIRITUAL GIFT OF SACRED DREAMS

At the October 1946 general conference, President Richards spoke of what he had been taught through personal revelation in the form of sacred dreams.

The Lord has revealed to me, by dreams, something more than I ever understood or felt before about the love for God and the love for fellow men. I believe in dreams, brethren and sisters. The Lord has given me dreams, which to me, are just as real and as much from God as was the dream of King Nebuchadnezzar that was the means of saving a nation from starvation, or the dream of Lehi who through a dream led his colony out of the old country, across the mighty deep to this promised land, or any other dreams that we read of in scripture. . . .

More than forty years ago I had a dream, which I am sure was from the Lord. In this dream I was in the presence of my Savior as he stood in mid-air. He spoke no word to me, but my love for him was such that I have not words to explain. I know that no mortal man can love the Lord as I experienced that love for the Savior unless God reveals it unto him. I would have remained in his presence, but there was a power drawing me away from him, and as a result of that dream I had this feeling, that no matter what might be required at my hands, what the gospel might entail unto me, I would do what I should be asked to do, even to the laying down of my life.

And so when we read in the scriptures what the Savior said to his disciples: 'In my Father's house are many mansions: . . . I go to prepare a place for you . . . that where I am, there ye may be also' (John 14:2, 3).

I think that is where I want to be. If only I can be with my Savior and have that same sense of love that I had in that dream, it will be the goal of my existence, the desire of my life.[14]

In the same address, President Richards went on to relate another dream.

Then a few years ago, at the closing of a conference of the St. Johns [Arizona] Stake, we had had a wonderful conference I thought, and I was very happy on retiring. I was sleeping in the home of the president of the stake, Brother Levi Udall, and that night I had a remarkable dream. I have seldom mentioned this to other people, but I do not know why I should not. It seems to me appropriate in talking along this line. I dreamed that I and a group of my own associates found ourselves in a courtyard where, around the outer edge of it, were German soldiers—and Fuhrer Adolph Hitler was there with his group, and they seemed to be sharpening their swords and cleaning their guns, and making preparations for a slaughter of some kind, or an execution. We know not what, but, evidently we were the objects. But presently a circle was formed and this Fuhrer and his men were all within the circle, and my group and I were circled on the outside, and he was sitting on the inside of the circle with his back to the outside, and when we walked around and I got directly opposite to him, I stepped inside the circle and walked across to where he was sitting, and spoke to him in a manner something like this:

"I am your brother. You are my brother. In your heavenly home we lived together in love and peace. Why can we not so live here on the earth?"

And it seemed to me that I felt in myself, welling up on my soul, a love for that man, and I could feel that he was having the same experience, and presently he arose, and we embraced each other and kissed each other, as kiss of affection.

Then the scene changed so that our group was within the circle, and he and his group were on the outside, and when he came around to where I was standing, he stepped inside the circle and embraced me again, with a kiss of affection.

I think the Lord gave me that dream. Why should I dream of this man, one of the greatest enemies of mankind, and one of the wickedest, but that the Lord should teach me that I must love my enemies, and I must love the wicked as well as the good?

Now, who is there in this wide world that I could not love under those conditions, if I could only continue to feel as I felt then? I have tried to maintain this feeling and, thank the Lord, I have no enmity toward any person in this world; I can forgive all men, so far as I am concerned, and I am happy in doing so and in the love which I have for my fellow men.[15]

President Spencer W. Kimball, as a much younger and newer member of the Quorum of the Twelve, sat in many meetings with President Richards. President Kimball stated the following, as a personal interpolation, while reading the above-quoted account as shared by President Richards with the general conference assemblage in October 1946. "I heard this [account of seeing the Savior] more than once in quarterly meetings of the Council of the Twelve when George F. Richards was my President of the Council of the Twelve."[16]

GLIMPSES OF ETERNITY

In 1946, Elder Bruce R. McConkie was called as a member of the First Council of Seventy, where his duties sometimes intersected with those of the President of the Twelve. He shared an experience he had with President Richards that contained some interesting doctrinal implications.

Years ago I was appointed to attend a quarterly [stake] conference that was holding forth in the Assembly Hall on Temple Square. At that time George F. Richards was the President of the Council of the Twelve. He did not have an assignment of his own, and so he came and attended my stake conference, and of course, was the concluding speaker in the various sessions. In one of the meetings I was talking about magnifying one's calling in the priesthood and thereby working out an inheritance of exaltation and receiving all that the Father hath—this in accordance with the statements in section 84 of the Doctrine and Covenants on the oath and covenant of the priesthood. President George F. Richards followed me and spoke on the same general theme. One of the things that he said was this in substance: "There are many people in the Church who hold no position at all but who in eternity will have higher positions than many of the Council of the Twelve." He was talking on this general theme that it does not matter where we serve but how. . . .

Now I do not have the slightest doubt that there will be a complete realignment of Church positions and responsibilities in the life to come. People who have low positions here will receive high ones there. It may be that some who have relatively high positions here will be in lesser positions there.[17]

During his last years, President Richards' health failed him, and he passed away in 1950. At his funeral, Elder Harold B. Lee said,

Brother Richards has lived close to the curtain that separates mortal beings from those in the spirit world. There were times, as he counseled the Twelve in our quarterly meetings, that we all knew that his counsel was stamped with the spirit of divinity. I am sure we shall long remember some of those precious things. His family tells some sacred things that they have suggested might well be repeated.

"He was sleeping in his bed only a week ago when he awoke his wife and said, 'I have just had the most glorious dream. I've been visiting with President [Joseph F.] Smith and President [Heber J.] Grant.' She asked him what they had discussed and he said, 'Oh, I was just explaining things, and we were discussing matters pertaining to the Church.' What a glorious experience. And through these last weeks there have been times when he would say, as he would awake from sleep, 'We are not alone in the room today.' And his Bessie would always, with a keen sense of humor, talk with him about these matters, but President Richards knew he was close to things heavenly."[18]

At the October 1950 general conference following his death, both President McKay and Elder Lee indicated they thought President Richards very near, influencing the proceedings, where many tributes were paid to him by his beloved associates in their addresses.

Notes

1. Dale C. Mouritsen, *A Symbol of New Directions: George Franklin Richards and the Mormon Church, 1861–1950* (unpublished doctoral dissertation, Brigham Young University, 1982), 53–54.
2. Ibid., 37.
3. Ibid., 56.
4. Ibid.
5. *Life of George F. Richards*, based on his personal diaries, with contributions from members of his family. Prepared by Minerva Richards Tate Robinson, Sarah Richards Cannon, and Mamie Richards Silver (Provo, Utah: J. Grant Stevenson, 1965), 41. See also *A Family of Faith: An Intimate View of Church History through the Journals of Three Generations of Apostles*, ed., Kent F. Richards (Salt Lake City: Deseret Book, 2013), 19, 283, 288, 292.
6. Ibid.
7. Ibid., 39–40.
8. Ibid., 40–41.
9. "'Earth's Crammed with Heaven': Reminiscences" (Brigham Young University devotional, October 11, 1977), speeches.byu.edu.
   The material inserted in brackets is from the voice recording of Elder LeGrand Richards' talk and was edited from the printed version. George F. Richards also wrote of his dream later in 1906. He recorded, "Attended Prayer Circle meeting at 6:19 p.m. President Francis M. Lyman presiding. I related a dream or vision I had wherein I saw and embraced the Savior on the 22nd or 23rd of March last. The seeing of him was something beautiful but that of itself would have been of little significance as compared with the results of my embracing him. My whole being seemed to be thrilled with the power of his love and I was indeed in heaven. The singing of the hymn—'I Need Thee Every Hour' brings this vision fresh to my mind, hence this my favorite hymn" (George F. Richards journal, July 26, 1906).
10. George F. Richards journal, October 6, 1907, as quoted in Mouritsen's *A Symbol of New Directions*, 66.
11. Mouritsen, *A Symbol of New Directions*, 76.
12. Ibid., 76–77.
13. Ibid., 199.
14. George F. Richards, in Conference Report, October 1946, 138–41. (See also George F. Richards' journal, November 8, 1938).
15. Ibid.
16. Spencer W. Kimball, "The Cause Is Just and Worthy," *Ensign*, May 1974. As of this writing (February 2017), the online text edition of the *Ensign* confused some of President Kimball's words with President George F. Richards'. Compare the quoted text

of President Richards' account herein with the video and text version of President Kimball at lds.org.

17. As quoted in Dennis B. Horne's *Bruce R. McConkie: Highlights from His Life and Teachings*, 2nd ed. (Salt Lake City: Eborn Books, 2010), 407–8.

18. Mouritsen, *A Symbol of New Directions*, 57.

15

PRESIDENT GEORGE Q. CANNON'S

SPECIAL WITNESS OF JESUS CHRIST

"I have seen the Savior Jesus Christ and conversed
with Him face to face, and He has talked with me."

President George Q. Cannon did not indicate when he received the personal revelation, but in 1882, he wrote in his journal that "it was revealed to me that I should be one of the Twelve Apostles, though I never breathed that to any human being—scarcely, in fact, to myself—until after I had been selected to be an Apostle. But when I look back at my life, it seems very marvelous what the Lord has done for me."[1]

Today, despite all the trials and setbacks he endured, along with the great successes and public accolades, Mormon historians regard George Q. Cannon as one of the most influential and prominent counselors to ever serve in the First Presidency.[2]

George Quayle Cannon was born in Liverpool, England, in 1827. He and his family heard the gospel taught by some of the earliest Mormon missionaries to England, and they were baptized in 1840. A couple of years later, they decided to emigrate from Great Britain to "Zion," or the headquarters of the Church at the time, then in Nauvoo, Illinois. George's mother died while crossing the ocean, and his father died a couple of years later. Thereupon George became part of John Taylor's family and learned the printing trade in Nauvoo. In 1846, he joined the rest of the Latter-day Saints in the long trek to the Great Salt Lake Valley, arriving in 1847.

Comes to Know God during Hawaiian Mission

From 1850 until his death, George Q. Cannon spent most of his time in the service of the Lord and His Church. He worked for some months at Sutter's Mill in California as a "Gold Missionary," as they were called (and which he did not like). Then he went with the first company of Mormon missionaries to Hawaii. He struggled to learn the language but eventually developed such an impressive facility that he was assigned to translate the Book of Mormon into Hawaiian, which he did at the close of his mission.

George's mission to Hawaii brought him experiences that became the foundation of his testimony and the spiritual anchor of his life. While aboard a ship, sailing to Hawaii, he received an inspired dream in which he saw and learned from the Prophet Joseph Smith.

> I dreamed last night that I was on board a vessel and that some of the brethren and myself were heaving with the windlass at an anchor that was fast in the mud; it did not seem to be of much use. At this time I thought Bro. Joseph Smith passed me and went forward on to the forecastle close by the bowsprit; I followed him up there; he knelt down and prayed a few minutes aloud that the anchor might be loosened, after he had done so I thought that one or two of the brethren took hold of the rope and pulled it up with the greatest ease. I thought that I spoke to him and said that I wished I was in possession of such Faith and he replied that it was my privilege and that I ought to have it; that I would need it to preserve me from pestilence and the judgments that were about to be sent forth on the Nations. When I awoke, I thought that it was given me as a warning, that Faith and prayer was of more effect than the windlass.[3]

Recounting his dream over three decades later, President Cannon publicly reflected on its impact: "The impression it made upon my mind has been a lasting one; I have never forgotten it; and through taking that lesson to heart I feel that I have been exceedingly prospered in my life. . . ."[4]

Throughout his Hawaiian mission, where he spent three and a half years, Elder Cannon noted in his journal many occasions when he felt the Spirit of the Lord come upon him powerfully as he preached to the native people. One example from his journal will suffice. Reflecting on his humble efforts to speak during a missionary meeting, he wrote,

> I felt weak and empty this morning and did not feel as though I could do anything. I requested their prayers, and I was truly blessed as I never preached with such power as I did this morning—the language came with ease and fluency and I was filled with the spirit with words and ideas. I never seen a more attentive congregation all wide awake with countenances and eyes beaming with pleasure and paying the best possible attention, drinking the words in greedily—the house was filled with the spirit the people all felt it. . . . I was filled with joy, I felt like shouting Glory, Glory, Glory to the Lord God of Israel for his goodness to me a poor weak instrument, a mere boy, to make me the bearer of such glad tidings and seal it by his spirit. The congregation seemed to be delighted—they were dressed very well and I could not help loving them—they seemed near and dear to me. . . . This day was as happy [a] day as I ever experienced I felt as I wished to feel.[5]

In commenting on his mission, President Cannon noted, "I was the first to preach the gospel in that [the Hawaiian] language and was the means of bringing many thousands of people to the knowledge of the truth. I also translated the Book of Mormon into the Hawaiian language. I have always felt very thankful to the Lord for impressing me to do what I did."[6] He also wrote, "Dreams, visions, and revelations were given to me, and the communion of the Spirit was most sweet and delicious."[7] Also, "When I prayed I could go unto God in faith; He listened to my prayers; He gave me great comfort and joy; He revealed Himself to me as He never had done before, and told me that if I would persevere, I should be blessed, be the means of bringing many to the knowledge of the truth, and be spared to return home after having done a good work. Many things were revealed to me, during those days, when He was the only friend we had to lean upon, which were afterwards fulfilled. A friendship was there established between our Father and myself, which, I trust, will never be broken nor diminished."[8]

On returning from his mission in 1854, Cannon began a writing and publishing career. He served a mission in San Francisco, California, publishing a small newspaper defending the Church. Then, in 1860, he was called and ordained by President Brigham Young as a member of the Quorum of the Twelve Apostles. He thereafter served a four-year term as President of the European Missions. In 1866–67 he established a magazine for the youth of the Church and also became the editor of the *Deseret News*. During these years he married, and at President Young's request, he entered plural marriage, eventually marrying six women.

SERVING AS A TERRITORIAL DELEGATE TO CONGRESS

From 1872 to 1882, he served as a Utah Territorial delegate to Congress, where his main duty was to do all in his power to oppose legislation harmful to the Church and plural marriage, and to lobby senators and congressmen in favor of Utah statehood. Too much anti-Mormon feeling existed in the halls of Congress to get them to pass such a bill at that time. As a delegate from a very unpopular territory, and without a formally recognized vote, Elder Cannon found himself a lonely man enduring fierce political opposition, most of it in behalf of the Church. In fact, President Brigham Young warned him that as he rose to prominence as a representative of the Mormon people and Utah, he would attract many enemies. George wrote,

> In conversation with President Young . . . he said that I ought to be careful about my movements in Washington—that I would be watched and everything I did scrutinized and I ought to keep a journal of my movements that I could prove where I was at any time. If anything should occur to Gen. [Ulysses S.] Grant, he (the President) would be accused of having prompted its commission, and I would probably be charged with having had it done. He said that next to himself I was the most hated of any of the authorities. . . . They would seek my life with the greatest anxiety after seeking his, and I ought to be careful of myself. In all the publications of our enemies there my name was generally held up to the public next to his own.[9]

In such circumstances, he went to the only source he could for strength. "I called upon Him mightily in prayer to help me. This is a great comfort to me. I am here without a man who is in sympathy with me; but I have a Friend more powerful than they all. In this I rejoice. I feel there are angels with me, and as one of old said they that are for us are more than they who are against us. When I pray I feel comforted and filled with joy. Of myself I feel very weak; but in my Lord I feel strong."[10]

Such were Elder Cannon's feelings on more than one occasion. It seemed that the intense opposition caused him to pray with but greater faith. He wrote, "It is a blessed thing to know that the Lord hears and answers prayer when offered aright. This has been my comfort and support here. I have never applied to him in vain. No matter how thick the clouds of darkness have been, or how much Satan and his servants have raged, the Lord has been my rock of refuge. He has given me peace, joy, and happiness and my life has been a great pleasure to me."[11]

Elder Cannon eventually lost several children to death as infants, and also a wife, which tried his soul deeply. Further, despite all he did, sometimes in blind hope, he had some children that left the Church. (One of them, his eldest, the silver-tongued Frank J. Cannon, lived a life of moral debauchery—drinking, smoking, prostitutes, adultery, and public slander and lies. After his father's death, when President Joseph F. Smith would not support his political or financial aspirations, Frank Cannon turned bitterly apostate and did all in his power to harm and oppose the Church.)

Elder Cannon eventually served as one of several counselors to President Young's First Presidency, and then in 1880, he was called as first counselor to President John Taylor. He would spend the rest of his life serving as first counselor in the First Presidency, except for a couple of years when the Quorum of the Twelve presided over the Church. He willingly gave all he had, consecrating his life and financial means to the Lord. In 1885, he wrote, "It is only a few days ago that, in communing with the Lord, his Spirit rested down upon me, and I was led to dedicate myself, my wives, my sons, and my daughters and my substance with great fervor to Him and his service, and I desired him to use me as he thought best. It is a great honor to work in any capacity for the Lord."[12]

From 1888 to 1889, he served a five-month term in the Utah Territorial Prison, having been convicted in the rabidly anti-Mormon courts of offenses related to plural marriage.[13] He was probably the most famous prisoner ever incarcerated there.

Because of favorable circumstances on occasion, relating to business and investments, President Cannon was able to acquire considerable wealth for a time. However, with the severe nationwide economic panic of the mid-1890s, his wealth disappeared, and he became heavily involved. With the help of his sons, he was able to continue the illusion of money, but his personal economic difficulties, and also those of the Church, became the great trial of his last years.

A SPECIAL WITNESS OF JESUS CHRIST

At some undetermined point or points in his life, President Cannon was given the supernal blessing of beholding the Lord Jesus, for in his later years he began to so testify. In his journal, in 1889, evidently referencing a meeting at which he had born his special witness, President Cannon wrote, "I testified that the Lord Jesus lived, for I had seen Him and heard His voice, and I had heard the voice of the Spirit [Holy Ghost], speaking to me as one man speaketh to another. I had been led to my present position by the revelations of the Lord, for He had pointed out to me the path to pursue."[14]

In April 1893, at a special priesthood meeting, held in the Salt Lake Temple in conjunction with the Temple's dedicatory services, President Cannon spoke to the general and local leaders in attendance. One of the President's office secretaries in attendance noted President Cannon's testimony then given. "I have seen the Savior Jesus Christ and conversed with him face to face and he has talked with me."[15] Verifying this statement, another meeting attendee entered very similar wording in his own journal. "I have been greatly favored of the Lord. My mind has been enrapt in vision and I have seen the beauties and Glory of God. I have seen and conversed with the Savior face-to-face."[16]

At the October 1896 general conference of the Church, as part of his address, President Cannon again bore his special witness. "I rejoice exceedingly in the testimonies that have been borne during this conference. I know that this is the work of God. I know that God lives. I know that Jesus lives; for I have seen Him. I know that this is the Church of God, and that it is founded on Jesus Christ, our Redeemer. I testify to you of these things as one that knows—as one of the Apostles of the Lord Jesus Christ that can bear witness to you today in the presence of the Lord that He lives and that He will live, and will come to reign on the earth, to sway an undisputed scepter."[17]

At another temple meeting, held on April 3, 1898, President Cannon was again recorded bearing his witness. "President George Q. Cannon began to speak at 11:30. He was saying or began to say that he knew that Jesus was the Christ, for he had seen his face and heard his voice. His emotions here overpowered him, and he had to stand and say nothing for a few moments until he could control himself. He also testified that he knew that God lived for he had seen his face and heard his voice. He also knew that the Holy Ghost was a *living being* for he heard his voice."[18]

Elder John Henry Smith, then serving in the Quorum of the Twelve Apostles and also present at this meeting, wrote in his diary that "President George Q. Cannon and I testified we had seen the Savior at the Temple meeting this morning."[19]

In this connection, an experience from the life of James E. Talmage is noteworthy. In 1899, Brother Talmage was not yet an Apostle but was still considered a highly valued and wonderfully serviceable asset to the Brethren and the Church in many matters. At the request of the First Presidency, he had been busily writing a book to be called *The Articles of Faith* and giving lectures on the same material. On the subject of the Holy Ghost, the question had arisen as to whether the Holy Ghost was a distinct personality with a spirit body. As Talmage indicates, this question soon came before the First Presidency, then consisting of President Snow, with George Q. Cannon as his first counselor and Joseph F. Smith as second. Brother Talmage wrote,

One of the questions referred to the First Presidency by the Committee was as to the advisability of reprinting the lecture entitled "The Holy Ghost," which appeared in the *Juvenile Instructor* soon after its delivery in the theology class at the Church University. I remember that considerable discussion attended the reading of the lecture before the former committee prior to its delivery. The question hung upon the expediency and wisdom of expressing views as definite as those presented in the lecture regarding the personality of the Holy Ghost, when marked ambiguity and differences of opinion appeared in the published writings of our Church authorities on the subject. The lecture was approved as it appeared in the *Instructor*. I have incorporated it in the prospective book in practically an unaltered form. President Snow took the article under advisement today. In conversation, President George Q. Cannon supported the view of the distinct personality of the Holy Ghost and stated that he had heard the voice of the third member of the Godhead actually talking to him.[20]

President Snow soon approved the lecture as written, and since then, the teaching of the distinctive personality of the Holy Ghost as a spirit being has become settled Church doctrine.

TEACHING ABOUT THE APOSTLESHIP

As a member of the First Presidency, President Cannon found himself teaching newly ordained Apostles (and also thereby a refresher for longer tenured Brethren) about their calling on many occasions. Sometimes this would occur as he participated in giving them their apostolic charge. Other times, the instruction was given during other meetings of the First Presidency and the Quorum of the Twelve. After the sustaining of the newly called Elders Matthias Cowley and Abraham Owen Woodruff at the October 1897 general conference, President Joseph F. Smith said that

> The calling of an Apostle . . . required a man to lay aside everything of a temporal character and hold himself ready to respond to any call which might be made upon him. He was to be a special witness of the gospel and of the Lord Jesus Christ. He must have a witness for himself that Jesus is the Christ, and that he committed the dispensation of the fulness of times to the Prophet Joseph Smith, and be ready to bear that testimony to all mankind. He should not engage in anything that would interfere with these duties without permission from the proper authority.[21]

Then President Cannon also spoke, saying that

> The apostleship was the highest authority the Lord bestows on man on the earth. It comprehends all the authority in the Priesthood. An Apostle should

be a prophet, a seer, and a revelator. . . . It was the privilege of an Apostle to live so as to have the revelations of Jesus personally. In Council, each Apostle should come with his mind as free as a child, without caucusing or planning how to have certain things done, so as to be free for the spirit of God to operate upon their minds. It was proper for each Apostle to express his views freely, but not his right to contend. When all had expressed themselves freely, it was the prerogative of the President of the Council to have the mind of the Lord and to decide that which was right; then all should be agreed and submit to that decision, and treat the President with the deference due to the man chosen to be the mouthpiece of God. When in Council, it was not right to leave during its session whenever it could be avoided. The word of God and the will of God should be sought for diligently. It was not proper to sit still, content with having received the apostleship, but it was necessary to progress, magnify the office, and realize the weight of the responsibility, seeking by prayer and faith to have the ministration of angels and the power of God. It was a solemn obligation the newly chosen brethren were about to take upon them, and they should not assume it unless they were determined to seek after every gift and power connected with it. They must not indulge in ambitious desires; when the sick were healed, when they were successful in preaching, they must not take credit to themselves but give the glory to God. They should be one with the Presidency and listen to the counsels of the man whom God had placed at the head.[22]

Concerning another occasion, during a meeting of the Presiding Brethren in the Temple, the following was recorded.

Before rising from the table, President Snow invited President Cannon to occupy the few remaining moments of unexpired time by speaking to the brethren as he might feel led. President Cannon, responding, said that he heartily endorsed the words of President Snow to the effect that we have the greatest cause to be thankful because of the blessings we enjoy. He referred to the pleasure experienced by him in his boyhood days when in the presence of the servants of God, and the respect he entertained towards them. This feeling had never left him, and he rejoiced in the society of the Apostles today, and in being in possession of their fellowship. He rejoiced in the feelings of union and good fellowship that exist, and there was no question in his mind but that this state of things would continue. He believed that greater power and gifts would be given to the Apostles, and that this would increase until they should meet face to face with the Savior himself. He felt that the day was not far distant when the Savior would meet with His Apostles and instruct them; and that they should prepare for the great events which were coming upon the earth. He knew the Savior was near to us, and that the day would come when the Apostles would be greatly honored of him.[23]

In 1900, while participating in giving the apostolic charge to Elder Reed Smoot, President Cannon said that "in case Brother Reed Smoot is ordained an Apostle, it is his privilege to see the Lord Jesus, if he so desires and shall live for it, that he may indeed become a special witness of Jesus. This privilege belongs to the apostleship."[24]

Despite all the trials and tribulations endured by President Cannon throughout a long and highly productive life, his testimony and reliance on God brought him more joy than sorrow. He rejoiced in his life's lot. He wrote, "I have been in poverty; I have been through the persecutions we all endured; I have been short of food; I have been in need of water; I have been destitute of clothing; I have preached the gospel without purse and scrip; I have been in prosperity; I have mingled with the leading men of the land, and have lived where I had everything I needed; and I bear testimony to you this day that the gospel of the Lord Jesus Christ is sufficient for every circumstance in life. It will make men happy in poverty and in adversity; it will make them happy in prosperity and in plenty."[25]

Such thoughts led him to speak as one who desired Translation, to leave this lone and dreary world of sorrow and pain and toil, and be changed and caught up to a better one (see 3 Nephi 28). He wrote, "Sometimes I have felt that I could not stay here on the earth, so happy have I been. I rejoice in this happiness and in these blessings. I would that all mankind could share in them. When I was a missionary, it was the great delight of my life to preach this gospel, and to entreat men to come to the Lord and receive the blessings I had received. I feel now that I would like to live until the Savior comes, if it were the Lord's will, to preach this gospel of salvation to mankind, and to make them sharers in the joys that I have partaken of."[26]

President George Q. Cannon eventually became one of the most well-known men in the United States during his lifetime. After enduring years of ill-will from many in the world, as his good works and integrity became known and appreciated, his name became celebrated. Those who once strove against him in journalism or the United States legislature, proclaimed their respect and esteem for him in his waning years. Most important, he had served God well, sharing his special witness with all who would listen.

President Cannon died in California on April 12, 1901.

Notes

1. George Q. Cannon journal, January 11, 1882; see churchhistorianspress.org.
2. Along with Cannon, Heber C. Kimball and J. Reuben Clark Jr. are generally considered to be among the greatest counselors to ever serve in the First Presidency.
3. George Q. Cannon journal, November 22, 1850; see churchhistorianspress.org.
4. George Q. Cannon, *Journal of Discourses* (London: Latter-day Saint's Book Depot, 1854–86 [June 27, 1881]), 22:289–90.
5. George Q. Cannon journal, July 27, 1851; see churchhistorianspress.org.
6. Ibid., November 22, 1900.
7. George Q. Cannon, *My First Mission* (Salt Lake City: Juvenile Instructor Office, 1879), 34; see archive.org.
8. Ibid., 18.
9. George Q. Cannon journal, January 4, 1873.
10. Ibid., December 1, 1873.
11. Ibid., June 16, 1880.
12. Ibid., August 10, 1885.
13. At this time, Utah Territorial Court judges were federal appointees, chosen by the anti-Mormon president of the United States. These appointees did all in their power to jail as many Mormons as possible, hoping thereby to harass and destroy the Church.
14. George Q. Cannon journal, November 4, 1889; see churchhistorianspress.org.
15. Wording given as quoted from the L. John Nuttall journal, April 20, 1893. Some authors have incorrectly attributed the experience to Nuttall instead of Cannon. Nuttall was the secretary to the First Presidency at the time, and was recording what Cannon said. The Abraham H. Cannon journal gives info about this meeting as follows: "A two-day meeting was held with the General Authorities and the presidents of stakes and their counselors on April [blank] and [blank]. There were 115 brethren present. . . . It was a very happy and never to be forgotten time. Our first day of meeting, and part of the second, were spent in speaking, each man being asked to express his feelings towards the authorities of the Church and the Saints generally" (Dennis B. Horne, *An Apostle's Record, The Journals of Abraham H. Cannon*, May 18, 1893 [Clearfield, Utah: Gnolaum Books, 2004], 268–69).
16. As quoted in the Francis Asbury Hammond Journal. Francis was present at this meeting on April 20, 1893, as cited in *Collected Discourses: Delivered by President Wilford Woodruff, His Two Counselors, the Twelve Apostles, and Others*, comp. and ed. Brian H. Stuy, 5 vols. (Woodland Hills, Utah: B.H.S. Publishing, 1987–1992), 3:285. The author has silently adjusted some poor grammar in this entry.
17. "Discourse delivered by President George Q. Cannon," October 6, 1896 (*The Deseret Weekly* [*News*], October 31, 1896), 610.

18. Joseph H. Dean journal, April 3, 1898, as quoted in David Bitton's *George Q. Cannon: A Biography* (Salt Lake City: Deseret Book, 1999), 415.

19. John Henry Smith journal, April 3, 1898, as quoted in *Church, State, and Politics: The Diaries of John Henry Smith*, ed. Jean Bickmore White (Salt Lake City: Smith Research Associates and Signature Books, 1990), 394.

    The author has expanded contractions in this entry for easier readability. Elder John Henry Smith did not on this occasion mean to imply that they had seen the Savior during that particular meeting but at earlier times in their lives. See also Dennis B. Horne, *Latter Leaves in the Life of Lorenzo Snow* (Springville, Utah: Cedar Fort, 2012), 255.

20. James E. Talmage journal, January 13, 1899. (See also Journal History of the Church, Church History Library, history.lds.org.)

21. Ibid.

22. Talmage journal, October 7, 1897.

23. Ibid., January 11, 1900.

24. Rudger Clawson journal, April 8, 1900; in *A Ministry of Meetings: The Apostolic Diaries of Rudger Clawson*, ed. Stan Larson (Salt Lake City: Signature Books and Smith Research Associates, 1993), 151–52.

25. George Q. Cannon, "The False Theories of Men," October 4, 1896, in *Collected Discourses: Delivered by President Wilford Woodruff, His Two Counselors, the Twelve Apostles, and Others*; comp. and ed. Brian H. Stuy, 5 vols. (Woodland Hills, Utah: B.H.S. Publishing, 1987–1992), 5:196–97.

26. Ibid.

16

THE PROPHET JOSEPH SMITH'S

SPECIAL WITNESS OF JESUS CHRIST

"For we saw him, even on the right hand of God; and we heard the voice bearing record that he is the Only Begotten of the Father."

Joseph Smith Jr. was the first and chief Apostle of this dispensation. Angelic ministrants gave him all the priesthood and keys necessary for the salvation and eternal life of mankind. These keys and powers were passed on to his successors and are fully active today. His life and ministry have been the subject of more written attention, by far, than any other leader of the Church. Because this is true, because Church leaders and scholars (and a host of others) have so closely examined everything connected with Joseph's life and work, no attempt to break new ground will be made here.

Instead, because so many of the Apostles quoted in this volume refer to Joseph Smith's special witness of Jesus Christ, a brief review of the highlights of his witness follows. This might refresh the memory of those who are already familiar with Joseph's experiences with the Godhead, and help those with less or no familiarity to understand why so many Apostles (and regular Church members) refer to Joseph's experiences and bear witness of them.

While Joseph Smith received scores of visions, manifestations, and visitations from heavenly beings, only four of them are recounted below, and they relate exclusively to his witness of the living reality of the Father and the Son.[1] These are the main four—the big four—the four most often referred to that constitute the majority of the reason why Joseph was *the* preeminent special witness of Jesus Christ. These are scriptural and have been sustained as such by the assembled membership of the Church. They are revelation to the Church and the world. They constitute the special witness of the head of the dispensation of the fulness of times, the last dispensation before the Second Coming of Christ. It is true that Joseph received visions of Jesus and even the Father at other times, but those accounts have not been canonized as have the ones included herein.[2]

THE FIRST VISION

The context of the First Vision is that Joseph Smith had applied the teachings of the Apostle James from the New Testament (James 1:5–6), that if a person lacked wisdom they could ask God for it, and if their faith did not waver, they could receive the guidance needed. Joseph felt the power of that direction sink into his soul as it had with no other person, and he eventually put James' direction to the test. Joseph explained what happened next.

> So, in accordance with this, my determination to ask of God, I retired to the woods to make the attempt. It was on the morning of a beautiful, clear day, early in the spring of eighteen hundred and twenty. It was the first time in my life that I had made such an attempt, for amidst all my anxieties I had never as yet made the attempt to pray vocally.
>
> After I had retired to the place where I had previously designed to go, having looked around me, and finding myself alone, I kneeled down and began to offer up the desires of my heart to God. I had scarcely done so, when immediately I was seized upon by some power which entirely overcame me, and had such an astonishing influence over me as to bind my tongue so that I could not speak. Thick darkness gathered around me, and it seemed to me for a time as if I were doomed to sudden destruction.
>
> But, exerting all my powers to call upon God to deliver me out of the power of this enemy which had seized upon me, and at the very moment when I was ready to sink into despair and abandon myself to destruction—not to an imaginary ruin, but to the power of some actual being from the unseen world, who had such marvelous power as I had never before felt in any being—just at this moment of great alarm, I saw a pillar of light exactly over my head, above the brightness of the sun, which descended gradually until it fell upon me.

It no sooner appeared than I found myself delivered from the enemy which held me bound. When the light rested upon me I saw two Personages, whose brightness and glory defy all description, standing above me in the air. One of them spake unto me, calling me by name and said, pointing to the other—This is My Beloved Son. Hear Him!

My object in going to inquire of the Lord was to know which of all the sects was right, that I might know which to join. No sooner, therefore, did I get possession of myself, so as to be able to speak, than I asked the Personages who stood above me in the light, which of all the sects was right (for at this time it had never entered into my heart that all were wrong)—and which I should join.

I was answered that I must join none of them, for they were all wrong; and the Personage who addressed me said that all their creeds were an abomination in his sight; that those professors were all corrupt; that "they draw near to me with their lips, but their hearts are far from me, they teach for doctrines the commandments of men, having a form of godliness, but they deny the power thereof."

He again forbade me to join with any of them; and many other things did he say unto me, which I cannot write at this time. When I came to myself again, I found myself lying on my back, looking up into heaven. When the light had departed, I had no strength; but soon recovering in some degree, I went home. (Joseph Smith—History 1:14–20)

Of this vision, commonly known in the Church as the First Vision, President Gordon B. Hinckley has said, "Our faith, our knowledge comes of the witness of a prophet in this dispensation who saw before him the great God of the universe and His Beloved Son, the resurrected Lord Jesus Christ. They spoke to him. He spoke with Them. He testified openly, unequivocally, and unabashedly of that great vision. It was a vision of the Almighty and of the Redeemer of the world, glorious beyond our understanding but certain and unequivocating in the knowledge which it brought."[3] In other words, this vision or appearance is one of the great foundational events establishing the Church. It testifies of the reality of the existence of God, and, of course, is therefore constantly and unsuccessfully attacked by critics. Nevertheless, as the apostles and prophets know, and as millions of members of the Church know, it happened in the spring of 1820, and it is true.

THE VISION OF THE DEGREES OF GLORY

The second great special witness received by the Prophet Joseph Smith was part of the vision of the degrees of glory found in section 76 of the Doctrine and Covenants. Joseph and Sidney Rigdon received the vision together in early 1832. The pertinent verses read,

And while we meditated upon these things, the Lord touched the eyes of our understandings and they were opened, and the glory of the Lord shone round about.

And we beheld the glory of the Son, on the right hand of the Father, and received of his fulness;

And saw the holy angels, and them who are sanctified before his throne, worshiping God, and the Lamb, who worship him forever and ever.

And now, after the many testimonies which have been given of him, this is the testimony, last of all, which we give of him: That he lives!

For we saw him, even on the right hand of God; and we heard the voice bearing record that he is the Only Begotten of the Father—

That by him, and through him, and of him, the worlds are and were created, and the inhabitants thereof are begotten sons and daughters unto God. (D&C 76:19–24)

When apostles and prophets testify of the Savior, they commonly quote the words of this vision, especially verses 22 and 23. One reason for this is that they have felt the confirming witness of the Holy Spirit in their soul that these words are true; that Joseph and Sidney did see the Son on the right hand of the Father and heard the Father's voice bearing record. Therefore, they know of a surety that this special witness is true. Other times they quote the wording for an even more significant reason.

The Vision of the Celestial Kingdom

The third major witness, a vision of the Father and the Son in the celestial kingdom, given to Joseph Smith in the Kirtland Temple in 1836, bears the same witness.

The heavens were opened upon us, and I beheld the celestial kingdom of God, and the glory thereof, whether in the body or out I cannot tell.

I saw the transcendent beauty of the gate through which the heirs of that kingdom will enter, which was like unto circling flames of fire;

Also the blazing throne of God, whereon was seated the Father and the Son.

I saw the beautiful streets of that kingdom, which had the appearance of being paved with gold. (D&C 137:1–4)

The Appearance of the Lord in the Kirtland Temple

The fourth vision occurred in 1836 in the Kirtland Temple. It was the glorious prelude to the bestowing of priesthood keys on Joseph Smith and Oliver Cowdery by the visiting ancient prophets who held them. The scripture says,

The veil was taken from our minds, and the eyes of our understanding were opened.

We saw the Lord standing upon the breastwork of the pulpit, before us; and under his feet was a paved work of pure gold, in color like amber.

His eyes were as a flame of fire; the hair of his head was white like the pure snow; his countenance shone above the brightness of the sun; and his voice was as the sound of the rushing of great waters, even the voice of Jehovah, saying:

I am the first and the last; I am he who liveth, I am he who was slain; I am your advocate with the Father.

Behold, your sins are forgiven you; you are clean before me; therefore, lift up your heads and rejoice. (D&C 110:1–5)

These four accounts are known to be actual events that transpired, as recorded by today's special witnesses. The Prophet Joseph Smith's special witness therefore becomes part of the witnesses of the other Apostles. However, be it known that once an Apostle receives his own special witness, he thereafter becomes an *independent* witness, meaning he is no longer dependent on the spiritual manifestations of Joseph or Brigham or Peter or Paul—or anyone else. He has learned for himself and requires no recourse to the witness of another. As Elder McConkie phrased it, "As pertaining to Jesus Christ, I testify that he is the Son of the Living God and was crucified for the sins of the world. He is our Lord, our God, and our King. This I know of myself independent of any other person."[4] Again, however, be it known that because the Spirit confirms the truth of these eyewitness scriptural accounts of the Prophet Joseph Smith to our modern Apostles, they do form part of their special witnesses in that sense, and both perspectives become valid.

THE CHURCH AND GOSPEL DOCTRINES ARE RESTORED, NOT RELOCATED

Joseph Smith obtained his knowledge of how to restore God's Church to the earth from the Father, His Son, and angelic ministrants, many of them named in scripture. He got it by receiving line upon line, precept upon precept, revelation upon revelation. He got it from translating the Book of Mormon and the Bible (the JST), and by receiving the revelations now found in the Doctrine and Covenants and Pearl of Great Price. He got it by exercising the keys of the mysteries of godliness.

He did not search among the sects of Protestantism (or Freemasonry or Catholicism) of his day, or obtain by a piecemeal process of discovery the doctrine and ordinances as some "scholars" now incorrectly teach. He was *the* Prophet, Seer,

Translator, and Revelator. His knowledge of the things of God came from Heaven, not from men or manmade organizations.

THE PROPHET JOSEPH SMITH STILL INFLUENCES THE CHURCH TODAY

As stated previously, the Prophet Joseph Smith is the chief Apostle of this final dispensation, and the fact that he has passed to the other side of the veil has not altered his status. He is still very much interested in the progress of the Church he restored at the Lord's behest, and despite how busy he is working for the salvation of the dead in the spirit world, he is still involved with its administration and oversight.

In a meeting of the Quorum of the Twelve Apostles, at which Spencer W. Kimball was sustained as the new President of the Church, some conversation was had among the Twelve relating to how the President of the Church is chosen. At that time, some interesting comments were made regarding Joseph Smith's continuing role in the process. The following brief quotation is from a description written by Elder Bruce R. McConkie. "[One] of the Twelve observed that in his view the Prophet Joseph Smith chooses the President of the Church. . . . Elder McConkie said that he agreed with what had been said about Joseph Smith choosing the President of the Church."[5] So—Joseph's involvement remains assured as he influences the Church, under the overall direction and authority of the Lord Jesus Christ, whose witness he was, and is, on both sides of the veil.

NOTES

1. One of the finest works recounting the original sources of the Prophet Joseph Smith's spiritual experiences is *Opening the Heavens: Accounts of Divine Manifestations, 1820–1844*, ed. John W. Welch and Eric B. Carleson (Provo, Utah: Brigham Young University, 2005). I recommend this work to anyone interested in further information about Joseph's interaction with the Father and the Son, as well as many other ancient prophets and apostles.
2. See the various accounts contained in *Opening the Heavens*.
3. Gordon B. Hinckley, "We Look to Christ," *Ensign*, May 2002.

4. Bruce R. McConkie, "The Purifying Power of Gethsemane," *Ensign*, May 1985.

5. Joseph Fielding McConkie, *The Bruce R. McConkie Story: Reflections of a Son* (Salt Lake City: Deseret Book, 2003), 368.

17

OTHER PROPHETS' AND APOSTLES'
SPECIAL WITNESSES OF JESUS CHRIST

"As the servants of the Almighty, as prophets and apostles in His great cause, we lift our voices in witness and testimony of our immortal Savior."

AUTHOR'S NOTE: This chapter contains a sampling of the testimonies of other prophets and apostles, many of them encountered during the research for this work.

THOMAS S. MONSON

With all my heart and the fervency of my soul, I lift up my voice in testimony as a special witness and declare that God does live. Jesus is His Son, the Only Begotten of the Father in the flesh. He is our Redeemer; He is our Mediator with the Father. He it was who died on the cross to atone for our sins. He became the firstfruits of the Resurrection. Because He died, all shall live again.[1]

GORDON B. HINCKLEY

As I have said many times before, and as I now say again, I know that God our Eternal Father lives. He is the great God of the universe. He is the Father of our spirits with whom we may speak in prayer.

I know that Jesus Christ is His Only Begotten Son, the Redeemer of the world, who gave His life that we might have eternal life and who rules and reigns with His Father. I know that They are individual beings, separate and distinct one from another and yet alike in form and substance and purpose. I know that it is the work of the Almighty "to bring to pass the immortality and eternal life of man" (Moses 1:39). I know that Joseph Smith was a prophet, the great Prophet of this dispensation through whom these truths have come. I know that this Church is the work of God, presided over, and directed by Jesus Christ, whose holy name it bears.[2]

I bear solemn witness of him and of his unique and singular place in the plan of eternal salvation of God our Eternal Father. I bear witness of these things by the power and authority of the holy apostleship in me vested.[3]

Howard W. Hunter

In our day, the Lord has again called Apostles. These Apostles have been ordained as special witnesses of Christ in all the world. They know of the reality of Christ and his redemption with a certainty born of the Spirit.

We are eternally grateful for the witness of Joseph Smith, "who was called of God, and ordained an Apostle of Jesus Christ" (D&C 20:2). In fulfilling his apostolic calling, Joseph Smith bore this powerful witness:

"And now, after the many testimonies which have been given of him, this is the testimony, last of all, which we give of him: That he lives!

"For we saw him, even on the right hand of God; and we heard the voice bearing record that he is the Only Begotten of the Father" (D&C 76:22–23).

The Prophet's witness, born of experience and of the Spirit, has been proclaimed throughout the world, and the Holy Ghost has confirmed the truthfulness of that witness in the hearts of millions who have received the word with gladness. The pattern for proving spiritual things has been reestablished in our day. And an unbroken chain of succession has ensured that the apostolic calling has been with us continually since it was restored to Joseph Smith.

As an ordained Apostle and special witness of Christ, I give to you my solemn witness that Jesus Christ is in fact the Son of God. He is the Messiah prophetically anticipated by Old Testament prophets. He is the Hope of Israel, for whose coming the children of Abraham, Isaac, and Jacob had prayed during the long centuries of prescribed worship.

Jesus is the Beloved Son who submitted to the will of his Father by being baptized by John in the river Jordan. He was tempted of the devil in the wilderness but did not yield to the temptations. He preached the gospel, which is the power of God unto salvation, and commanded all men everywhere to repent and be baptized. He forgave sins, speaking as one having authority, and he demonstrated his power to do so by healing the lame and the halt and by opening the eyes of the blind and unstopping the ears of the deaf. He changed water to wine, calmed the troubled waters of Galilee, and walked on that same water as if on solid ground. He confounded the wicked rulers who sought his life and brought peace to troubled hearts.

Finally, he suffered in the Garden of Gethsemane and died on the cross, giving his sinless life as a ransom for every soul who enters mortality. He did in very fact rise from the dead on the third day, becoming the firstfruits of the Resurrection and overcoming death.

The resurrected Lord has continued his ministry of salvation by appearing, from time to time, to mortal men chosen by God to be his witnesses, and by revealing his will through the Holy Ghost.

It is by the power of the Holy Ghost that I bear my witness. I know of Christ's reality as if I had seen with my eyes and heard with my ears. I know also that the Holy Spirit will confirm the truthfulness of my witness in the hearts of all those who listen with an ear of faith.[4]

EZRA TAFT BENSON

Because He was God—even the Son of God—he alone had the power of resurrection. And so on the third day following His burial, He came forth from the tomb alive and showed Himself to many. There were witnesses then who saw Him. Many in this dispensation have seen Him. As one of those special witnesses so called in this day, I testify to you that He lives. He lives with a resurrected body. There is no truth or fact of which I am more assured or more confident than the truth of the literal Resurrection of our Lord.[5]

SPENCER W. KIMBALL

Elder George Q. Cannon, who was in the presidency of the Church at one time, said this: "I know that God lives. I know that Jesus lives, for I have seen Him. I know that this is the Church of God, and that it is founded on Jesus Christ, our Redeemer. I testify to you of these things as one who knows—as one of the Apostles of the Lord Jesus Christ that can bear witness to you today in the presence of the Lord that He lives. . . ."

Brethren and sisters, we come now to the close of this great conference. You have heard from most of the Brethren, as I have said, and their testimonies have been inspiring. What they have told you is true. . . .

Brethren and sisters, I want to add to these testimonies of these prophets my testimony that I know that He lives. And I know that we may see him, and that we may be with him, and that we may enjoy his presence always if we will live the commandments of the Lord and do the things which we have been commanded by him to do and reminded by the Brethren to do.[6]

"I know that God lives. I know that Jesus Christ lives," said John Taylor [George Q. Cannon], my predecessor, "for I have seen him." I bear this testimony to you brethren in the name of Jesus Christ.[7]

David O. McKay

I then fell asleep, and beheld in vision something infinitely sublime. In the distance I beheld a beautiful white city. Though far away, yet I seemed to realize that trees with luscious fruit, shrubbery with gorgeously tinted leaves, and flowers in perfect bloom abounded everywhere. The clear sky above seemed to reflect these beautiful shades of color. I then saw a great concourse of people approaching the city. Each one wore a white flowing robe, and a white headdress. Instantly my attention seemed centered upon their Leader, and though I could see only the profile of his features and his body, I recognized him at once as my Savior! The tint and radiance of his countenance were glorious to behold! There was a peace about him which seemed sublime—it was divine!

The city, I understood, was his. It was the City Eternal; and the people following him were to abide there in peace and eternal happiness.

But who were they? As if the Savior read my thoughts, he answered by pointing to a semicircle that then appeared above them, and on which were written in gold the words:

"These Are They Who Have Overcome The World—Who Have Truly Been Born Again!"

When I awoke, it was breaking day over Apia harbor.[8]

Brethren and sisters, I have cherished from childhood the truth that God is a personal being and is, indeed, our Father whom we can approach in prayer and receive answers thereto. My testimony of the risen Lord is just as real as

Thomas', who said to the resurrected Christ when he appeared to his disciples: "My Lord and my God." I know that he lives. He is God made manifest in the flesh; and I know that "there is none other name under heaven given among men, whereby we must be saved."

I know that he will confer with his servants who seek him in humility and in righteousness. I know because I have heard his voice, and I have received his guidance in matters pertaining to his kingdom here on earth.

I know that his Father, our Creator, lives. I know that they appeared to the Prophet Joseph Smith and revealed to him the revelations which we now have recorded in the Doctrine and Covenants and in other Church works. This knowledge is as real to me as that which occurs in our daily lives. When we lay our bodies down at night, we know—we have an assurance—that the sun will rise in the morning and shed its glory over all the earth. So near to me is the knowledge of Christ's existence and divinity of this restored Church.[9]

George Albert Smith

God does live; Jesus is the Christ; Joseph Smith is a prophet of the Living God; and the authority of the priesthood is with this Church today and will continue to administer to those who are willing to be ministered unto under the inspiration of our Heavenly Father. I bear you this testimony tonight, knowing the seriousness, if it were not true, of saying it, and I bear it in love and kindness and gratitude to God, and say that I know these things are true, and I bear you that witness in the name of Jesus Christ our Lord.[10]

Heber J. Grant

The Lord gives to many of us the still, small voice of revelation. It comes as vividly and strongly as though it were with a great sound. It comes to each man, according to his needs and faithfulness, for guidance in matters that pertain to his own life. For the Church as a whole it comes to those who have been ordained to speak for the Church as a whole. . . .

I bear witness to you that I do know that God lives, that he hears and answers prayer; that Jesus is the Christ, the Redeemer of the world; that Joseph Smith was and is a prophet of the true and living God; and that Brigham Young and those who have succeeded him were, and are, likewise prophets of God.

I do not have the language at my command to express the gratitude to God for this knowledge that I possess. Time and time again my heart has been melted, my eyes have wept tears of gratitude for the knowledge that he lives and that this gospel called Mormonism is in very deed the plan of life and salvation, that it is in very deed the gospel of the Lord Jesus Christ.[11]

JOSEPH F. SMITH (AS DECLARED TO THE QUORUM OF THE TWELVE)

The name of Jesus of Nazareth, the only begotten Son of the Father in the flesh, appeals to my soul, to my judgment, to my reason. . . . With what I know I could not help but believe, irrespective of the testimonies of the ancient Apostles, or irrespective of any testimony of the Prophet Joseph. The Spirit and mission of Jesus of Nazareth, as declared and explained by himself appeals to me with irresistible power and without a single doubt that he is my Savior and my Master. Then when we add the testimonies of those who were eye and ear witnesses to his mission and ministry, and later, the testimonies of those on this continent which have come to us through the Book of Mormon, the conviction of His divine mission, of His origin and birth are absolutely beyond question of doubt or power of denial. I feel that I can say with all my soul, I know that my Redeemer lives, and that I shall stand in the latter days upon the earth, and, if faithful, shall be associated with those with whom we have labored, loved and suffered in this life, and with our loved ones whom He has given to us, and that too through the endless ages of eternity. I never read the New Testament history containing the teachings of Jesus Christ without experiencing a feeling calculated to soften the heart and fill the soul with reverence and faith in them. And this testimony, the living, abiding testimony that Jesus is the Christ, the Son of the living God, should ever be found dwelling in the hearts of this body of men. You, my brethren, should know for yourselves that Jesus is the Christ, and you should be able to bear this testimony at all times and under all circumstances, as though you had seen with the eye and heard with the ear; also that the plan of salvation revealed through the Prophet Joseph is of God and not of man.[12]

Again, and without desire to multiply words, I bear my testimony to you, my brethren and sisters, that God lives, that his Son lives, and I say to you in connection with this thought and this testimony that I accept without recourse, without any hesitancy or doubt upon my mind, the statement that was made by the Prophet Joseph Smith with reference to God and to his only begotten Son, that "The Father has a body of flesh and bones as tangible as man's; The Son also: but the Holy Ghost has not a body of flesh and bones, but is a personage of Spirit," and man is made in their image.[13]

LORENZO SNOW

I was baptized by Elder John Boynton, then one of the Twelve Apostles, June 1836, in Kirtland, Ohio. Previous to accepting the ordinance of baptism, in my investigations of the principles taught by the Latter-day Saints, which I proved, by comparison, to be the same as those mentioned in the New Testament taught by Christ and His Apostles, I was thoroughly convinced that obedience to those principles would impart miraculous powers, manifestations and revelations. With sanguine expectation of this result, I received baptism and the ordinance of laying on of hands by one who professed to have divine authority; and, having thus yielded obedience to these ordinances, I was in constant expectation of the fulfillment of the promise of the reception of the Holy Ghost.

The manifestation did not immediately follow my baptism, as I had expected, but, although the time was deferred, when I did receive it, its realization was more perfect, tangible and miraculous than even my strongest hopes had led me to anticipate.

Some two or three weeks after I was baptized, one day while engaged in my studies, I began to reflect upon the fact that I had not obtained a *knowledge* of the truth of the work—that I had not realized the fulfillment of the promise "he that doeth my will shall know of the doctrine," and I began to feel very uneasy. I laid aside my books, left the house, and wandered around through the fields under the oppressive influence of a gloomy, disconsolate spirit, while an indescribable cloud of darkness seemed to envelop me. I had been accustomed, at the close of the day, to retire for secret prayer, to a grove a short distance from my lodgings, but at this time I felt no inclination to do so. The spirit of prayer had departed and the heavens seemed like brass over my head. At length, realizing that the usual time had come for secret prayer, I concluded I would not forego my evening service, and, as a matter of formality, knelt as I was in the habit of doing, and in my accustomed retired place, but not feeling as I was wont to feel.

I had no sooner opened my lips in an effort to pray, than I heard a sound, just above my head, like the rustling of silken robes, and immediately the Spirit of God descended upon me, completely enveloping my whole person, filling me, from the crown of my head to the soles of my feet, and oh, the joy and happiness I felt! No language can describe the almost instantaneous transition from a dense cloud of mental and spiritual darkness into a refulgence of light and knowledge, as it was at that time imparted to my understanding. I then received a perfect knowledge that God lives, that Jesus Christ is the Son of God, and of the restoration of the holy Priesthood, and the fulness of the gospel. It was a complete baptism—a tangible immersion in the heavenly principle or element, the Holy Ghost; and even more real and physical in its effects upon every part of my system than the immersion by water; dispelling forever, so long as reason and memory last, all possibility of doubt or fear in relation to the fact handed down to us historically, that the Babe of Bethlehem is truly the Son of God; also the fact that He is now being revealed to the children of men, and communicating knowledge, the same as in the apostolic times. I was perfectly satisfied, as well I might be, for my expectations were more than realized, I think I may safely say in an infinite degree.

I cannot tell how long I remained in the full flow of the blissful enjoyment and divine enlightenment, but it was several minutes before the celestial element which filled and surrounded me began gradually to withdraw. On arising from my kneeling posture, with my heart swelling with gratitude to God, beyond the power of expression, I felt I *knew* that He had conferred on me what only an omnipotent being can confer that which is of greater value than all the wealth and honors worlds can bestow. That night, as I retired to rest, the same wonderful manifestations were repeated, and continued to be for several successive nights.[14]

Early in the spring of 1840, I was appointed to a mission in England, and I started on or about the twentieth of May. I here record a circumstance which occurred a short time previous—one which has been riveted on my memory, never to be erased, so extraordinary was the manifestation. At the time, I was at the house of Elder H. G. Sherwood; he was endeavoring to explain the parable of our Savior, when speaking of the husbandman who hired servants and sent them forth at different hours of the day to labor in his vineyard.

While attentively listening to his explanation, the Spirit of the Lord rested mightily upon me—the eyes of my understanding were opened, and I saw as clear as the sun at noonday, with wonder and astonishment, the pathway of God and man. I formed the following couplet which expresses the revelation, as it was shown me, and explains Father Smith's dark saying to me at a blessing meeting in the Kirtland Temple, prior to my baptism, as previously mentioned in my first interview with the Patriarch.

As man now is, God once was:
As God now is, man may be.

I felt this to be a sacred communication, which I related to no one except my sister Eliza, until I reached England, when in a confidential private conversation with President Brigham Young, in Manchester, I related to him this extraordinary manifestation.[15]

[May 1846, soon after arriving at Mt. Pisgah, Iowa] I never had such a severe fit of sickness before since my recollection. My friends and family had given up most all hopes of my recovery. Father Huntington, the president of the place, called on his Congregation to pray for me. He also with Gen. Rich and some others clothed themselves in the garments of the Priesthood and prayed for my recovery. I believe it was through the continued applications [supplications] of my family and friends to the throne of Heaven that my life was spared. In my sickness I went through in my mind the most singular scenes that any man ever did. My family generally believed that I was not in my right mind. But the scenes through which my spirit travelled are yet fresh in my memory as though they occurred but yesterday. And when my people supposed me in the greatest pain and danger, I am conscious of having a great many spiritual exercises sometimes partaking of the most acute suffering that heart can conceive, and others the most rapturous enjoyment that heart ever felt or imagination ever conceived.

I suppose at first I must have been left in the hands of an evil spirit, in fact I was administered to upon this supposition. I was led into the full and perfect conviction that I was entirely a hopeless case in reference to salvation; that eternities upon eternities must pass and still I saw my case would remain the same. I saw the whole world rejoicing in all the powers and glories of salvation without the slightest beam of hope on my part, but doomed to a separation from my friends and family, all I loved most here, to eternity upon eternity. I shudder even now at the remembrance of the torments and agony of my feelings. No tongue can describe them or imagination conceive. Those who were attending me at that time describe me as being in a [near-dead] condition of body. I remained several hours refusing to speak. My body was cool, and my eyes and countenance denoted extreme suffering.

After this scene ended I entered another of an opposite character. My spirit seems to have left the world and introduced into that of Kolob. I heard a voice calling me by name saying, "he is worthy, he is worthy, take away his filthy garments." My clothes were then taken off piece by piece and a voice said, "let him be clothed, let him be clothed." Immediately I found a celestial body gradually growing upon me until at length I found myself crowned with all its glory and power. The ecstasy of joy I now experienced no man can tell, pen cannot describe it. I conversed familiarly with Joseph, Father [Joseph] Smith [Sr.] and others, and mingled in the society of the Holy One. I saw my family all saved and observed the dispensations of God with mankind, until at last a perfect redemption was effected, though great was the sufferings of the wicked, especially those that had persecuted the Saints. My spirit must have remained, I should judge, for days enjoying the scenes of eternal happiness.[16]

Experience Recounted by Alice Armeda Snow Young Pond

One evening while I was visiting grandpa Snow in his room in the Salt Lake Temple, I remained until the doorkeepers had gone and the night watchmen had not yet come in, so grandpa said he would take me to the main front entrance and let me out that way. He got his bunch of keys from his dresser. After we left his room and while we were still in the large corridor leading into the celestial room, I was walking several steps ahead of grandpa when he stopped me and said, "Wait a moment, Allie. I want to tell you something. It was right here that the Lord Jesus Christ appeared to me at the time of the death of President Woodruff. He instructed me to go right ahead and reorganize the First Presidency of the Church at once and not wait as had been done after the death of the previous presidents, and that I was to succeed President Woodruff."

Then grandpa came a step nearer and held out his left hand and said, "He stood right here, about three feet above the floor. It looked as though He stood on a plate of solid gold."

Grandpa told me what a glorious personage the Savior is and described His hands, feet, countenance and beautiful white robes, all of which were of such a glory of whiteness and brightness that he could hardly gaze upon Him.

Then he came another step nearer and put his right hand on my head and said, "Now, granddaughter, I want you to remember that this is the testimony of your grandfather, that he told you with his own lips that he actually saw the Savior, here in the Temple, and talked with Him face to face."[17]

RUSSELL M. NELSON

The living Lord leads His living Church! The Lord reveals His will for the Church to His prophet. Yesterday, after we were invited to sustain Thomas S. Monson as President of the Church, we also had the privilege to sustain him, the counselors in the First Presidency, and members of the Quorum of the Twelve Apostles as prophets, seers, and revelators. Think of that! We sustain 15 men as prophets of God! They hold all the priesthood keys that have ever been conferred upon man in this dispensation.

The calling of 15 men to the holy apostleship provides great protection for us as members of the Church. Why? Because decisions of these leaders must be unanimous. Can you imagine how the Spirit needs to move upon 15 men to bring about unanimity? These 15 men have varied educational and professional backgrounds, with differing opinions about many things. Trust me! These 15 men—prophets, seers, and revelators—know what the will of the Lord is when unanimity is reached! They are committed to see that the Lord's will truly will be done. The Lord's Prayer provides the pattern for each of these 15 men when they pray: "Thy will be done on earth as it is in heaven."

The Apostle with the longest seniority in the office of Apostle presides. That system of seniority will usually bring older men to the office of President of the Church. It provides continuity, seasoned maturity, experience, and extensive preparation, as guided by the Lord.

The Church today has been organized by the Lord Himself. He has put in place a remarkable system of governance that provides redundancy and backup. That system provides for prophetic leadership even when the inevitable illnesses and incapacities may come with advancing age. Counterbalances and safeguards abound so that no one can ever lead the Church astray. Senior leaders are constantly being tutored such that one day they are ready to sit in the highest councils. They learn how to hear the voice of the Lord through the whisperings of the Spirit.[18]

DALLIN H. OAKS

I know that we have a Heavenly Father, whose plan brings us to earth and provides the conditions and destiny of our eternal journey. I know that we have a Savior, Jesus Christ, whose teachings define the plan and whose Atonement gives the assurance of immortality and the opportunity for eternal life. I know that the Father and the Son appeared to the Prophet Joseph Smith to restore the fulness of the gospel in these latter days. And I know that we are led today by a prophet, President Thomas S. Monson, who holds the keys to authorize priesthood holders to perform the ordinances prescribed for our progress toward eternal life.[19]

M. RUSSELL BALLARD

I know that Jesus is the Christ. Brothers and sisters, you simply cannot do the work that members of the Council of the Twelve and other General Authorities are called upon to do if you do not know that Christ lives. He is very close to this work, and I love him. No greater honor could ever come to a man than to be asked to bear witness of our Savior's name throughout all the nations of the earth. I do that with great humility and gratitude. I witness to you tonight that he is the Son of God. This is his Church. The plan of salvation that we have been talking about is from our Father in Heaven and our Lord Jesus Christ.[20]

I know that this work is true. I cannot comprehend any blessing that could ever come to a man that would be remotely as precious as being called to witness and testify of Jesus Christ throughout the earth. I love the Lord. I know that he lives. I know this is his Church. I know that President Ezra Taft Benson is his prophet. I know that President Gordon B. Hinckley and President Thomas S. Monson are the prophet's counselors. I know that my beloved brethren of the Twelve are Apostles of the Lord Jesus Christ. We witness and testify to the world boldly and fearlessly and yet humbly that Jesus Christ lives and this is his Church.[21]

ROBERT D. HALES

I have found one of the great joys of being in the Quorum of the Twelve—we all have the same purpose. There is no doubt that many of us will go on different highways and byways to get to our destination. But when we get there, I know I'll find eleven other Brethren there. That's why we come together and why we're one. . . .

I leave you with my testimony. I know that God lives and that Jesus is the Christ. Part of what I've learned, that I know it with a surety, came as a result of what I've had to go through. I would not have been as open with you 38 years ago. But what I've learned is the only thing I can give to you is how I've been taught and what I've learned in hopes that it will help you. I know that God lives, that Jesus is the Christ.[22]

JEFFREY R. HOLLAND

I testify that the living God is our Eternal Father, and that Jesus Christ is His living and Only Begotten Son in the flesh. I testify that this Jesus, who was slain and hanged on a tree, was the chief Apostle then and is the chief Apostle now, the chief cornerstone of His Church in this last and greatest of all dispensations. I testify that He lives, that the whole triumph of the gospel is that He lives, and because He does, so will we. . . .

I am more certain that He and His Father appeared to Joseph Smith than I am that you sit there and I stand here. I testify with President John Taylor that "Joseph Smith, the Prophet and Seer of the Lord, has done more, save Jesus only, for the salvation of men in this world, than any other man that ever lived in it" (D&C 135:3).[23]

In my lifetime I have had a thousand spiritual witnesses—ten thousand of them?—that Jesus is the Christ, the Everlasting Son of the Everlasting God. In that lifetime I have also learned that the gospel of Jesus Christ, once lost to mankind through apostasy, has been restored to the earth and is found in its fulness in The Church of Jesus Christ of Latter-day Saints. This is the one church on the face of the earth that Christ himself has restored, authorized, and empowered to act in his name. With a commission that could not have been imagined in the days of my youth, I myself am now called as a witness of these facts, a special witness "of the name of Christ in all the world."[24]

QUENTIN L. COOK

The great responsibility of an Apostle is to be a special witness of Jesus Christ. I want you to know that the Savior lives. I want you to know that He is divine. I want you to know that he did atone for our sins. I want you to know that the doctrine of Christ, which you are taking to the world, is the most important thing you could be doing. I want you to know that the Savior guides the Church today. I'm so grateful for the blessings I have had in my life, of both feeling the Holy Ghost, and also knowing the voice of the Savior.[25]

I want you to know that Jesus Christ lives. I want you to know that He is divine. I want you to know that this is His work. I want you to know that you are His emissaries and that you are doing what you ought to do. I want you to know that because of great blessings from the Holy Ghost, but beyond that, spiritual experiences too sacred to share, I know the Savior's voice. I know who He is. I testify to you that He lives and that He guides the Church today.[26]

I know His voice. I know His face. I know He lives and He is divine.[27]

D. TODD CHRISTOFFERSON

But the head of the Church is Jesus Christ, and I bear witness that He is an active leader, that He's personally very much involved in the direction of the work. . . . And He is real. He is the resurrected Lord, and His Resurrection makes all the difference. Everything changes because He is literally resurrected. And He is the Son of God. He is the Redeemer. He lives. . . . It's my privilege to bear witness of Him and His reality as the Son of God who makes everything else possible, every good thing. And of Him I bear the witness that Joseph bore, that He lives. [See D&C 76:22–23.][28]

NEIL L. ANDERSEN

Nothing is more important; I tell you with absolute sureness that I know Jesus is the Christ. I know that. He is resurrected. He is a God but He is a being. I am now a member of the Twelve. Many [spiritual] experiences have come to me. But I assure you that I knew long before, by the power of His Spirit, that He is the Lord Jesus Christ. . . .

I confirm to you that Jesus is the Christ, the Son of God; He lives. We will all kneel at his feet. . . . He is resurrected. He guides this holy work. He appeared to the Prophet Joseph Smith. He guides His prophet today, President Thomas S. Monson. I sit in the senior councils of the Church and I assure you that He is not far from His prophets and apostles; that He leads us and guides us and that this is His holy work. And that before He comes [again] it will be in every nation, among every people, among every culture, spoken by every language; that as He comes there may be a righteous people to receive Him. I know He lives. I witness He lives. I am His witness and I so declare.[29]

RONALD A. RASBAND

I can't ever remember not believing in Jesus Christ. I have loved him since I learned of Him from the knees of my mother sharing scriptures with me and reading stories. I have just grown up in the Lord. I've always loved Him. I've always had a desire to serve Him. I love the Lord; I know He is God's living Son, Jesus the Christ. I'm honored beyond my words to express to have been called to serve Him up to this very moment, and I will devote my time, my talents, everything I have now till the day I die. I'm committed to do it. I'm honored to do it.[30]

RICHARD G. SCOTT

As one of His Apostles, authorized to bear witness of Him, I solemnly testify that I know that the Savior lives, that He is a resurrected, glorified personage of perfect love. I witness that He gave His life that we might live with Him eternally. He is our hope, our Mediator, our Redeemer. I know that He lives.[31]

Joseph B. Wirthlin

As a special witness of our Lord and Savior Jesus Christ, I testify with all my heart that the gospel of Jesus Christ is restored to Earth again. I testify that a young boy retired to a grove of trees and sought the answers to the questions of his heart. God the Father and Jesus Christ appeared to Joseph Smith, and so began the great work of restoration that unveiled the gospel in all its fulness.

Jesus the Christ lives. He loved us so much that He paid the ultimate price to save us from our sins.

Jesus the Christ lives today. He is not aloof or uninterested in our lives. He has told us, "Behold, I stand at the door, and knock: if any man hear my voice, and open the door, I will come in to him, and will sup with him, and he with me" (Revelation 3:20).

The heavens are not closed. The Master of ocean, earth, and skies speaks to prophets and apostles today.

All who approach Him with humility and real intent, seeking to know of Him, surely shall find Him.[32]

Neal A. Maxwell

Occasionally, a few in the Church let the justified caveat about the Bible—"as far as it is translated correctly" (Articles of Faith 1:8)—diminish their exultation over the New Testament. Inaccuracy of some translating must not, however, diminish our appreciation for the powerful testimony and ample historicity of the New Testament.

Latter-day Saints gladly share in the Holy Bible with all Christians. Since, alas, the Old Testament is so very, very little read in Christendom, what we end up sharing with other Christians, practically speaking, are the four Gospels and the precious epistles of the New Testament. Even so, these pages are a treasure trove testifying of Jesus.

On occasion, the pages of the New Testament come especially alive for me. A year ago, in the midst of certain Pauline pages, it was as if the cultures and centuries that stood between Paul and me were melted away by the warmth of the Spirit. Paul's words flowed into my mind unimpeded, and I understood as never before. They seemed to fall upon my ear and soul, not printed words being processed by my brain, but communication, friend to friend. It was an experience lasting perhaps no more than twenty minutes, but it was one I shall never forget. . . .

So when we read and turn the pages of the precious New Testament, there is a barely audible rustling like the quiet stirrings of the Spirit, something to be "spiritually discerned" (1 Cor. 2:14). The witnessing words came to us—not slowly, laboriously, or equivocally through the corridors of the centuries, but rather, swiftly, deftly, and clearly. Upon the wings of the Spirit these words proclaim, again and anew, *"Jesus lived. Jesus lives!"*

And likewise, I humbly so proclaim![33]

LeGrand Richards

I feel very honored . . . to share my testimony . . . because, with all my heart and soul, I know this is the Lord's work, that Jesus Christ is the Redeemer of the world, the head of His Church, that Joseph Smith was His prophet, for the establishment of His kingdom here upon this earth in the latter days to prepare the way for His Second Coming.

. . . I had to spend a few weeks at home with a little ailment. It gave me an opportunity to read a few books, and I read my patriarchal blessing and the blessings that I received from Presidents of the Church when I was set apart as mission president twice; when I was set apart as the Presiding Bishop of the Church; and last of all when President David O. McKay, assisted by his counselors and the members of the Quorum of the Twelve, laid his hands upon my head twenty-four years ago last April in the holy temple and ordained me an Apostle of the Lord Jesus Christ.

In the blessing, President McKay gave me a charge that I should be a witness of Him, and that I should bear witness of His divine calling and the divine calling of His prophet Joseph Smith and of the truths of the restored gospel. And my, the joy I have had in these 24 1/2 years trying to respond and be obedient to the charge that President McKay gave me upon that occasion. I have had great joy and happiness therein.

I have come to feel the meaning of the words of the prophet Nephi when he said, "[The Lord] hath filled me with his love, even unto the consuming of my flesh" (2 Ne. 4:21).[34]

Hugh B. Brown

I leave with you my own testimony as to the divinity of this work. God has been so good to me as to make known to me, in ways that I cannot explain, that Jesus of Nazareth is the Son of God. I know that he is the Redeemer of this world. I have been close enough to him to get from him a convincing testimony of that fact, which has been sealed upon my soul. I leave you this testimony, and I say, as Peter of old said in answer to the question, "Whom say ye that I am?" "Thou art the Christ, the Son of the living God" (see Matt. 16:15–16). I know it. I know it better than I know anything else, and for that knowledge I am grateful to him. I would like to continue faithful to the end if I can.[35]

One of the things President McKay says to all the men who are called to the Quorum of the Twelve is this: You are to become a witness of Jesus the Christ; a special witness. Wherever you go you are to bear that witness, and bless the people. My young friends, with all the solemnity of my soul, speaking from the very center of my heart, I say to you, knowing that I am on the very brink of eternity, I say to you, Jesus of Nazareth is the Son of God; the redeemer of the world. . . . He is the Son of the Living God and He has come again in our time; and he will come again and rule and reign on this earth for a thousand years of universal peace known as the Millennium.[36]

J. REUBEN CLARK JR. (AS RELATED BY GLEN L. RUDD)

About thirty years ago I received a phone call in my office at Welfare Square from Elder Harold B. Lee. He wanted me to drop everything and come immediately to his office. When I arrived, he introduced me to a very splendid gentleman from England. He was a member of the British cabinet—the solicitor general of Great Britain. He was a man in his early fifties. Brother Lee took this gentleman and me into the First Presidency's reception room where we were joined by President J. Reuben Clark Jr. of the First Presidency. President Clark was past ninety years of age and was having difficulty walking. However, he was in complete control of his faculties. He seated Brother Lee at one end of the large table in this room, and me at the other end. He sat on one side at the middle of the table and asked the gentleman from England to sit directly across from him. I thought to myself, "What will they talk about? I am sure he will ask how the Prime Minister is and how legal matters are going in Great Britain." I thought that President Clark, being interested in international affairs, might ask about those matters. However, President Clark, without any apologies and without any hesitation, began to bear his testimony of the reality of the First Vision. He told in simple terms how and why Joseph, as a boy, went into the Sacred Grove. He then told what actually happened, how Joseph knelt in prayer and how the power of Satan almost overcame him. Then President Clark told of the light appearing and the appearance of God the Father and the Son. Never once did he apologize or say, "We believe this." He spoke in absolute facts and in such a manner that the three of us listening were completely captivated by the simplicity in which he told this marvelous experience. At that moment I thought nobody on this earth could deny that testimony. The man from England listened intently. President Clark spoke with great intent. It was a great moment in my life as I listened to a ninety-year-old prophet of God tell the magnificent account of one of the greatest events that has ever taken place on this earth. I am sure the man from England never forgot that great experience. I surely have not and quite likely never will.[37]

N. Eldon Tanner

And to you young people today I should like to bear my own personal testimony that by the power of the Holy Ghost I know as I know I live that God lives; that Jesus is the Christ, the Redeemer of the world; that he came and dwelt among men; that he willingly gave his life for you and me; that he was literally resurrected; that he and God the Eternal Father did actually appear to Joseph Smith in answer to his prayer.[38]

Joseph F. Merrill

For myself I am very sure that just as certainly as you are sitting there and I am standing here, I know that God lives and that this is his Church. He, himself, through the Holy Ghost, has revealed this to me. In answer to prayer I have been the happy recipient several times of revelation direct from God, given verbally, once orally. Hence I positively know that he lives. In recent years I have publicly related some of these experiences many times.[39]

Orson F. Whitney

One night, or rather early in the morning I dreamed as follows:

I thought I was in the garden of Gethsemane. I saw the Savior and his Apostles, Peter, James, and John, enter from the direction to my right, and, leaving them there in a group, praying, He passed to the other side and also knelt down. He seemed to be in great mental distress and his face, which was turned towards me, was streaming with tears. He prayed to the Father: "Let this cup pass from me; nevertheless, Thy will, and not mine, be done." Finishing He arose and crossing to where his Apostles were, shook them—for they had fallen asleep—and rousing them up, reproved them for neglecting to watch and pray. He then returned to his former place and kneeling down prayed again. Unseen of them I watched their movements from behind a tree. My heart was so full of sympathy for Jesus and his sorrow that I wept in unison with him and my whole soul as if melted, went out to him. Pretty soon He arose and beckoning his companions to him, seemed about to take his departure. The whole circumstance of the dream then changed, though the scene remained the same. The only difference was in time; instead of before the Crucifixion, it was after, and the Son of God, having made the sacrifice required, was about to go to the Father, taking the three disciples with Him. I could stand it no longer, and rushing out from my concealment fell down at his feet, clasped him about the knees, and begged Him to take me with him also. He gazed upon me with inexpressible tenderness, then stooped and lifted me up into his arms and embraced me with all the affection of a father or an elder brother. I could feel the beating of his heart and the warmth of his bosom against mine. With a voice full of sweetness and compassion and slowly swaying his head in denial, he said, "No, my son; your work is not finished yet. These have done their work and they can go with me, but you must stay and finish yours." These words uttered in all kindness only made me more anxious to go, though I did not repeat my request, but clinging to him besought him further: "Well, promise me that I will come to you hereafter." Again, he shook his head and sadly and sweetly said, "That will depend entirely on yourself." I awoke with a sob, and it was morning.

I was profoundly impressed and related the dream to Brother Musser. He told me it was from the Lord. Of this, I had no doubt, for the lesson it taught was full of wisdom and warning, and it was stamped upon my mind eternally. I could not forget it, and hope I shall always profit by its instruction.[40]

Notes

1. Thomas S. Monson, "I Know That My Redeemer Lives," *Ensign*, May 2007.
2. Gordon B. Hinckley, "We Look to Christ," *Ensign*, May 2002.
3. Gordon B. Hinckley, "Special Witnesses for Christ," *Ensign*, May 1984.
4. Howard W. Hunter, "An Apostle's Witness of Christ," *Ensign*, January 1984. From an address delivered at a friendshipping and fellowshipping fireside satellite broadcast from the Tabernacle on Temple Square, October 30, 1983.
5. Ezra Taft Benson, "Jesus Christ: Our Savior, Our God," *Ensign*, April 1991, 4.
6. Spencer W. Kimball, "The Cause Is Just and Worthy," *Ensign*, May 1974.
   According to another account, a sister missionary was present at a meeting wherein Spencer W. Kimball felt prompted to share an additional sacred detail (beyond what is given in his journal and biography) of the culmination of his call to the apostleship.

Elder Kimball testified that at that great time of spiritual struggle, he "saw the Lord Jesus and heard from the mouth of the Savior Himself the soul-cheering affirmation, 'I have called you to be my witness to the world. Doubt not, but be of good cheer.'" (See Justin Collings, a grandson, "Grandma Burton's Witness," familysearch.org.)

7. Spencer W. Kimball, "Strengthening the Family—the Basic Unit of the Church," *Ensign*, May 1978.

President Kimball meant to refer to President George Q. Cannon in his statement, not to President John Taylor (a minor error) in his use of this meaningful quotation.

8. Taken from President McKay's world tour journal, May 10, 1921, as quoted in David O. McKay, *Cherished Experiences from the Writings of President David O. McKay*, comp. Claire Middlemiss (Salt Lake City: Deseret Book, 1955), 101–2.

9. David O. McKay, in Conference Report, April 1968, 9–10.

10. George Albert Smith, in Conference Report, April 1946, 126.

11. Heber J. Grant, in Conference Report, April 1945, 9–10.

12. Joseph F. Smith, January 8, 1914. In commenting in his journal on the remarks of President Joseph F. Smith related in a meeting of the First Presidency and the Twelve, Elder James E. Talmage wrote, "At our meeting today, after the administering of the sacrament, an unusual outpouring of the Spirit of God was manifest. It was a remarkable meeting, the memory of which will never fade from the minds of those present" (James E. Talmage journal, January 8, 1914; see Journal History of the Church, Church History Library, history.lds.org).

13. Joseph F. Smith, in Conference Report, October 1916, 6.

14. As quoted in Dennis B. Horne's *Latter Leaves in the Life of Lorenzo Snow* (Springville, Utah: Cedar Fort, 2012), 64. Another account of this marvelous manifestation, when the spirit personage of the Holy Ghost entered and enveloped the mortal body of Lorenzo Snow, is the following:

"I laid my pride, worldly ambition and aspirations upon the altar, and as humble as a child went to the waters of baptism, received the ordinance administered by an Apostle and afterward the laying on of hands.

"One evening, a few days after this, when alone, engaged in earnest prayer, the heavens were opened, the veil was rent from my mind, and then and there I received the most wonderful manifestations, grand and sublime, I believe, as man was ever permitted to receive, and beyond the power of language fully to describe. It was shown me in that vision that there truly existed a Son of God—that Joseph Smith was really a prophet of God.

"The first intimation of the approach of that marvelous vision, was a sound just above my head like the rustling of silken robes, when immediately the Holy Spirit descended upon me enveloping my whole person, filling me from the crown of my head to the soles of my feet, which was a complete baptism as tangible an immersion in a Heavenly principle or element—the Holy Ghost—infinitely more real, physical in its effects upon every part of my system then was the immersion when I was baptized in water. That night after retiring to rest the same wonderful manifestations were repeated, and continued to be several successive nights. From that time to the present on numerous occasions, miraculous manifestations of the divine power have followed me and my administrations of the gospel ordinances" (ibid., 443–49).

15. As quoted in Horne's *Latter Leaves in the Life of Lorenzo Snow*, 68–69; also 431–42.

16. Maureen Ursenbach Beecher, ed., "The Iowa Journal of Lorenzo Snow," *BYU Studies* 24:3 (1984), 268–69; see byustudies.byu.edu. Lightly edited by the author for modern punctuation and spelling.

17. LeRoi C. Snow, "An Experience of My Father," as quoted in Horne, *Latter Leaves in the Life of Lorenzo Snow*, 261–65. Some (usually critics) who are familiar with the loose and often unreliable writings of LeRoi C. Snow have attempted to cast doubt on this account. For this reason, both this chapter and my *Latter Leaves in the Life of Lorenzo Snow* contain thorough examination and documentation of the experience as recorded and substantiated in several sources. There is no question it occurred. Elder John A. Widstoe, of the Quorum of the Twelve, was assigned by that body to investigate the matter further. A few years after Allie's death, Widstoe contacted her husband, Noah Pond. In reply, Elder Widstoe received the following letter from Pond:

"We talked about the great privilege that was hers in visiting her grandfather, President Lorenzo Snow, in the Salt Lake Temple on the memorable evening of his narrative of the Heavenly visitation of the Savior to him and the instructions given him to proceed forthwith in the reorganization of the First Presidency of the Church.

"The reason for Allie going to the Temple [was] . . . the taking of the 'gruel,' a favorite food item of the President. On the evening of the occurrence he had taken time to tell her many interesting experiences, and the hour became late, so late in fact that the watchman had locked the doors and the Temple was silent with only the two within.

"President Snow led Allie to the large front door, and in passing from his room, he halted at the designated spot, and placing his arm on her shoulder he said, 'I want you to remember, my daughter, that here the Savior appeared to me in answer to my prayers, and instructed me to proceed with the reorganization of the First Presidency.' That this was pleasing to the Lord and blessings upon the Church would follow President Snow's administration. President Snow's statement was very definite that he saw the Savior, and heard his voice." For a complete review of this entire experience with documentation, see Horne, *Latter Leaves in the Life of Lorenzo Snow*, 261–66 and 515–16 notes.

18. Russell M. Nelson, "Sustaining the Prophets," *Ensign*, November 2014.

19. Dallin H. Oaks, "Testimony," *Ensign*, May 2008.

20. M. Russell Ballard, "Keeping the Commandments—Right Now" (Brigham Young University fireside, September 6, 1987), 8, speeches.byu.edu.

21. M. Russell Ballard, "Respond to the Promptings of the Spirit" (address to Church Educational System religious educators, January 8, 1988), 8.

22. Robert D. Hales, "Organize the Work/Accomplish the Work," Leadership Enrichment Series, November 13, 2012, 17.

23. Jeffrey R. Holland, "Our Consuming Mission" (address to Church Educational System religious educators, February 5, 1999), 8.

24. Jeffrey R. Holland, *Christ and the New Covenant* (Salt Lake City: Deseret Book, 1997), 343.

25. Quentin L. Cook, transcribed excerpt from address given at the Provo, Utah, Missionary Training Center, June 10, 2014.

26. Quentin L. Cook, transcribed excerpt from address given at the Provo, Utah, Missionary Training Center, March 3, 2015.

27. Quentin L. Cook, as quoted in "Leaders Address Members of the Jerusalem District," *Church News*, November 17, 2016; see lds.org.

28. D. Todd Christofferson, "The Journey to Lead like the Savior," Leadership Enrichment Series, November 6, 2013, 16–17.

29. Neil L. Andersen, transcription of excerpt of address given at Provo, Utah, Missionary Training Center, April 8, 2014.

30. "Elder Ronald A. Rasband: Prepared for a Lifetime of Service," Church newsroom, mormonnewsroom.org.

31. Richard G. Scott, "He Lives," *Ensign*, November 1999. Elder Scott repeated part of the concluding paragraph of this witness word-for-word in the October 2001 general conference.

32. Joseph B. Wirthlin, "The Two Guiding Lights" (Brigham Young University fireside, February 1, 2004), speeches.byu.edu.

33. Neal A. Maxwell, "The New Testament—A Matchless Portrait of the Savior" (quotation taken from an edited, condensed version of a talk delivered February 23, 1985, at the New Testament Symposium held at Brigham Young University), publications.mi.byu.edu/fullscreen/?pub=1023.

34. LeGrand Richards, "The Simplicity in Christ," *Ensign*, November 1976.

35. Hugh B. Brown, in Conference Report, April 1969, 114..

36. Hugh B. Brown, "Father Are You There?" (Brigham Young University address, October 8, 1967); audio version available at speeches.byu.edu.

37. J. Reuben Clark Jr., as quoted in *Thoughts on Welfare from the Words of President Harold B. Lee*, comp. Glen L. Rudd (Salt Lake City: privately published, n.d.), 142.

38. N. Eldon Tanner, in Conference Report, October 1964, 48.

39. Joseph F. Merrill, in Conference Report, October 1950, 125–26.

40. As quoted in Dennis B. Horne, *The Life of Orson F. Whitney: Poet, Historian, Apostle* (Springville, Utah: Cedar Fort, 2014), 31–32, 405–9.

INDEX

G

H

ABOUT THE AUTHOR

Dennis B. Horne was born in Salt Lake City, Utah, and grew up in Bountiful, Utah. He served in the Missouri Independence Mission and then attended both Brigham Young and Weber State Universities, earning a bachelor of science in communications. While finishing his degree, he met and married the late Celia Rae (Benson) Horne. They had two daughters together before she passed away. He later met and married Karin Chelsey Nelson, with whom he has one daughter. He worked for a number of years in television broadcasting and then with the Materials Management Department of the LDS Church as a technical writer. He has lived in several locations in Davis County, Utah, and currently resides in Woods Cross.

Dennis is the author of a number of doctrinally and historically oriented works, including *Bruce R. McConkie: Highlights from His Life and Teachings* (now in 2nd ed.), *Called of God by Prophecy, An Apostle's Record: The Journals of Abraham H. Cannon, Determining Doctrine, Faith to Heal and Be Healed, Latter Leaves in the Life of Lorenzo Snow,* and *The Life of Orson F. Whitney.* He also presented papers at the 2012 and 2014 BYU Church History Symposiums and was published in *Mormon Historical Studies.*

ALSO AVAILABLE AS AN
EBOOK

CFI

CEDAR FORT
Publishing & Media

AN IMPRINT OF CEDAR FORT, INC.

WWW.CEDARFORT.COM

ISBN 978-1-4621-2115-1   USA $22.99 CAN $26.99

9 781462 121151   52299